THE BAPTISM OF THE HOLY SPIRIT

THE BAPTISM OF THE HOLY SPIRIT

Don Van Steele

The Views of A.B. Simpson and His Contemporaries

Richard Gilbertson

CHRISTIAN PUBLICATIONS
CAMP HILL, PENNSYLVANIA

Christian Publications
3825 Hartzdale Drive, Camp Hill, PA 17011

The mark of ✝ *vibrant faith*

ISBN: 0-87509-520-8
LOC Catalog Card Number: 93-70746
© 1993 by Christian Publications
All rights reserved
Printed in the United States of America

93 94 95 96 97 5 4 3 2 1

Cover Design: Step One Design

Table of Contents

Thanks

Numerous people have made the writing of this book possible. It is with profound gratitude that I acknowledge their help.

The vision of the Board of Directors of Christian Publications in instituting the Pardington Prize for material of an academic nature written by Alliance authors has afforded me this opportunity to share my research and insights with the worldwide Alliance family. I have been honored as a winner of the Pardington Prize.

My thanks goes as well to the Editorial Office of Christian Publications, and in particular to Jonathan Graf, its director. He and his associates have performed an outstanding job in shepherding my manuscript through the long process to finished book. I especially appreciate H. Robert Cowles for his outstanding work in enhancing my style without changing my intent.

The contents of this book began as a thesis for the Master of Theology degree at Regent College, Vancouver, British Columbia, Canada. Dr. J. I. Packer, Professor of Theology, served as midwife for the project. I am indebted to him for his constructive criticism. I want also to thank my second reader, Dr. Glen Scorgie, Academic Dean at North American Baptist College, Edmonton, Alberta, Canada, for his helpful critique.

When I first considered a study of Simpson's view regarding the baptism of the Holy Spirit, two individuals gave me valuable encouragement: Dr. David F. Hartzfeld, then Dean and Associate Professor of Old Testament at Canadian Theological Seminary, Regina, Saskatchewan, and Dr. Charles Neinkirchen, then Associate

Professor of Church History at the same school. Mr. Harry ("Sandy") Aire, Director of Library Services at Canadian Bible College/Canadian Theological Seminary, granted me ready access to the archives containing Albert B. Simpson's writings. His graciousness and desire to help made my research a pleasurable experience.

More recently, Dr. Gerald E. McGraw, Director of the School of Bible and Theology at Toccoa Falls (Georgia) College, has provided me with very helpful interaction on my manuscript.

Throughout the long gestation period, my family members have been great cheerleaders! I especially want to thank Ruth-Anne, my wife. Her willingness to share me with my computer has been an appreciated sacrifice. Her encouragement and support have helped me to persevere.

Richard P. Gilbertson
April, 1993

Introduction

Purpose, Method, Scope

Mention of the phrase "the baptism of the Holy Spirit" seems to produce controversy. In the 1990s there continues to be varied opinion as to its meaning and significance for the Christian.

In the time of Albert Benjamin Simpson, founder of The Christian and Missionary Alliance, this expression and experience was no less controversial. Simpson was not afraid to use the term, however, and was prepared to argue persuasively for his particular interpretation of it. In an article entitled "The Baptism of the Holy Spirit, a Crisis or an Evolution?," Simpson maintained that this blessing of God held great significance for the Christian:

> Is the baptism of the Holy Spirit a distinct blessing or is it simply a deeper development of the experience of conversion? Is the indwelling of the Christ in the believer's heart a definite promise to the consecrated believer, or is it received at regeneration and simply revealed and manifested as a later stage of progressive Christian experience? This is a question of much practical importance and divides the teachers of deeper spiritual truth. . . .
>
> So long as people think they have it all, there is little incentive to rouse themselves and claim their full inheritance. But when God's people see that like Israel of old, they are still toiling in the wilderness under God's displeasure, that they are neglecting a great salvation, . . . they are led to heart searching, humiliation and unceasing prayer.

A new impulse comes into their lives like a great tidal wave over the ocean of love, and an experience comes to the soul as much higher than conversion as conversion was better than the old life of flesh and sin.

This is the deepest need of the church today. One such consecrated, Spirit-filled life means a score of souls for God.[1]

The baptism of the Holy Spirit, accordingly, was a significant experience in Simpson's life and a dominant motif in his writing and teaching. Yet what he had to say about it has received only minor attention in Christian and Missionary Alliance (C&MA) writing.[2] Studies outside C&MA circles, however, indicate that Simpson played a significant role in the dissemination of teaching regarding the baptism of the Holy Spirit.[3] Unfortunately, most of these studies mention Simpson only briefly and cite a limited selection of his writings. Consequently, the investigation in this book will serve to provide new light on the impetus behind the early C&MA movement. A new generation of Alliance people and those interested in the origins of this denomination should greatly benefit from Simpson's rich teaching on the subject.

In order to understand Simpson's thinking and teaching, it is best to see him in relation to his era. Investigation into the work of the Holy Spirit was of intense interest to many people in the late 1800s, Simpson among them. Moreover, a number of Christian leaders during that period wrote concerning their understanding of the baptism of the Holy Spirit. Much may be learned by comparing Simpson's teaching with that of his evangelical contemporaries. *It is the thesis of this book that Simpson's views on the baptism of the Holy Spirit shared many commonalities with the views of his contemporaries, but also displayed significant differences.* These differences reflect Simpson's attempt to define himself in relation to the positions of his contemporaries. Of course Simpson believed that his position was scriptural. *The objective of this study, then, will be to demonstrate that Simpson's views were distinct though not unique.*

In developing this thesis, a number of critical questions need to be asked and answered:

1. What factors prompted the rise of interest in the person and work of the Holy Spirit during the late 19th century?
2. What issues were associated with the baptism of the Holy Spirit?
3. What was Simpson's view of the baptism of the Holy Spirit?
4. How did Simpson's immediate contemporaries view it?
5. What similarities exist between Simpson's view and the views of his contemporaries?
6. In what ways does Simpson's view differ from the views of his contemporaries?
7. Why does Simpson differ from his contemporaries?

Hopefully we will find answers to these questions in the course of this study.

Our principal intent will be to explore in the writings of Simpson and his contemporaries the Holy Spirit's relationship to the believer at the crisis experience of the baptism of the Holy Spirit. This study, therefore, will focus primarily on the ministry of the Spirit. We will demonstrate that sanctification and empowering for service are closely linked to the experience of the "baptism." Although both sanctification and empowering are important, they will receive attention only as they relate to the experience of the baptism of the Holy Spirit.

Our method of inquiry will involve an extensive investigation of Simpson's writings. These we will compare with the principal works on this subject from 1850 to 1910. (Most of Simpson's significant writings were completed prior to 1909.)

The historical-theological trends of the late 1800s form the backdrop of this investigation. We will look to secondary sources in analyzing this milieu and examining its effects on the writers of that era.

Chapter Outline

Here, in brief, is a "road map" to what lies ahead. Hopefully it will indicate the route we are taking and help to make the trip more pleasurable.

Chapter 1 explores the historical-theological factors that contributed to the increased interest in the late 1800s in the doctrine of the Holy Spirit. In particular, we will note the emergence of concern for sanctification and power for service.

Chapter 2 will introduce A. B. Simpson. We will survey his spiritual journey, highlighting the events that were seminal to the development of his understanding of the Holy Spirit's work.

Chapters 3-6 undertake an extensive exposition of Simpson's writings on the baptism of the Holy Spirit. We will be devoting particular attention to how the baptism of the Holy Spirit relates to sanctification and power for service.

Chapters 7-8 examine the views of Simpson's contemporaries on the baptism of the Holy Spirit. The intent of this survey will be to provide a basis for comparing Simpson's views with the views of these others.

Chapters 9-10 will make that comparison, highlighting both the similarities and the dissimilarities between Simpson and his contemporaries.

Chapter 11 looks at the teachings of the early Pentecostal movement on the baptism of the Holy Spirit. We will also look at Simpson's response to the Pentecostal movement and its teachings.

Finally, **Chapter 12** undertakes an assessment of Simpson's formulations on the baptism of the Holy Spirit. We will try to understand why Simpson differed from his contemporaries. And, in addition, we will look at the strengths of Simpson's doctrinal position.

With that road map in hand, let's embark on our journey!

End Notes

1. A. B. Simpson, "The Baptism of the Holy Spirit, a Crisis or an Evolution?" *Living Truths,* (Sep 1905) 705, 714-715

2. These are the only academic works that explicitly explore the subject:

   Mark Lee, "The Biblical View of the Doctrine of the Holy Spirit in the Writings of A. B. Simpson" (M.A. thesis, Wheaton Col, 1952) 29-34, 66-70. A very broad study using a Reformed theological grid to examine Simpson's Pneumatology. The indicated pages deal with the baptism of the Holy Spirit.

Charles Nienkirchen, "A. B. Simpson: Forerunner and Critic of the Pentecostal Movement," *The Birth of a Vision*, David F. Hartzfeld and Charles Nienkirchen, eds. (Beaverlodge, AB: Buena Book Services, 1986). An examination of Simpson's views and their influence on early Pentecostalism.

Gerald E. McGraw, "The Doctrine of Sanctification in the Published Writings of Albert Benjamin Simpson" (diss., New York U, 1986). Pages 285-293 deal with Simpson's understanding of the baptism of the Spirit.

(It should be noted that most of the research on Simpson's "Deeper Life" teaching broadly covers his view of sanctification in general, rather than the baptism of the Holy Spirit specifically.)

3. A representative survey includes, among Pentecostal writers:

Carl Brumback, *A Sound from Heaven* (Springfield, MO: Gospel Publishing House, 1977). Brumback is an Assemblies of God historian.

Harold Hunter, *Spirit Baptism: A Pentecostal Alternative* (New York: University Press of America, 1983)

Non-Pentecostal writers include:

Frederick Dale Bruner, *A Theology of the Holy Spirit: The Pentecostal Experience and the New Testament Witness* (Grand Rapids, MI: Wm B. Eerdmans, 1970)

Donald W. Dayton, *The Theological Roots of Pentecostalism* (Grand Rapids, MI: Zondervan, 1986)

George M. Marsden, *Fundamentalism and American Culture: The Shaping of Twentieth-Century Evangelicalism, 1870-1925* (New York: Oxford University Press, 1980)

Chapter 1

The Rise to Prominence
of the Doctrine of the Holy Spirit
in 19th Century America

For most of 18 centuries, the church seems to have regarded the Holy Spirit as the silent member of the Godhead. People granted Him recognition; He was a part of the baptism formula and sometimes mentioned in the benediction. But God the Father and Jesus Christ the Son had preeminence.

Quite suddenly, in the latter part of the 19th century, all of that changed. The Holy Spirit came into prominent view, as this 1899 quotation from C. I. Scofield attests:

> The church is in the midst of a marked revival of interest in the Person and work of the Holy Spirit. . . . Within the last twenty years more has been written and said upon the doctrine of the Holy Spirit than in the preceding eighteen hundred years.[1]

With that assessment, Albert Benjamin Simpson, founder of The Christian and Missionary Alliance, agreed. Half a dozen years later, writing in his magazine *Living Truths,* he had these words for his readers:

> The person and work of the Holy Spirit are always intensely interesting to the devout Christian. This is especially so at a time when He is manifesting Himself in

unwonted power in the life and work of His people. The last quarter of a century has brought a revolution in the literature of the Holy Ghost. There is no more hopeful sign in the Christian life of our time than the intense interest with which God's children are looking to the doctrine of the Holy Spirit.[2]

Why This Sudden Prominence?

Why this sudden recognition and prominence given to the Holy Spirit in the latter part of the 19th century? The purpose of this chapter will be to explore the factors which contributed to the rise of this interest in the Holy Spirit in America,[3] particularly in the years 1870 to 1900. The emerging concept of the "baptism of the Holy Spirit" will be noted as well, though an extensive treatment of this theme occurs in subsequent chapters.

Several theories have been put forward to explain the rise and growth of interest in the doctrine of the Holy Spirit in 19th century America. One theory suggests that in God's eternal plan it was foreordained that there would be a renewed outpouring of the Holy Spirit immediately prior to the return of Christ. The rise to prominence of the doctrine of the Holy Spirit, accordingly, was viewed as a restoration of the "apostolic faith."[4] Such a view was a common one during the early part of the 20th century.

Another hypothesis holds that the rise of interest in the Spirit came about as a result of the impact of Methodism on America.[5] According to the proponents of this view, the Methodist tradition brought to the forefront the role of the Spirit in conversion and sanctification. Within such a context, goes the argument, it was natural to have more emphasis devoted to the nature of the Holy Spirit's work.

More recent scholarship, particularly the work of Donald W. Dayton, has argued that a complex number of interrelated developments contributed to the rise of this doctrine's prominence in America.[6] These developments included major shifts in the American cultural milieu which caused many to seek God in a new way. At the same time, there was renewed interest by many in issues like holy living and power to serve God.[7]

Likely this latter theory provides the most inclusive means for exploring the ethos out of which the resurgence of interest in the doctrine of the Holy Spirit arose. From such a survey of 19th century America we want to uncover the important trends emerging which influenced Simpson and his contemporaries.

The Doctrine of the Holy Spirit in Pre-Civil War America

Although this study is primarily concerned with the period from 1870 to 1910, we must first go to pre-Civil War America to uncover several influential trends. These trends laid the foundation for postwar developments.

There are two significant aspects of pre-Civil War America that have a direct relationship to the later emphasis on the doctrine of the Holy Spirit. First, there arose an interdenominational quest for "holiness," particularly from the 1820s onward. In addition to renewing interest in experiential Christianity, this quest served to spark activity in the areas of evangelism and social reform. Second, there existed a prevailing theological and cultural optimism which placed great faith in human agency.

At the onset of the 1800s, America was still basking in the glow of the Second Great Awakening. By the late 1820s, however, the spiritual vitality of many churches had begun to wane.[8] In the Wesleyan wing of the church this decline prompted a renewed interest in discovering Methodist roots, particularly Wesley's doctrine of Christian Perfection. Anthologies of the writings of Wesley and his contemporary John Fletcher were circulated among Methodist ministers.[9] In 1839, Timothy Merritt began to publish *The Guide to Christian Perfection,* a popular magazine disseminating Wesleyan holiness teaching.[10] Second- and third-generation believers read this material with great interest. Many people found the material to be effective in bringing new spiritual vitality to their Christian experience.[11]

John Wesley's doctrine of Christian Perfection is elusive and has been the subject of ongoing debate as to its precise interpretation.[12] Referring to this doctrine, Wesley himself wrote:

> Entire sanctification or Christian perfection is neither more or less than pure love; love expelling sin and governing both the heart and life of a child of God. The Refiner's fire purges out all that is contrary to love.[13]

One writer described the primary focus of Wesley's view as "pure, Godly attention."[14] Central to this doctrine is the belief that, since God has commanded believers to "be perfect," there must be some means of becoming so.[15] An experience distinct from and subsequent to conversion, sometimes called "entire sanctification" or the "second blessing," was thought to impart this provision of God.[16] Receiving this "blessing" involved the consecration of the believer to God and faith to believe that God would give freedom from the inner disposition to sin willfully.[17] Accordingly, it was important in Wesley's view that believers recognize this blessing and respond to God's gracious gift. Moreover, Wesley believed that as a result of this blessing Christians could live in a state of "perfection."[18] Sin, in Wesley's opinion, was to be viewed primarily as a voluntary act of the will.[19] For this reason, Methodists have often been called "eradicationists," the theological position that teaches that man's sinful nature may be rendered inoperative (eradicated) in the Christian.[20]

Phoebe Palmer: American Modifications to Wesley

Wesley's theological formulations underwent several alterations in the American milieu. Phoebe Palmer was the most instrumental in this respect. Together with her husband, Palmer gained widespread influence in Methodist circles with her "Tuesday Meetings for the Promotion of Holiness" and various revival conference tours. Though they affirmed continuity with Wesley's teaching, "their shift in emphasis and terminology ultimately produced significantly different results."[21]

Three principal changes occurred. First, there was a shift from Wesley's focus on "pure, Godly attention" to one on power to live the sanctified life. Second, even greater emphasis was placed on the act of consecration as a distinct experience. As a consequence, much greater focus was placed on the instantaneous aspect of sanctification, almost eclipsing mention of subsequent, progressive sanctification. Third, the terminology of "claiming the blessing" became a new part of seeking sanctification.[22] Whereas Wesley placed greater emphasis on the Spirit's bearing witness to change, Palmer put primary focus on the human dimension of "believing" that the transformation had occurred as a result of "claiming the blessing."[23]

It has been suggested that the teachings of Wesley, along with these shifts introduced by Palmer, served to prepare the soil for subsequent emphases in the doctrine of the Spirit.[24] Foremost was the belief in a conscious appropriation of the blessing of sanctification subsequent to conversion. Having met certain requirements, one could "claim the blessing." Furthermore, this experience was held to bring instantaneous results in the believer's life. These features later became integral aspects of teaching in America on the baptism of the Holy Spirit.

Charles G. Finney: "Arminianizing" Calvin

In the 1830s there had been a concurrent quest for holiness in Calvinist circles. Some analysts see this as one of the outworkings of the Second Great Awakening which supposedly marked the beginning of the "Arminianization" of Calvinist theology.[25] Charles G. Finney is the figure most often associated with popularizing perfectionist teachings in Reformed circles, along with the Arminian emphasis on free salvation and human choice.

Though Finney will be the subject of exploration in a later chapter, several of his key contributions should be noted here. Several years after a significant encounter with God, Finney began to teach that a "second blessing" of holiness was possible in this life. He and his colleagues at Oberlin College propagated what became known as "Oberlin Perfectionism." He also was the first to employ "means" or techniques to promote revival, based on his presuppositions regarding God's ordering of human psychology.[26] This was a marked departure from the earlier view that revivals occurred solely as a result of divine sovereignty.[27] As a result Finney is viewed as the father of modern revivalism.[28] Furthermore, through Finney's ministry, there existed by the 1850s a large "Revivalist Calvinist" group.[29]

Like Palmer, Finney shifted focus from process to the immediacy of religious experience. William W. Sweet observes that this new revivalism "made salvation the beginning of religious experience in contrast to the older revivalism which made conversion the end."[30] Whereas in 18th century America evangelistic preaching tended to load many requirements into salvation, the revivalist tradition went to the opposite extreme by merely emphasizing "believing faith." This "easy believism," as it is sometimes called, separated salvation from the call to holy living.[31] Richard Lovelace suggests that this resulted in people having deficient conversion experiences and hence the need for a second spiritual crisis.[32]

The interdenominational concern for Christian perfection did not privatize belief but flowed into many forms of activity. Evangelism, particularly as found in Finney's itinerant crusades, was viewed as the logical outworking of revival.[33] The work of Timothy Smith has also revealed widespread concern for social reform as a result of this revivalistic impetus.[34] Christians created manifold agencies which served both to improve society and to spread the gospel. Activism was the order of the day.

These developments occurred against the backdrop of a young and vibrant nation. The United States was a land of optimism. The spirit of the age was to establish an American Utopia, free from the evils of the old world.[35] Part of the emerging American mentality was a belief in the unlimited potential of the individual and his ability to make voluntary choices to determine his destiny.[36] These prevailing ideals could not help but affect the religious context and were well suited to the rise of "Christian Perfectionism." Similarly, post-millennialism reigned in theological circles, giving the hopeful prospect of the church triumphantly making progress in this world, bringing in the Kingdom of God.[37] Together with the optimistic outlook of society and the millennial hope of the church, the vision of a "Christian America" looked to be within reach.[38]

Several Summary Observations

Before moving to the post-Civil War era in America, we need to make several summary observations about the doctrine of the Holy Spirit. As intimated earlier, teaching directly related to the Holy Spirit was rare in this pre-1860 era. Oberlin Perfectionism and the American version of Wesleyan Perfectionism focused their primary concerns on how Christ had provided the means for holy living.[39] Moreover, the term "baptism of the Holy Spirit" was seldom employed. The periodicals *Oberlin Evangelist* and *Guide to Holiness* (a Methodist publication) did nonetheless sometimes use this term. When the phrase "the baptism of the Holy Spirit" occurred, it was generally used (1) to refer to a revival or spiritual awakening in which the Holy Spirit is poured out on the church, with reference to the day of Pentecost as the archetypal event of this kind; (2) to denote the numerous "baptisms" or "anointings" believers may experience during their lives; or (3) to describe the "unction" that a preacher or evangelist needs from God to accomplish more than he could by mere human effort.[40] All these usages, however, were infrequent.

There was a marked intensification of interest in the doctrine of the Holy Spirit shortly before the Civil War. Seminal to this rise was a growing consensus among Christians that there was a need to recover the vitality of the early church.[41] The quest for "vitality" flourished in the context of the revivalism and social reform optimism of the 1840s and 1850s. Interest was further fueled by the publishing in 1856 of *The Tongue of Fire* by the British Methodist William Arthur, a work which quickly gained widespread readership in America.[42] Arthur cited the remarkable effects that Pentecost had on the early church and stressed that a revival could have the similar effect of creating a new "Pentecost" then. The striking feature of *The Tongue of Fire* is that it focuses exclusively on the work of the Spirit. This was a marked change. Indeed, Arthur's book concluded with the prayer:

> And now, adorable Spirit, proceeding from the Father and the Son, descend upon all the Churches, renew the Pentecost in this our age, and baptize thy people generally—O, baptize them again with tongues of fire! Crown this nineteenth century with a revival of "pure and undefiled religion" greater than that of the last century, greater than that of the first, greater than any "demonstration of the Spirit" even yet vouchsafed to men![43]

Shortly after this book was published, the 1857-58 revival occurred. Revival at that time served to further spread the belief that God was about to pour out His Spirit for the renewal of His Church in a way similar to the day of Pentecost. Desire for this "Pentecostal" outpouring of the Holy Spirit received additional impetus from cultural and theological developments after the Civil War. It is to these developments that our investigation now turns.

The Doctrine of the Holy Spirit in Post-Civil War America

The end of the Civil War in 1865 marked the beginning of extensive transitions in American society. The horror of the conflict dispelled some of the country's utopian optimism. The United States was also becoming an increasingly complex society. From the 1870s onward, the nation experienced rapid urbanization. Cities such as New York, Boston and Chicago became large metropolises. Expanding urbanization not only resulted in a shifting demography but also introduced the sociological problems that accompany city living.[44] Industrialization was also on the rise, further accelerating societal change and contributing to the problems of urban life. In addition, waves of immigrants landed on the shores of the country in the 1880s and 1890s.[45] The majority of them were from non-Anglo-Saxon backgrounds. They tended to congregate in the larger urban areas.

These societal developments posed significant challenges for the church. At about this time Protestantism was also beginning to experience the inroads of Continental theology, higher biblical criticism, and Darwinism.[46] The assault of these forces appeared to overwhelm the defenders of orthodoxy. Many believed that the only hope was divine intervention. This conviction was further supplemented by a decreased faith in human agency. The horrors of the 1861-1865 Civil War had brought to the forefront the innate evil in mankind. A new humility and awareness of human limitations marked the era beginning in the 1870s.[47] In the light of factors like these, it is not difficult to understand why Christians were especially interested in the "power" aspect of the Holy Spirit's ministry. Seeking God's enabling to meet these new challenges naturally led to a greater interest in the work of His Spirit.

The rise of the doctrine of the Spirit was further fueled by the perceived impotence of the church to inspire people to either holy living or evangelism. Indeed, many within the mainline churches sensed that spiritual vitality was at a low ebb. Part of this decline was attributed to the increasing affluence in many denominations. Wealth seemed to result in a corresponding decrease in concern for holiness and evangelism.[48] Increasing intellectualism in the mainstream seminaries, particularly those in the Reformed tradition, was also perceived to be a cause for the decline.[49] Moreover, many within the mainline denominations sought to reject the formalism and superficiality that characterized much of church life.[50]

Secular society displayed a concurrent interest in the spiritual realm.[51] The problems of urban living as well as reaction to materialism sparked this concern. Hence, from the 1870s onward, the United States saw the rise of spiritualism. There was Mary Baker Eddy's Christian Science movement and the Theosophical Society. There was renewed interest in gnostic philosophy.[52] Thus in both Christian and non-Christian circles, there was a marked quest for spiritual reality and vitality.

Mass Evangelism, World Evangelization, Premillennialism

The years after 1870 saw the development of mass evangelism, most notably through the ministry of Dwight L. Moody. Urban centers became the new focus for evangelistic crusades since they had a high concentration of unchurched people.[53] The problems mentioned previously of America's cities indicate the complexity of this task, and Christians sought new means to reach the unchurched.[54] Concurrent with this evangelistic interest was a renewed concern for world missions. Many new missionary sending agencies came into being during the late 19th century.

The magnitude and complexity of these evangelistic efforts at home and abroad made those involved aware of their need for divine resources. Quite naturally this prompted interest in the Holy Spirit, for He was the divine Agent who equipped believers to spread the gospel. Moreover, this quest for effectiveness in ministry accordingly became one of the prime motivating forces in developing the "power" emphasis which marked the teaching on the Holy Spirit at that time.

The upsurge in the popularity of Premillennialism that began in the mid-1870s also had a very profound effect upon the American theological milieu.[55] The Civil War had dealt Postmillennialism a severe blow. Clearly the church must overcome deep-rooted problems if it was to establish God's kingdom on earth. The resurgence of premillennialism reflected this postwar ethos and had a significant influence on American evangelical theology.

First, it imparted a much more pessimistic view regarding the transformation of the world. D. L. Moody's well-known comment expresses the prevailing attitude: "I look upon this world as a wrecked vessel. God has given me a lifeboat and said to me, 'Moody, save all you can.' "[56] Therefore, concern for evangelism received further impetus.

Second, the rise in concern for foreign missions was closely tied with the premillennial movement. Citing Matthew 24:14 as their theme text, many in this movement believed that worldwide missions would hasten the return of Christ.[57]

Third, the supposedly imminent culmination of human history spawned the belief in this movement that there would be an unprecedented outpouring of the Holy Spirit to pave the way for the return of Christ.[58] This expectation is sometimes called the "latter rain."[59] Invoking the prophecy from Joel alluded to by Peter on the day of Pentecost, this view held that the spring and fall rains (Joel 2:23) in Palestine parallel the history of the church.[60] The fall rains that facilitated the planting of crops corresponded to the Spirit's outpouring in the beginning century of the church. The spring rains that prepared Palestine crops for harvest exemplified the expected outpouring of God's Spirit just prior to the final chapter of church history.[61]

A New Emphasis on the Holy Spirit Emerges

Within such a cultural and theological milieu emerged the new emphasis on the doctrine of the Holy Spirit. Prior to the 1870s there was almost a binary understanding of the Godhead, the Holy Spirit seldom being mentioned. The upsurge of interest in the Holy Spirit was a corrective to these years of neglect.[62] Furthermore, in the period from 1840 to 1860, concern for personal intimacy with the person of Christ had received much attention.[63] As focus shifted to the Holy Spirit, attention was given to the ministry of the Spirit in revealing Christ to the individual.[64] Moreover, acknowledging the personhood of the Holy Spirit was increasingly seen as the key to communion with God.[65]

The Pentecost archetype introduced by Arthur in *The Tongue of Fire* continued to gain prominence after the Civil War. The term "Pentecost" was affixed to many spheres of ministry: "Pentecostal Pulpit," "Pentecostal Testimonies" and "Pentecostal Choirs" are but a few examples.[66] Indeed, even the Wesleyan journal *Guide to Holiness* changed its title in 1897 to *Pentecostal Life* to reflect, as the magazine noted,

> . . . the signs of the times, which indicate inquiry, research, and ardent pursuit of the gifts, graces, and power of the Holy Spirit. The Pentecostal idea is pervading Christian thought and aspiration more than ever before.[67]

This upsurge of the Pentecost archetype served to bring to the forefront the activity of the Spirit, reinforcing the common view that,

> ... the coming of a new age of the Holy Spirit would restore primitive Christianity to the churches; they, in turn would recover the purity and the power to overcome the forces of formalism, worldliness, materialism, higher criticism and all the other "isms" which increasingly seemed to threaten everything the first Pentecost had promised.[68]

Rethinking Salvation History

The perception of salvation history accordingly underwent a transition. The traditional view focused on the two covenants of law and grace, with Christ's atonement forming the line of demarcation between the two.[69] However, after the 1870s, a threefold view of history developed. The three eras, or dispensations, were the Old Testament, the life of Christ, and the age of the Holy Spirit.[70] The day of Pentecost became the new fulcrum of history. Rather than demeaning Christ's work for salvation, this view sought to emphasize Christ's continuing work in the church through the Holy Spirit.

One of the consequences of this shift was the assertion that the age of miracles had not passed and that God would continue to perform "signs and wonders" to authenticate the gospel.[71] This view clashed with more traditional Protestant positions, such as that held by the traditional Princeton theology.[72] Those who held to the three-era position expected the supernatural as part of the era of the Spirit, a view that fitted well the rising premillennial movement mentioned above.

The upsurge of the doctrine of the Holy Spirit was also marked by a shift in exegetical foundations. Prior to the 1860s, the central focus had been on sanctification; hence, passages such as Matthew 5:48, Second Corinthians 7:1, First Thessalonians 5:23-24 and John 17:20-23 were primary.[73] With the resurgence of the doctrine of the Holy Spirit came an attendant rise of interest in the book of

Acts. Acts 1:8, 2:4 and 19:2 were seen as particularly weighty texts.[74] Also the Old Testament prophecies recorded in Acts, particularly those in Joel, received special attention.[75] Hence, there occurred a shift of interest from the didactic passages found in Paul's writings to the narrative material found in Luke's writings.[76]

One of the consequences of the shift to the book of Acts was the popular view that certain experiences of believers in the early church were normative. The pattern of a person's becoming a disciple and then being baptized with the Spirit was the perceived scriptural foundation for the idea of a two-step conversion process involving two distinct and separate experiences.[77] Moreover, there was a rise in the treatment of the Old Testament *Heilsgeschichte* (salvation history) as typifying Christian experience, particularly by the "Higher Life" movement.[78] The exodus from Egypt, the wilderness wanderings and the crossing of the Jordan River into the Promised Land were all seen as stages in the individual's spiritual pilgrimage.[79]

A New Look at the Baptism with the Holy Spirit

After 1870 exploration of the work of the Spirit centered upon delineating the "baptism of the Holy Spirit."[80] Discussion of this experience in a believer's life took place along two related lines of investigation.

The one axis explored the work of the Holy Spirit in the ongoing quest for holiness. After the Civil War there was a marked move away from Christocentric sanctification. This shift is seen most clearly in the writings of Asa Mahan. His *Scripture Doctrine of Christian Perfection* (1846) was for the most part a Wesleyan view of sanctification, with significant emphasis on Christ's work in sanctification. But in *Baptism of the Holy Spirit* (1870), the Holy Spirit's work in applying sanctification became primary.[81]

Numerous reasons have been put forward for this shift. Some have suggested that an emphasis on the Holy Spirit best expressed what Wesley had been straining to articulate.[82] Others viewed the book of Acts and Pentecost as offering the most convincing and biblical way of defending a normative two-step conversion process.[83]

Though conjecture may not have established the precise reasons for this shift, the fact remains that after 1870 teaching on sanctification put greater emphasis on the Holy Spirit.

The other axis of inquiry explored the "empowering" work of the Spirit. As we observed above, the decreased faith in human ability, along with the increased problems facing the church, intensified desire for "power." Moreover, Christian workers like D. L. Moody stressed the prime importance of being "empowered for service."

Various theological streams developed their own nuances of interpretation on how these two axes related to the baptism of the Holy Spirit. Many in the Wesleyan-Holiness camp held that at Pentecost, in the baptism of the Spirit, the disciples were both sanctified and empowered by the Spirit for Christian service.[84]

Another camp, primarily composed of Revivalistic Reformed leaders, deemphasized the sanctification aspect of this event and stressed the power-for-service aspects of Pentecost.[85] They used the term "baptism of the Holy Spirit" to denote this empowering subsequent to conversion. They did, however, include a strong emphasis on God's provision for holy living.

A third position, far less prevalent, was the so-called "third blessing" view.[86] Those who held this view divided the baptism into two experiences, one for sanctification and one for empowering.[87] While the nuances within these views will be explored in a later chapter, it should be noted that each position argues for the work of the Spirit subsequent to conversion.

Summary

We have seen some of the background of the world A. B. Simpson lived and worked in. Americans had lost faith in human ability to deal adequately with the nation's cultural problems. Many within the churches sensed that Christianity was powerless and struggling. It desperately needed divine provision to meet the challenges it faced. Out of those concerns arose a sizeable group of Christian leaders who believed that the solution lay in a rediscovery of the power and work of the Holy Spirit. A. B. Simpson was one of those leaders.

MI: Zondervan, 1986). Also Dayton, "The Doctrine of the Baptism of the Holy Spirit: Its Emergence and Significance," *Wesleyan Theological Journal* (Spring, 1978) 114-126.

7. See William G. McLoughlin, *The American Evangelicals, 1800-1900: An Anthology* (New York: Harper & Row, 1968) 26. The author asserts, "The history of American evangelicalism is . . . more than the history of a religious movement. To understand it is to understand the whole temper of American life in the nineteenth century."

Leonard I. Sweet, ed., *The Evangelical Tradition in America* (Macon, GA: Mercer University Press, 1984) offers an excellent survey of the historical analysis which has been done on this period in American church history (see pages 1-86).

8. Vinson Synan, *The Holiness-Pentecostal Movement in the United States* (Grand Rapids, MI: Wm B. Eerdmans, 1971) 42

9. Syn, *Holiness-Pentecostal Movement* (see note 8 above) 42

10. Cha E. Jones, *Perfectionist Persuasion* (Metuchen, NJ: Scarecrow Press, 197 In 1845 the name of the magazine was changed to *Guide to Holiness*.

11. Day *Theological Roots* (see note 6 above) 64

12. For *le, the Wesleyan Theological Journal* devoted two years of issues to the over the interpretation of Wesley's doctrine of Christian perfection ious issues in volumes 13 and 14).

13. Thon son, ed., *The Works of John Wesley* XII (Grand Rapids, MI: Zond 59) 432

14. Edith ogel-Blumhoefer, "The Overcoming Life: A Study in the Refor elical Contribution to Pentecostalism," (diss. Harvard U, 1977)

5. See W in Account of Christian Perfection" in *The Works of John Wesley* MA: Hendrickson Publications, 1986) 380-382. Wesley appeal injunction in Matthew 5:49 to support his contention that an becoming perfect must be provided by God. George E. Mar this theological concept made a profound impact on the An *Americ* gical milieu [see Marsden, *Fundamentalism and* 1925 (N *Shaping of Twentieth-Century Evangelicalism, 1870-* d University Press, 1980) 73].

6. See, for of Pieti *A Plain Account* 368-369. Bruce Shelley in "Sources plores th m," *Fides et Historia* (Fall/Spring, 1972) 69, exing had upon America.

It is to his biography that we now turn.

End Notes

1. C. I. Scofield, *Plain Papers on the Doctrine of the Holy Spirit* (New
   Fleming H. Revell, 1899) 9

2. A. B. Simpson, "Some Aspects of the Holy Spirit," *Living Truths* (Nov.
   384

3. Prior to surveying the progress of this doctrine in America, we shou
   brief mention to its expression in the history of the church.

   Until the Reformation, the Holy Spirit received but little attention (
   99, Thomas 990). His person and work were eclipsed by the imp
   concern to explicate the nature of Christ and to articulate the
   understanding of the Godhead. It was mainly within these co
   discussion of the person of the Holy Spirit occurred.

   During the Reformation, however, the work of the Spi
   extensive treatment, particularly in Calvin's magisterial *I*
   Christian Religion. Indeed, B. B. Warfield asserted in the
   Kuyper's *The Person and Work of the Holy Spirit*, "The devel
   the work of the Holy Spirit is an exclusively Reformatio
   it is to John Calvin that we owe the first formulation of t
   developed] it especially in the broad departments o
   'Regeneration,' and the 'Witness of the Spirit' " (page

   The 17th century Puritan writers John Owen and T
   exemplary works on the Holy Spirit, particularly wi
   tion of redemption. Abraham Kuyper indicates tha
   was very little written in English in this area.

4. Frank Bartleman, *How Pentecost Came to L*
   Beginning (Los Angeles: Privately printed, 192

5. For example, Frederick Dale Bruner, *A T*
   Pentecostal Experience and the New Testam
   Wm B. Eerdmans, 1970) 37-38. See also H
   Wesleyans and the Charismatic Renewal
   1986).

   The so called "two-stage" salvation
   held by Bruner to have contributed t
   work of the Holy Spirit subsequent

6. Donald W. Dayton, *The Theologi*

17. See *Plain Account* (see note 15 above) 370-372. Wesley emphasized that sin was pushed aside as a believer was increasingly filled with divine love.

18. W. E. Boardman makes the following statement on the nature of "perfection": "The Wesleyans admit the claims of the law of God as requiring absolute perfection, like the spotless purity of Jesus and the holy angels, and *make no profession of it* (emphasis mine) but only of *Christian* (emphasis his) perfection, making a broad distinction between Christian and angelic perfection." [Boardman, *The Higher Christian Life* (Boston: Henry Hoyt, 1871). In 1859 edition, 41.] In my understanding, Wesley did not claim absolute sinlessness but the perfecting of an attitude of love to God with the total personality and a love to neighbor that matched love to self—in other words, perfect love.

19. Wesley describes this belief in *Plain Account* (see note 15 above) 435 and 445.

20. Wesley, *Plain Account* (see note 15 above) 69. See also Waldvogel-Blumhoefer (see note 14 above) 4. Eradicationism holds that the sin nature is completely removed from the believer as a result of a second work of divine grace.

21. Waldvogel-Blumhoefer (see note 14 above) 4; Jones (see note 10 above) 4-7.

22. Waldvogel-Blumhoefer (see note 14 above) 4-6; also Dayton, *Theological Roots* (see note 6 above).

23. Donald Wheelock, "Spirit Baptism in American Pentecostal Thought" (diss. Emory U, 1983) 1-56, explores this contrast between Palmer and Wesley.

24. Wheelock (see note 23 above) 81-82; Bruner (see note 5 above) 38-39.

25. Melvin Easterly Dieter, *The Holiness Revival of the 19th Century* (Metuchen, NJ: The Scarecrow Press, 1980) 21. Warfield satirically called this trend "the Pelagianizing of American theology," [*Perfectionism* vol. 2, (Philadelphia: The Presbyterian and Reformed Pub. Co., 1971) 464]. See also James E. Hamilton's informative analysis, "Academic Orthodoxy and the Arminianizing of American Theology," *Wesleyan Theological Journal,* (Spring, 1974) 52-59. Nathaniel Taylor, founder of the "New Haven Theology," is generally recognized as introducing shifts in traditional Calvinist soteriology [Mark A. Noll, "The Great Awakenings," *Evangelical Dictionary of Theology,* ed. Walter A. Elwell (Grand Rapids, MI: Baker Book House, 1984) 484]. Seminal was the discussion on the place of man's will. Jonathan Edwards, perhaps influenced by Lockean psychology, asserted the traditional Augustinian-Calvinist view of man's will. [See McLoughlin (see note 7 above) 6-7, who

suggests that Edwards was influenced by John Locke. The philosophical trends in Taylor's times had brought Scottish Common Sense philosophy to the forefront, a movement which had a much different view of human psychology.] From this perspective, the human will is viewed as not being an independent faculty but rather the outflow of basic human motivations (Noll 484). Since human nature is incurably depraved, all choices will be selfish; hence, divine grace is needed to produce disinterested choice for God (McLoughlin 7). Taylor, influenced by Scottish Common Sense philosophy, saw the will as an independent faculty which simply made choices based on input from the mind and the emotions [W. A. Hoffecker, "Nathaniel William Taylor," *Evangelical Dictionary of Theology* (see this note above) 1070]. Taylor believed that God constituted man this way so that man would have moral responsibility (McLoughlin 7). The result of Taylor's conjectures was a reinterpretation of the extent of human responsibility within God's sovereignty.

26. Garth E. Rosell in "Charles G. Finney: His Place in the Stream of American Evangelicalism," *Evangelical Tradition,* (see note 7 above) gives an informative overview of Finney's understanding of faculty psychology (mind, will, emotions).

27. Finney's use of technique has come under severe criticism. For example, see chapter entitled "Oberlin Perfectionism" in B. B. Warfield, *Perfectionism.* Rosell (see note 26 above) argues that records by eyewitnesses of Finney's meetings portray him much differently than do his antagonists.

28. *Evangelical Tradition* (see note 7 above) contains a collection of essays exploring the effect of Finney on the formation of American evangelicalism.

29. According to Timothy L. Smith, *Revivalism and Social Reform: American Protestantism on the Eve of the Civil War* (New York: Harper & Row, 1965) 32, these included "New School Presbyterians," most Congregationalists, low church Episcopalians and the Regular Baptists.

30. William W. Sweet, *The American Churches: An Interpretation* (New York: Cokesbury, 1947) 126

31. Richard F. Lovelace, *Dynamics of Spiritual Life: An Evangelical Theology of Renewal* (Downers Grove, IL: Intervarsity Press, 1979) 250

32. Lovelace (see note 31 above) 120

33. See *Evangelical Tradition* (see note 7 above) 140

34. Grant Wacker, "The Holy Spirit and the Spirit of the Age in American Protestantism, 1880-1910," *Journal of American History* (Jun 1985) 48.

Wacker refutes the idea that Christians of the evangelical wing were never active in social reform. His thesis is that both the liberal social gospel movement and the evangelical movement were children of the same father: pre-Civil War revivalistic Christianity, particularly the efforts of Finney. It was not until the 1910-1920s that Fundamentalists/Evangelicals abandoned these concerns. Smith, in his *Revivalism and Social Reform* (see note 29 above) provides an additional examination of evangelical social involvement.

35. Smith, *Revivalism and Social Reform* (see note 29 above) 105, 113

36. David F. Wells and John D. Woodbridge, *The Evangelicals: What They Believe, Who They Are, Where They Are Changing* (Grand Rapids, MI: Baker, 1975) 155

37. McLoughlin (see note 7 above) 12-13

38. Rosell (see note 26 above) 147

39. Dayton, "The Doctrine of the Baptism" (see note 6 above) 115. In Wesley's *Plain Account* (see note 16 above) he makes very little reference to the book of Acts. Moreover, he does not discuss the work of the Holy Spirit in detail. Palmer, as noted above, focused the majority of her attention on the "experience" of the blessing rather than the theological origins of this supposed provision of God.

40. Dayton, "Doctrine of Baptism" (see note 6 above) 117

41. Dayton, *Theological Roots* (see note 6 above) 73

42. Dayton, *Theological Roots* (see note 6 above) 74. Dayton also mentions Henry C. Fish, an American Baptist minister, as one who wrote a book with similar themes. Fish called for "a return of the scene of apostolic days, especially those of the ever memorable Pentecost," asking, "Why may we not anticipate the return of the Pentecostal seasons? Why may not Christians now be filled with the Holy Ghost, as were they in primitive times?" [*Primitive Piety Revived: Or, the Aggressive Power of the Christian Church* (Boston: Congregational Board of Publication, 1855) 244-245].

43. William Arthur *The Tongue of Fire; or, the True Power of Christianity* (New York: Harper and Brothers, 1856) 354. Quoted in Dayton, *Theological Roots* (see note 6 above) 74.

44. Marsden, *Fundamentalism* (see note 15 above) 21

45. Smith, *Called Unto Holiness: The Story of the Nazarenes* (Kansas City, MO: Nazarene Publishing House, 1962) 13

46. These challenges were principally from Schleiermacher and, in the later

1800s, Ritschl. Horace Bushnell is viewed by many as the father of American liberalism.

47. Smith, *Revivalism* (see note 29 above) 236

48. Dieter (see note 25 above) 204

49. Wacker (see note 34 above) 60. Wacker asserts that, although there were certainly streams of vitality remaining in the Edwardsean and Princeton tradition, renewal forces came to believe "that encrusted scholasticism in the main stream seminaries and formalism and lovelessness in the mainstream churches" called for significant spiritual renewal. It should be noted that Wacker uses the term "scholasticism" to denote the excessive rationalistic focus on systematics that sometimes marked this theological tradition. It is interesting to observe that the majority of the people who became leaders in the rise of the doctrine of the Holy Spirit came from within the ranks of the Reformed churches. For example, A. J. Gordon was a Baptist, A. T. Pierson and A. B. Simpson were Presbyterians and R. A. Torrey was a Congregationalist.

50. A. T. Pierson, *Forward Movements of the Last Half Century* (New York: Funk and Wagnalls, 1900) vii

51. Dayton, *Theological Roots* (see note 6 above) 78

52. Dayton, *Theological Roots* (see note 6 above) 78-79. See also Wacker (note 34 above) 56 and McLoughlin (note 7 above) 14-20.

53. In *Forward Movements* (see note 50 above) 230-232 Pierson mentions the rise of city evangelism.

54. At least two factors made city evangelism difficult: (1) rural ministers did not easily adapt to the challenges of the city, (2) the majority of existing city churches had been long established, their membership largely of the educated upper classes, so neither their structure nor perspective were geared to evangelism. Immigrants and the poorer classes did not assimilate well into the existing city churches.

55. Marsden (see note 15 above) 46. Much has been written on the rise of premillennialism in North America. Timothy P. Weber's *Living in the Shadow of the Second Coming: American Premillennialism 1875-1982* (Grand Rapids, MI: Zondervan, 1983) offers a helpful overview. It should be noted that premillennialism was not a unified homogenous movement nor was it identified solely with dispensationalism, the movement which dominated the premillennial camp from 1900 onward.

56. Quoted by McLoughlin (see note 7 above) 24

57. Dayton, *Theological Roots* (see note 6 above) 145, and Pierson (see note 50 above) 416.

58. See Wacker (note 34 above) 57 and Smith, *Revivalism* (see note 29 above) 227-329. It is interesting to observe in this context that throughout church history there has always appeared to be a direct correlation between a heightened awareness of the work of the Spirit and a heightened yearning for the return of Christ.

59. Although popularized by the Pentecostal movement, this view of church history was common near the turn of the century. See Bruner, *A Theology of the Holy Spirit,* (note 5 above) 28.

60. Although Peter in Acts 2 quotes only Joel 2:28-32, the word picture reaches back into the preceding verses, particularly Joel 2:23, where the King James Version reads "the former rain, and the latter rain."

61. See Dayton, *Theological Roots* (note 6 above) 27; Bruner (note 5 above) 28-29; Pierson (note 50 above) 401; Simpson, "What is Meant by the Latter Rain?" *The Christian and Missionary Alliance Weekly* (19 Oct 1907) 323-324."

62. Waldvogel-Blumhoefer (see note 14 above) 2

63. McLoughlin (see note 7 above) 19-20 postulates that philosophical Romanticism contributed to the proliferation of interest in Christ. McLoughlin cites the sentimental hymns and sermons composed in this era as support for his thesis. Charles Finney and Asa Mahan devoted a great deal of their theological discussions to the work of Christ in sanctification.

64. McLoughlin (see note 7 above) 25. Waldvogel-Blumhoefer (see note 14 above) 26 specifically points to Simpson as the one who best developed this aspect of the Holy Spirit's ministry.

65. Waldvogel (see note 14 above) 6

66. Dayton, *Theological Roots* (see note 6 above) 92

67. "Pentecost—What Is It?" *Guide to Holiness* (Jan 1897) 37. Quoted in Dayton, *Theological Roots* (see note 6 above) 119.

68. Synan (see note 8 above) 67

69. Synan (see note 8 above) 48

70. Synan (see note 8 above) 48. Also see Dayton, *Theological Roots* (see note 6 above) 92-93.

71. Dayton, *Theological Roots* (see note 6 above) 24

72. The leading proponent of this view was B. B Warfield. Speaking of the miraculous, he wrote: ". . . it belonged therefore exclusively to the Apostolic age. . . . These gifts . . . were part of the credentials of the apostles as the authoritative agents of God in founding the church. Their function thus confined them distinctly to the Apostolic Church, and they necessarily passed away with it" [*Counterfeit Miracles* (New York: Charles Scribner's Sons, 1918) 5-6]. Those who opposed Warfield's position did not deny the special miraculous abilities of the Apostles but vehemently denied that God had ceased to authenticate the gospel by miracles.

73. W.E. Sangster has studied the common themes which emerge from the exegesis of these passages in his book *The Path to Perfection* (New York: Abingdon-Cokesbury, 1943) 37-52.

74. Synan (see note 8 above) 49

75. Synan (see note 8 above) 49. Later in the chapter we will note that Joel 2 became the key text of the "Latter Rain" movement.

76. Dayton, *Theological Roots* (see note 6 above) 23

77. Dayton, *Theological Roots* (see note 6 above) 24

78. Dayton, *Theological Roots* (see note 6 above) 23

79. Perhaps the best example of this is Martin Wells Knapp's *Out of Egypt into Canaan: Or, Lessons in Spiritual Geography* (Boston: McDonald and Gill, 1889). A. B. Simpson wrote a book entitled *The Land of Promise: or, Our Full Inheritance in Christ* (New York, Christian Alliance Publishing Co., 1888). The intent of this book was to show the importance of a believer's entering fully into all the aspects provided in his salvation.

80. Dayton is seemingly the only person who has done extensive work on the transition in the meaning of this term prior to 1900 and the Pentecostal movement. See his aforementioned works (note 6 above). Wheelock (note 23 above) and Waldvogel-Blumhoefer (note 22 above) make occasional references to this term in their dissertations but they do not track its development.

81. Synan (see note 8 above) 48

82. Dayton, "Doctrine of the Baptism" (see note 6 above) 119

83. Dayton, "Doctrine of the Baptism" (see note 6 above) 119

84. Dayton, "Doctrine of the Baptism" (see note 6 above) 120-122

85. Dayton, "Doctrine of the Baptism" (see note 6 above) 120-122. Ministers

such as D. L. Moody, R. A. Torrey and A. J. Gordon are included in this section.

86. B. H. Irwin and R. C. Horner were two of the prominent proponents of this "third blessing" teaching [Dayton, *Theological Roots* (see note 6 above) 97-100].

87. John the Baptist's expression, "He will baptize you with the Holy Spirit and with fire" (Luke 3:16) is a key verse in the formulation of this view.

Chapter 2

A Biography of Albert B. Simpson

In the previous chapter we looked at some of the trends occurring in 19th century America. Turning our focus to Albert B. Simpson, we now want to discover what influences shaped his life and thought. In particular we want to examine his spiritual journey, especially those events which helped him formulate his theological convictions concerning the Holy Spirit.

Albert Benjamin Simpson was born December 15, 1843, in the town of Bayview, Prince Edward Island. In 1847 his family moved to Chatham, Ontario, and it was there that Simpson spent his formative years. His parents were staunch Presbyterian Calvinists who actively sought to promote a devout environment in their home.[1] Simpson's father followed Puritan practices for family nurture, emphasizing family prayer, worship and memorization of the Westminster Shorter Catechism. Moreover, his father would read to his children from Puritan classics such as Boston's *Fourfold State* and Richard Baxter's *Saints' Everlasting Rest.* Simpson comments:

> Looking back on these early influences, . . . the religious knowledge, which was crammed into my mind even without my understanding it, furnishing me with forms of doctrine and statements of truth which afterwards became illuminated by the Holy Spirit and realized in my own experience, and thus became ultimately the precious vessels for holding the treasures of divine knowledge.[2]

Simpson's Conversion Experience

Despite this appreciation for his early religious training, Simpson expressed regret that it also imparted to him a caricature of God as one who was very severe and distant. Furthermore, like many who grew up in such a Calvinist tradition, Simpson was very troubled over the assurance of salvation. He recounted how in his early teens he was plagued continually by fears that he was not among the elect.[3] After a period of intense pleading that God would save him, Simpson one day happened on Walter Marshall's *Gospel Mystery of Sanctification.*[4] Simpson wrote of the experience:

> As I turned the leaves, my eyes fell upon a sentence which opened for me the gates of life eternal. It is this in substance: "The first great work you will ever perform is to believe on the Lord Jesus Christ." . . . To my poor bewildered soul this was like the light from heaven that fell upon Saul of Tarsus.[5]

For the first time, Simpson apprehended God's promise of forgiveness and salvation for those who trust in Christ's finished work. Then and there he followed the prescription of the book. Although emotional assurance was only gradual in coming, Simpson asserted that he now knew his salvation was sure.

Simpson Becomes a Presbyterian Minister

It is noteworthy to observe the stages of Simpson's salvation experience, for they formed a pattern which was to mark later spiritual crises in his life. First there was a period of seeking, brought about by the awareness of his spiritual need. Second, he became cognizant of divine provision. Finally, he saw the need to specifically appropriate the divine provision.

Sensing the call of God to enter the ministry, Simpson found his spiritual convictions intensifying. At the conclusion of high school he taught for a year to earn money for university. During this time he read Philip Doddridge's *The Rise and Progress of Religion in the Soul.*[6] In response to the book's call to its readers to enter into a covenant of dedication to God, Simpson drew up a document pledging himself to God and to a life of service in vocational ministry. Simpson gained from this book a further conviction that believers need to actively and decisively respond to divine invitations.

Having passed the rigorous entrance process of the Presbyterian Synod, he was admitted in 1861 to Knox College, Toronto, with advanced standing, needing only one year of studies prior to entering the three year theological training program.[7] While at the university Simpson showed considerable academic aptitude, winning several prizes and scholarships.[8] Moreover, he gained prominence as a gifted preacher.[9] In 1865, at age 21, he completed his studies and passed the comprehensive examinations of the Presbytery.[10]

That September Simpson accepted a call to Knox Presbyterian Church in Hamilton, Ontario. At the time Knox Presbyterian was a very prominent church with a seating capacity of 1,200.[11] Simpson's youth did not prevent the congregation from quickly respecting their devout new minister. Knox Session minutes indicate that during his nine year ministry significant advances occurred in the church, including the addition of 750 new members.[12]

The Louisville Years

The period from 1874 to 1881 involved several crucial developments in Simpson's life, both professionally and personally. In 1874 he was called to pastor a Presbyterian church in Louisville, Kentucky. This transition catapulted Simpson into a difficult situation. He described his new parish as a "wealthy, fashionable church without spiritual life."[13] Moreover, there in the heartland of the American Civil War, the bitterness of the past conflict continued to cause division both within Simpson's church and among the other churches in Louisville.[14]

Concurrent with these circumstances was Simpson's growing frustration with his own spiritual life. Besides a desire for greater holiness, Simpson sensed a lack of power in his life and ministry.[15] Later, in the third person style he often used to describe his own spiritual journey, he recounted this experience of despondency:

> He struggled long and vainly with his own intense nature, his strong self-will, his peculiar temptations, and his spiritual life had been constant humiliation. He had talked to his people about the deeper things of the Spirit but there was a hollow ring, and his heart was breaking to know the Lord Jesus as a living bright reality.[16]

The combination of these yearnings and circumstances culminated in 1874 in a spiritual crisis.[17] Following a period of intense searching,[18] Simpson read W. E. Boardman's book, *The Higher Christian Life,*[19] and came to the realization that what he was seeking could not be accomplished by self-effort. It would come only through divine provision.[20] In his own words he shares the impact of that realization:

> As he pored over that little volume, he saw a new light. The Lord Jesus revealed Himself as a living and all-sufficient presence, and he learned for the first time that Christ had not saved us from future peril and left us to fight the battle of life as best we could, but He who had justified us was waiting to sanctify us, to enter into our spirit and substitute His strength, His holiness, His joy, His love, His faith, His power, for all our worthlessness, helplessness, and nothingness, and make it an actual and living fact, "I live, yet not I, but Christ liveth in me." It was indeed a new revelation. Throwing himself at the feet of that glorious Master, he claimed the mighty promise, "I will dwell in you and walk in you." Across the threshold of his spirit there passed a Being as real as the Christ who came to John on Patmos, and from that moment a new secret has been the charm, and glory, and strength of his life and testimony.[21]

Thus, Simpson dedicated himself to God and appropriated what he perceived as God's provision. The familiar pattern noted earlier repeats itself here: awareness of need, apprehension of God's provision and the appropriation of it.

Simpson's discovery led to a renewed study of the Scriptures. He came to the conviction that many "refuse the workings of the Holy Spirit," whether out of ignorance, faulty theology or disobedience.[22] As a result they fail to enter into God's full provision for their salvation. Simpson viewed the Holy Spirit as the divine agent of appropriating Christ's sanctifying righteousness, declaring, "The baptism of the Holy Spirit is simultaneous with our union with the Lord Jesus; the Spirit does not act apart from Christ, but it is His to take the things of Christ and show them to us."[23] Although Simpson's view of the baptism of the Holy Spirit will be the subject of the next chapter, it should be noted that he used the term here in the context of experiencing "sanctification" and the indwelling of Christ.[24] Moreover, his comment suggests that the benefits of union with Christ do not become effectual until appropriated.

Shortly after this experience, Simpson urged his fellow ministers in Louisville to reconcile their differences and hold a joint evangelistic crusade.[25] The year was 1875, and Major D. W. Whittle and P. P. Bliss were the invited evangelists.[26] In the course of the crusade 5,000 people were converted. Equally important, revival came to the churches of Louisville.

Simpson himself was much impacted by the campaign. Not only was he surprised by the effectiveness of mass evangelism, but he was impressed with the spiritual power of Whittle's preaching. Although Simpson nowhere explicitly describes the influence Whittle had on him personally, he seems to have been made newly aware that effective ministry can only be through the power of the Holy Spirit.[27] Simpson's remaining years in Louisville were devoted to crusade evangelism, an activity quite different from his ministry in Hamilton.

Simpson Moves to New York City

In 1879 Simpson was offered a pastorate in New York City. That large metropolis of course afforded great opportunities for mass evangelism.[28] Moreover, Simpson had a growing commitment to world evangelization, and New York would be an excellent base. He accepted the call to 13th Street Presbyterian Church on condition that the members would agree to reach out to the unchurched.[29]

Following a year of intense ministry in New York, Simpson had a recurrence of a heart problem that had plagued him throughout his life. On health leave from his ministry, Simpson happened to hear Dr. Charles Cullis speak on divine healing.[30] He was particularly impressed by testimonies some of the audience gave to physical healings they had experienced. After the meeting, Simpson began to examine the Scriptures to see if there was validity to divine healing. He became convinced that "this was part of Christ's glorious Gospel for a sinful and suffering world."[31] He claimed God's provision and dedicated himself to promulgating this aspect of the gospel message.[32] Later, Simpson experienced the healing of his heart disease. He remained free of any symptoms until his death in 1919.

During 1881 Simpson also acquired what he viewed as a fuller and deeper understanding of the Holy Spirit's work. He came to recognize a correlation between water baptism and baptism with the Spirit. Because this insight is so fundamental to our understanding of Simpson's religious experience and formation of doctrine, we include his lengthy commentary here:

> It was in the autumn of 1881, while cherishing no thought of any change in his theological views, but very earnestly looking out upon the fields, and asking, "Lord, what wilt Thou have me to do?" He was giving a course of lectures to his congregation in the city of New York, and he had come to that passage describing the crossing of the Red Sea by the Israelites under Moses. . . . Along with this there was suddenly flashed into his mind that striking passage in I Cor. x. 2: "And they were all baptized unto Moses in the cloud and in the sea," and like a vision there arose before him the picture of Israel's host passing through the flood while at the same time

the cloud representing the Holy Spirit fell upon them and covered them with its heavenly baptism. Thus there was a double baptism. They were baptized in the flood; they were baptized in the cloud. . . .

Then simultaneously arose another vision that seemed to unfold as a panorama. It was that of Christ entering the Valley of Jordan in baptism, and as He passed through that sacred rite and came forth like Israel crossing the Sea, in like manner the Spirit descended upon Him and abode, and He received the double baptism of the water and the Spirit at the same moment. . . .

Then a third vision seemed to arise. It was the multitude at Pentecost, heart-stricken and convicted by the power of God, and crying out under Peter's sermon, "Men and brethren, what must we do?" And then came the answer of our text: "Repent and be baptized, every one of you, in the name of Jesus Christ for the remission of sins, and ye shall receive the gift of the Holy Ghost." There again the water and the Spirit were inseparably linked. The outward baptism was but a stepping stone to the higher baptism of the Holy Ghost and they were all expected to enter into both, as though neither was complete without the other. . . . And indeed, there was but one baptism, for the water and the Spirit were each but part of a greater whole, and both were linked in the divine appointment, the one as the sign, and the other as the divine reality of a great crisis act by which we passed through death to life and become united through the Holy Ghost henceforth to the living God as the source and power of our new and heavenly life.[33]

Several features of this citation are noteworthy. First, Simpson acquired these convictions apparently independently of other influences. Second, Simpson came to see that there was a logical interrelationship between the two baptisms. Water baptism was a sign of complete dedication to God, symbolizing identification with Christ in His crucifixion and resurrection. Baptism with the Spirit was the divine reality imparted by God to provide the resources for holy living.[34] This "great crisis act" of complete dedication was normative and intended for all. Third, it was only through this complete dedication that the divine resources were actualized in the believer's life.

Like many in his theological tradition, Simpson had viewed water baptism primarily as initiation into the church or a covenantal step of parents dedicating their children.[35] Hence, water baptism's importance was not always understood by the person being baptized. For this reason this crisis of the baptism of the Holy Spirit sometimes occurred at a point in life subsequent to water baptism. This experience involved a distinct dedication to God and the baptism with the Spirit.

Simpson Launches Out

Something else happened in 1881. Simpson decided to leave the Presbyterian ministry. He writes this about his decision:

> After an experience of two years in this city church pastorate, marked by unbroken harmony between himself and his church, and much spiritual blessing every way, he became convinced of the impossibility of reaching the masses by the old conventional church methods, and determined, after much prayerful consideration, to retire from his pastorate and begin an evangelistic campaign along nondenominational lines and by simple methods of church work and life, on the principle of a free church without pew rents, where all classes and denominations would be equally welcome.[36]

In November, 1881, Simpson resigned from his church, and shortly thereafter he began evangelistic meetings among the urban poor.[37] Over the ensuing years large numbers of people were converted, an independent church body organized, a permanent facility established. The Gospel Tabernacle became a base for evangelistic meetings, the promotion of world missions and popular conferences on the Christian life. The church as well supervised an orphanage, several rescue missions and a home for unwed mothers.[38]

In 1884 Simpson also began to hold conferences in various parts of the United States and Canada. His objectives were several:

- to gather Christians of common faith and spirit for fellowship
- to study the Word of God
- to promote a deeper spiritual life among Christians
- to seek a better understanding of the Scriptures respecting our physical life in Christ
- to wait upon the Lord for a special baptism of the Holy Spirit for life and service
- to encourage each other's hearts in the prospect of the glorious appearing of the Lord
- to promote the work of evangelization at home and missions abroad.[39]

Simpson encapsulated the message of this movement in his expression "The Fourfold Gospel": Christ Our Savior, Christ Our Sanctifier, Christ Our Healer and Christ Our Coming King. It was a slogan that captured the convictions Simpson had himself acquired. It was also expressive of the larger theological trends which were sweeping across the land in his day.[40]

In 1887 Simpson began two complementary organizations that would merge a decade later to become The Christian and Missionary Alliance. The Christian Alliance was a fellowship of those who shared Simpson's doctrinal views. The Evangelical Missionary Alliance was comprised of those who, like Simpson, desired the world's evangelization. Alliance "branches" sprang up throughout the United States and eastern Canada. These in turn produced and supported Alliance missionaries who went to many parts of the world. To provide rudimentary training for these eager volunteers, Simpson had established in 1883 the Missionary Training Institute, a school that continues today as Nyack (New York) College.[41]

At the beginning Simpson did not intend to form a new church denomination, but it became apparent in his later years that the need to establish overseas churches for the converts of his missionary efforts called for an ecclesiastical structure at home.[42] Simpson continued to give active leadership in the C&MA until the year before his death in 1919.

Simpson's Place in His Era

Prior to concluding this survey of Simpson's life and work, we need to make some mention of his place within the various theological streams of his era. There have been frequent attempts to categorize Simpson and the C&MA. Often the assertion is made that Simpson held to a Keswick-type view of sanctification.[43] More precisely, Simpson should be seen as having been influenced by Boardman's *The Higher Christian Life*, a book which also impacted the Keswick movement. Other than in an 1885 invitation to speak at one of their conferences, Simpson had little formal contact with the British Keswick movement.[44] It is true that prominent Keswick leaders such as F. B. Meyer and Charles Inwood spoke in Simpson's conventions.[45] But it was Simpson's policy to invite speakers from a wide spectrum of theological persuasion.

Edith Waldvogel-Blumhoefer offers perhaps the most accurate categorization of Simpson. She asserts that he belonged to a group within the Reformed tradition who called for the need of an "overcoming" Christian life and a reaffirmation of the importance of both the person and the ministry of the Holy Spirit.[46] People such as A. J. Gordon, R. A. Torrey and D. L. Moody belonged to this group—men who also were frequently invited to speak at Simpson's conventions.[47] Articles on the Holy Spirit by both Torrey and Gordon appeared in Simpson's periodicals.[48] Thus, this group of contemporaries provides us with helpful reference points for comparing and contrasting Simpson's views on the Spirit with theirs. We shall look at some of these men in later chapters.

In this chapter we have discovered that in the course of Simpson's personal life and ministry he found it necessary to grapple with many of the issues impacting North American Protestantism in his day—issues we have introduced in chapter 1. In those encounters, Simpson frequently found himself at issue with his theological heritage. Once convinced of biblical truth, he unhesitatingly embraced it, even if it meant moving away from the comfort of tradition. These shifts were not made easily or quickly. This was especially so in regard to the person and work of the Holy Spirit. But as he walked step by step with God in obedience to His leadership, Simpson became increasingly certain that a gracious God had made every provision for a victorious Christian life.

In the chapters that follow, we shall try to see, through the eyes of this extraordinarily gifted man, how a Christian may enter into these divine provisions.

End Notes

1. Referring to his father, Simpson wrote: "My father was a good Presbyterian elder of the old school, and believed in the Shorter Catechism, the doctrine of foreordination, and all the conventional principles of a well ordered Puritan household. He was himself a devout Christian and most regular in all his religious habits." [Cited in A. E. Thompson, *The Life of A. B. Simpson* (New York: Christian Alliance Pub. Co., 1920) 8.] A. E. Thompson was a Simpson contemporary and was commissioned by the C&MA to produce Simpson's official biography. Thompson's book is helpful in that it contains information on Simpson which cannot be obtained elsewhere. Moreover, it is fairly objective, free of hagiography.

2. Thompson (see note 1 above) 10-11

3. Simpson wrote, "My whole religious training had left me without any conception of the sweet and simple Gospel of Jesus Christ. The God I knew was a being of great severity, and my theology provided in some mysterious way for a wonderful change called the new birth or regeneration, which only God could give to the soul. How I longed and waited for that change to come, but it had not yet arrived. . . . How I cried in utter despair for God to spare me just long enough to be saved" [Thompson (see note 1 above) 15-16].

4. Thompson (see note 1 above) 16-17. Very little has been written either on

Walter Marshall's book or its author. Marshall was an English Puritan who lived from 1628 to 1680. William Cowper commented of Marshall, "I think Marshall one of the best writers and one of the most spiritual expositors of Scripture I have ever read." Gerald E. McGraw, "The Doctrine of Sanctification in the Published Writings of Albert Benjamin Simpson" (diss., New York U, 1986) 134-138, explores some contents of this book and their effect upon Simpson. Simpson quotes extensively from *The Gospel Mystery of Sanctification* in chapter 2 of his own book *The Cross of Christ* (New York: Christian Alliance Publishing Co., 1910), particularly the sections concerning sanctification and the nature of union with Christ.

5. Thompson (see note 1 above) 16-17. Simpson continued this quote from Marshall: "Until you do this, all your works, prayers, tears and good resolutions are vain. To believe on the Lord Jesus is just to believe that He saves you according to His word, that He receives and saves you here and now, for He has said—'Him that cometh to me I will in no wise cast out.' The moment you do this, you will pass into eternal life, you will be justified from all your sins, and receive a new heart and all the gracious operations of the Holy Spirit."

6. Doddridge (1702-1751) was an English Non-Conformist minister. The title of his book suggests its contents and flow. Doddridge explains how one may gain assurance of salvation and then develop increasing Christlikeness. A key feature of this book is a call to make a covenant of complete dedication to God as an apt response to the glories of salvation.

7. Thompson (see note 1 above) 31. During this era the usual process was to complete three years of university prior to embarking on a three-year theological program. Simpson was exempted from the first two years of university.

8. Thompson (see note 1 above) 33-34. Simpson humorously noted that one of the awards was for a defense of the practice of infant baptism and baptism by sprinkling. Later he wrote, "Through God's great goodness I won the prize, but in later years I had to take back all the arguments and doctrinal opinions which I so stoutly maintained in my youthful wisdom" (see page 37).

9. Thompson (see note 1 above) 34-35, 39

10. Thompson (see note 1 above) 42. Of the examination Thompson says: "This old-time presbytery subjected these college graduates to a searching examination in Biblical Hebrew and Greek, theology, Church History and Church Government, as well as personal religion. Moreover, Mr. Simpson's examination included a discourse on II Timothy 1:10, read before the presbytery,

and the following papers submitted for criticism: a Latin thesis, *an filius dei ab eterno sit genitis a Pater* [sic]; an excursus on Romans 7; a popular sermon on Romans 1:16, and a lecture on Matthew 4:1-11. After this procedure the candidates were licensed as ministers of the Presbyterian Church of Canada."

11. Thompson (see note 1 above) 43

12. Thompson (see note 1 above) 50. Simpson also instituted weekly prayer meetings in the various regions of the cities.

13. Simpson, "Prevailing Prayer," *The Alliance Weekly* (27 Mar 1915) 51

14. Thompson (see note 1 above) 54-55

15. Thompson (see note 1 above) 65

16. Simpson, "A Personal Testimony," *The Alliance Weekly* (2 Oct 1915) 11

17. There is much debate over the chronology of these spiritual crises in Simpson's life. McGraw (see note 4 above) attempts to establish a precise sequence by examining Simpson's sources along with previous interpretations rendered by A. E. Thompson, A. W. Tozer and S. J. Stoesz.

18. Simpson explored numerous unsatisfactory sources for help. The turning point was the realization of the sufficiency of Christ. Simpson writes of this journey in his own words in an oft reprinted article, "Himself" [*The Word, the Work and the World* (Jun 1885) 258]: "Having searched for a theory or something to hang on to, I prayed a long time to get sanctified, sometimes I thought I had it. On one occasion I felt something, and I held on with a desperate grip for fear I should lose it, and kept awake the whole night fearing it would go, and of course, it went with the next sensation and the next mood. Of course, I lost *it* because I did not hold on to *Him*. I had been taking a little water from the reservoir, when I might all the time have received from *Him* His fullness through the channels open. I went to meetings and heard people speak of joy. I thought I would have joy, but I did not keep it because I had not Himself as my joy. At last He said to me—O, so patiently, 'My child, just take Me, and let Me be in you the constant supply of all this Myself.' And when at last I got my eyes off my sanctification, and my experience of it, and just placed them on Christ in me, I found, instead of an experience, I had a Christ larger than the moment's need, the Christ that had all that I should ever need, who was given to me all at once, and for ever!"

19. Boardman's book was published at the height of the 1857-1858 revival. Though Boardman was familiar with Wesleyan and Oberlin teaching, he sought to express holiness in different terms. His book gained widespread

readership, particularly in Reformed circles, because of its avoidance of Methodist and Oberlin terminology [Melvin Easterday Dieter, *The Holiness Revival of the 19th Century* (Metuchen, NJ: The Scarecrow Press, 1980) 57].

20. Simpson, "Personal Testimony" (see note 16 above) 11. McGraw (see note 4 above) 144-149, 159-162 explores the impact of Boardman on Simpson's thought.

21. Simpson, "Personal Testimony" (see note 16 above) 11

22. Thompson (see note 1 above) 66

23. Thompson (see note 1 above) 67. Thompson does not cite the origin of this quote from Simpson.

24. Simpson's linking of sanctification, the indwelling of Christ, and the baptism of the Holy Spirit is seen in "Prevailing Prayer" (see note 13 above) 51. (The same article contains another account of his personal spiritual crisis while in Louisville along with details of the subsequent revival which occurred in that city.) Referring to his experience, Simpson wrote: "Just at that time God poured out His Spirit upon my own heart. It was then that I received for the first time the new light of the indwelling Christ and the baptism of the Holy Ghost, and it became a fire in my bones, and so possessed me that nights long I waited before God crying to Him for a great revival."

25. Simpson, "A Story of Providence," *Living Truths* (Mar 1907) 150. Simpson wrote, "The Baptism of the Holy Spirit . . . awakened in his heart an intense longing for the salvation of souls."

26. Thompson (see note 1 above) 54 and Simpson, "Prevailing Prayer" (see note 13 above) 51

27. McGraw (see note 4 above) 71-72 examines the impact of Whittle on Simpson. Having compared their teachings, McGraw asserts there are significant differences in their views of sanctification. However, Whittle's views on the empowering of the Spirit are akin to Simpson's. A. T. Pierson, a contemporary of Simpson, said that as a result of seeing Whittle's spiritual fervor, Simpson "claimed to be conscious of the Holy Spirit in his life and ministry" (quoted in McGraw 56).

28. Thompson (see note 1 above) 82

29. Simpson, "Story of Providence" (see note 25 above) 150. Although the elders agreed to this ministry goal, they were later hesitant to accept the practical implications such a program had for church life: for example, the entry of the poorer, uneducated classes into church membership.

30. Thompson (see note 1 above) 75

31. Thompson (see note 1 above) 75

32. Thompson (see note 1 above) 76. Thompson quotes the covenant Simpson made with God.

33. Simpson, "Baptism, and the Baptism of the Holy Spirit," *The Christian and Missionary Alliance Weekly* (17 May 1902) 286

34. Simpson also said, "The ordinance of baptism, while the initiatory rite of the Christian church, looks forward to entire sanctification, and reaches its full significance only in complete death with Jesus Christ to self and sin" ["Sanctification in Romans," *The Christian Alliance and Missionary Weekly* (30 Jun 1893) 406].

35. Simpson, "Baptism, and Baptism" (see note 33 above) 286

36. Simpson, "Story of Providence" (see note 25 above) 150

37. Of this transition, Simpson wrote elsewhere: "[He] resigned the pastorate of that church for the purpose of more effectively preaching the Gospel to the masses in this great city, who go to no church, and are not reached by the Gospel through ordinary channels. For nearly twenty years he had been a pastor in various Presbyterian churches, and his pastorates had been pleased and useful. His withdrawal did not therefore arise from any personal disappointment or alienation, but from a deep and solemn conviction that the religious needs of the great masses of the population demanded a work more simple, direct, and aggressive than had been or perhaps could be accomplished by usual methods. The population of the city had increased in the past ten years by nearly one half a million, and yet there had scarcely been added a single church to the Protestant denominations" ["The Spirit of the Lord is Upon Me," *The Word, the Work and the World* (Mar 1883) 45].

38. Thompson (see note 1 above) 92-102. For an insightful overview of Simpson's social concern, see John V. Dahms, "The Social Interest and Concern of A. B. Simpson," *The Birth of A Vision*, David F. Hartzfeld and Charles Nienkirchen, eds. (Beaverlodge, AB: Buena Book Services, 1986) 49-74.

39. Thompson (see note 1 above) 105-106

40. In Donald W. Dayton's *The Theological Roots of Pentecostalism* (Grand Rapids, MI: Zondervan, 1986), there is a helpful survey of theological trends. Dayton credits Simpson with coining the phrase "The Fourfold Gospel." Simpson describes his journey to premillennialism in "How I was Led to

believe in Premillennialism," *The Word, the Work and the World* (Nov 1885) 305. Once again Simpson had to turn away from his theological background. He notes there his reasons for rejecting postmillennialism.

41. Robert L. Niklaus, John S. Sawin and Samuel J. Stoesz, *All for Jesus: God at Work in The Christian and Missionary Alliance Over One Hundred Years* (Camp Hill, PA: Christian Publications, 1986) 103

42. See, for example, *All For Jesus* (note 41 above), which traces the transition of the C&MA from an interdenominational fraternity to a denomination.

43. William Menzies, "The Non-Wesleyan Origins of the Pentecostal Movement," *Aspects of Pentecostal-Charismatic Origins,* Vinson Synan, ed. (Plainfield, NJ: Logos International, 1975) 87-96

44. It should be noted that at this conference Simpson preached the sermon "Himself" (see note 18 above) as a corrective to what he perceived as imbalances in the Keswick message. George M. Marsden, *Fundamentalism and American Culture* (New York: Oxford University Press, 1980) 94-95 asserts that while "Keswick teachers, A. B. Simpson, the Salvation Army, and the Holiness camp meeting movement" were largely "allies" in the quest for sanctification, by 1900 their differences of opinion "were becoming noticeably sharp."

45. Thompson (see note 1 above) 110

46. Edith L. Waldvogel-Blumhoefer, "The Overcoming Life: A Study in the Reformed Evangelical Contribution to Pentecostalism" (diss. Harvard U, 1977) 1

47. Thompson (see note 1 above) 110. Thompson gives an extensive list of Simpson's contemporaries.

48. See R. A. Torrey in *Living Truths* (Sep 1904) 503-507 and A. J. Gordon, "The Holy Spirit," *The Word, the Work and the World* (Apr 1885) 241-246.

Chapter 3

The Baptism of the Holy Spirit in the Writings of A. B. Simpson, Part 1: Christ, *Our Sanctifier*

Thus far we have examined some of the history related to the rise of interest at the end of the 19th century in the doctrine of the Holy Spirit. We have also surveyed the spiritual journey of Albert B. Simpson, particularly those aspects of his biography that illuminate his concern over the work and ministry of the Holy Spirit. We are now at the point where we can explore in precise terms Simpson's theological formulations.

The purpose of this chapter is to lay a foundation for understanding Simpson's view of the baptism of the Holy Spirit. To do this we must identify several problems related to such an understanding of Simpson and propose a method to overcome them. Later we will investigate the issues in Simpson's teaching that directly relate to his views concerning the baptism of the Holy Spirit.

Any investigation into Simpson's thought must provide adequate methods for allowing his material to speak for itself. In other words, we must derive what Simpson intended to say and not read into his writings ideas which were not his. As in biblical exegesis, there is always a danger of misinterpreting the original intent of an author.

In addition to our concern for an adequate methodology, there are several factors which make the analysis of Simpson's material difficult. First, A. B. Simpson was a prolific writer. He used the written word as an inexpensive way to spread the teachings and activities of the C&MA movement.[1] Simpson published over 100 books, the majority of them compilations of sermons that had been stenographically recorded.[2] In addition he edited and wrote for a series of periodicals from 1880 until his death in 1919. Appendix 1 shows the magnitude of these endeavors. The large volume of primary sources presents a formidable task for anyone who examines specific areas of Simpson's thought.

Second, the genre of Simpson's writing presents difficulties for theological inquiry. Since Simpson's books in large part were sermons and not theological treatises, they are popularly slanted and tend to be theologically imprecise. His more cogent writing appears in his editorials and magazine articles.[3] However, these too are written on the popular level and were addressed to an audience that was acquainted with and sympathetic to his teachings.

Third, Simpson's use of terminology often was marked by the injection of meanings other than those held in popular usage. It is important, therefore, to define terms as Simpson used them. To import alien definitions of these terms may not only obscure Simpson's teaching but also lead to erroneous conclusions.[4]

The 1906 Conference on Alliance Doctrine

There is, however, a solution for these concerns. In the spring of 1906, C&MA leaders convened "Alliance workers throughout the country" for what was referred to as "The 1906 Conference for Prayer and Counsel Respecting Uniformity in the Testimony and Teaching of the Alliance." For this conference, A. B. Simpson and a select committee consisting of Henry Wilson, J. D. Williams, A. E. Funk and F. H. Senft produced a working paper that contained in outline form the general distinctives of the early C&MA movement. If Simpson, as C&MA president, did not himself write the paper, we may be sure it reflected his personal views. (Appendix 2 is the complete text of this document.) Section II of the paper succinctly spells out the Alliance position concerning the ministry of the Spirit, including the baptism of the Holy Spirit. It therefore provides us an interpretive key for unlocking Simpson's teaching on this important subject.

In using this 1906 document as an interpretive guide, we have a means of overcoming the difficulties already mentioned in the study of Simpson's work:

- By providing a framework for analysis, it helps us sift through the enormous volume of Simpson's material
- It offers an analytical framework that flows from *within* Simpson's material
- Because its phrases and the relationship between various facets of his teaching are formally laid out, it helps us understand the genre of Simpson's writing

Anticipating Some Possible Objections

Before we examine the contents of this document, we should anticipate several objections to its use as an interpretive guide to Simpson's thought. The major objection springs from the possibility that his viewpoint on the baptism of the Holy Spirit might have been different either before or after he and his colleagues produced this document.[5] It is possible, however, to demonstrate satisfactorily that Simpson's view was the same prior to 1906, and that it remained consistent until his death in 1919.

Perhaps the strongest evidence that Simpson did not change his views is found in a paper, "The Work of The Christian and Missionary Alliance," that he produced in 1893 and published that same year in *The Word, Work and World.* The article was republished in 1916 just prior to the annual C&MA summer convention as a reminder to Alliance people of the original goals and impetus of the movement.[6]

One section of the article outlines the "four great truths" that the C&MA movement affirmed. The segment on sanctification is essentially the same as Section II of Simpson's 1906 working paper, although the term "baptism of the Holy Spirit" is not explicitly used.[7] Simpson, however, had used the term earlier than 1893, for it appears in an article Simpson wrote in 1892.[8] Moreover, in *Walking in the Spirit,* a book containing sermons preached by Simpson in 1889, not only does he use the term "baptism of the Holy Spirit," but he outlines essentially the same areas as those that appear in the 1906 statement.[9] In an even earlier primary source—1885—Simpson without specifically using the term "baptism of the Holy Spirit," nevertheless describes the experience in virtually the same language as he uses in the 1906 document[10] (see section II.b. in Appendix 2).

In addition to the 1893 paper and article, republished in 1916, there is additional evidence that Simpson's teachings on the baptism of the Holy Spirit remained unchanged after 1906. In a 1918 *Alliance Weekly* article, Simpson articulates his views on the work of the Spirit, using statements very similar to those he had made earlier.[11] Simpson articles in the years 1907, 1909 and 1912 contain statements that are almost identical to those found in the 1906 document[12] (again, see section II.b. in Appendix 2).

The primary sources indicate, therefore, that Simpson's teaching on the baptism of the Holy Spirit and other areas related to sanctification were relatively constant in the years prior to and after the 1906 conference. Thus, the use of the conference's working paper, prepared by Simpson and his fellow C&MA leaders, constitutes a valid interpretive guide.[13]

A second objection to the reliance on the 1906 document might arise from the tremendous backlash against the 1907 "Pentecostal outbreak," which saw several groups in the so-called "Keswick-Holiness" stream alter their positions on the Holy Spirit. It could be argued that, after the Pentecostal controversy, no pre-1907 view of the baptism of the Spirit could really remain the same. But, as we have already noted, Simpson's material after 1906 contains no apparent departures from his earlier position on the baptism of the Holy Spirit. Indeed, Simpson wrote an article lamenting the retreat of some evangelicals from this and related doctrines.[14] Despite his opposition to the teaching that glossolalia were the primary initial evidence of the Holy Spirit's baptism,[15] his views on the Holy Spirit remained unaltered.[16]

Background to the 1906 Conference

Having anticipated—and replied to—some of the possible objections to our use of the document Simpson presented to the 1906 Conference for Prayer and Counsel Respecting Uniformity in the Testimony and Teaching of the Alliance, we now must explore its background. This will facilitate our use of the material as an interpretive guide to Simpson. It also will help us understand the somewhat ambiguous nature of certain of its assertions.

The first mention of the proposed conference is an editorial in the December 30, 1905, issue of the denomination's official publication, by then named *The Christian and Missionary Alliance*. It indicates there was a growing consensus among the Alliance constituents that a conference should be held "for the purpose of comparing views and endeavoring to secure perfect harmony of opinion and testimony in connection with the great truths committed to us."[17]

In the March 31, 1906 issue, Simpson again refers to the conference, pointing out that it was not an attempt "to establish for the Alliance a cast-iron creed."[18] He wrote:

> It is not possible in a movement like this, which represents all evangelical denominations, and which is fraternal rather than ecclesiastical, to formulate an exact statement of doctrinal belief on all questions which could satisfy all the parties of opinion among us. It will be the aim of the Conference, we presume, rather to define the lines on which we allow liberty of individual opinion, and the lines on which more exact uniformity is expected. . . .[19] The points essential to our initial testimony are Salvation, Sanctification, Divine Healing, and the Lord's Coming. And even on these great themes there is much variety of expression and opinion. It can hardly be expected that all the teachers on sanctification could agree about phases and phrases. But it surely can be an understanding that all antagonisms will be avoided and that those who hold extreme views either on the "eradication" or "suppressionist" side will avoid attacking those who differ. . . .[20]

It is evident, therefore, that there existed a diversity of views within the C&MA, particularly regarding how sanctification was defined. Simpson seems to stress the need for uniformity in distinctives while allowing for diversity in the expression of those distinctives.[21]

The paper prepared by Simpson and his committee was mailed in March, 1906, to Alliance workers.[22] It indicates that position papers were to be presented on each of the distinctives, with time allowed for discussion.

Unfortunately, no records or minutes have ever been recovered from the actual proceedings of the Conference.[23] It is known, however, that the Conference ratified the distinctives. Simpson writes in the June 2, 1906, issue of *The Christian and Missionary Alliance*:

> These words express the sense of privilege and opportunity which we have all felt profoundly during the conference of the Christian and Missionary Alliance, which is just closing as we go to press. The discussions of the past few days have brought out with great emphasis and vividness the glorious message which the Lord has given us to proclaim to our fellow men and live out in the world. . . . The spirit of the conference has been exceptional. Some of the questions before it were anticipated with some apprehension, especially those relating to the varied components of the doctrine of sanctification. But the great Teacher has guided us into the truth with singular unity of spirit and judgment. . . .[24]

There being no reported objections by the gathered Alliance workers to Simpson's paper, we can assume that it remains a valid interpretive tool for our study of Simpson's views on the baptism of the Holy Spirit.

The Key Statement: *Christ, Our Sanctifier*

We come, then, to an examination of the actual content of this

1906 document. Contained within it are presentations on each element of the Fourfold Gospel: Christ our Savior, Christ our Sanctifier, Christ our Healer and Christ our Coming King. The section pertaining to Christ our Sanctifier will of course be the focus of our investigation. Section II.2 reads:

II. Our Distinctive Testimony

2. Christ, our Sanctifier, assuming the following essential points:

a. a definite second blessing, *distinct in nature*, though not necessarily far removed in time, from the experience of conversion;

b. the baptism of the Holy Ghost as *a distinct experience*, not merely for power for service, but for personal holiness and victory over the world and sin;

c. the indwelling of Christ in the heart of the consecrated believer *as a distinct experience*;

d. sanctification by faith *as a distinct gift* of God's grace to every open and surrendered soul;

e. growth in grace and the deeper filling of the Holy Spirit *as distinct from* and the result of the definite experience of sanctification.

It is understood that all our Alliance officers and teachers are at liberty to present the truth of sanctification in such phases and phrases as his own convictions warrant, in general accordance with the above specifications, but with the understanding that such extreme views as are sometimes taught under the name of "eradication" or "suppression" shall not be presented in an aggressive or controversial spirit toward those who differ. (Emphases in the original document.)[25]

The nature of the paper as a whole was such that only general statements were made under each of the distinctives. In the case of this section, "Christ, Our Sanctifier," we have five points asserted with little elaboration. It should be possible to examine Simpson's most lucid material in their light in order to establish exactly what he meant by what he wrote. Through such an examination of Simpson's writings, we should be able to flesh out the intentions in these 1906 statements.

Although our study will focus primarily on Section II.2.b—Simpson's understanding of the baptism of the Holy Spirit—our first object is to explore what Simpson and his colleagues meant by the broader phrase, "Christ, our Sanctifier," that heads this part of the section. Specifically, how did Simpson view Christ's work in sanctifying a believer?

Christ Is Our Model

One of Simpson's most popular themes in preaching and writing was the significance of Christ's earthly life for believers. In fact, understanding Simpson's presentation of Jesus' life and ministry on earth is central to unlocking his understanding of the work of the Holy Spirit, including sanctification, in the Christian's life.

First, Simpson saw Christ Jesus as "our model." Simpson accented the importance of knowing God's purposes in His saving plan. Pointing to First Peter 1:2 and Romans 8:29, he wrote:

> It would throw a flood of light on the perplexing doctrine of election if we would remember, when thinking of this subject, that we are elected by God, not unto salvation unconditionally and absolutely, but unto holiness. We are predestinated to be conformed to the image of His Son.[26]

While not denying Christ's forensic work in salvation,[27] Simpson emphasized that the purpose of God in our salvation was to increasingly conform us to "the likeness of his Son" (Romans 8:29). Simpson therefore believed it was very important to understand the earthly life of Jesus. He wrote:

> In our zeal for the great doctrines connected with [Christ's] death, let us never depreciate the value of His life, and the importance of His perfect example, both as a revelation of God and as an ideal for humanity.[28]

To Simpson, Christ's earthly life was to be a believer's pattern or model for holiness. Part of the conforming to the likeness of God's Son was to emulate this pattern Jesus had provided us.

Simpson presented a number of aspects of how Jesus was the pattern Man. In an article entitled, "Christ: Our Model, Motive and Motive Power," Simpson asserts that Jesus provided believers with the definitive pattern for a relationship with God.[29] He supremely models the believer's purpose in life: "devotion to the will and the glory of God."[30] Christ is the embodiment of love "for the Father, . . . for His own, . . . for the sinful, . . . for His enemies."[31] Christ established a pattern of living by the standards of the Scriptures as the expression of God's will. Simpson asks,

> Whence did [Jesus] derive the strength for His perfect example? Was it from some source beyond our reach? Was it through His own divine nature? Or was it through sources which are as available for us as they were for Him? [The last] would seem so. Listen to His own confession: "The Son can do nothing of himself, but what he seeth the Father doing. . . . I can of Mine own self do nothing, as I hear I judge. . . . As the living Father hath sent Me, and I live by the Father, so he that eateth Me, even he shall live by Me" [John 5:19, 30; 6:57]. This is remarkable language. And it makes it certain that our Lord derived His daily strength from communion with God, from a life of faith and prayer, from constantly receiving the Holy

Spirit and the gracious help of His Father, just as we must.[32]

In Simpson's view, Christ is the believer's model of dependence on God.

Christ also illustrated the ministry of the Holy Spirit in the life of the believer. It is in these two areas that Simpson believed the majority of Christians had a deficient Christology. He believed that when people thought of Christ they tended to dismiss His life because they assumed He had

> . . . some special and individual advantage over us through His divine nature, perhaps to say, "Christ could do that because He was the Son of God, but I cannot be expected to do such things."[33]

Simpson certainly did not deny that Jesus was "truly God in His divine nature, 'very God of very God.' "[34] However, he asserted that these powers were set aside to provide the believer with an example of dependence on God and to show forth the ministry of the Holy Spirit.[35] The same Holy Spirit that indwelt Jesus has been given to believers so that they may share in the "enduement of power from God," even as Christ did.[36]

The Holy Spirit's Relationship to Christ

Second, Simpson held that it was imperative to understand the Holy Spirit's ministry in Jesus' life. He asserted:

> This is a subject that is worthy of the closest study, for it teaches us much practical truth not only in connection with the Master, but also with our own spiritual life. For if [Jesus] was our Forerunner, and if it be true that "as he is so are we also in this world" [1 John 4:17], then the definite steps of our Lord's experience should be repeated and fulfilled in the lives of His followers.[37]

Simpson saw Christ's life as a model with respect to the ministry of the Holy Spirit. Since believers are to be conformed to the image of Christ—a process which involves following the example of Christ's life—Christ's experience with the Holy Spirit is normative and to be reproduced in His followers. In Simpson's writings he frequently alludes to "the definite steps of our Lord's experience."

The baptism of Jesus at the Jordan River constitutes, in Simpson's view, the greatest event among these "definite steps." Accordingly, the exploration of this event holds a prominent place in Simpson's writings.[38] His comments on Jesus' baptism show a marked consistency in explicating its significance. The first feature he pointed to was the significance of water baptism at the hands of John the Baptist. Referring to the meaning of Christ's action he wrote:

> At thirty years of age [Jesus] consecrated Himself to His ministry of life and suffering and service, and went down into the waters of the Jordan, in the token of His self-renunciation and His assumption of death.[39]

Simpson viewed Jesus' water baptism as both expressing His dedication to the will of the Father and a symbolic act, prefiguring His crucifixion and resurrection. The parallel Simpson saw in the experience of believers is the decisive dedication that needs to be made at some point in their lives. This matter will be elaborated on in chapter five.[40]

Simpson explored the significance of the coming of the Holy Spirit upon Christ. The following quotation typifies Simpson's presentation of what occurred at this baptism:

> The baptism of Jesus Christ with the Holy Ghost marks an epoch in His earthly life. From this moment all His public ministry began and all His work was accomplished in dependence upon the Holy Ghost.[41]

> The Holy Ghost as a Person actually removed from the heavens and came down to earth, and henceforth resided as

a distinct Person in union with the Son of Man. From this time forward there were two Persons united in the life and ministry of Jesus Christ; all He said and did was in the power of the Spirit.[42]

The first of the above two quotes emphasizes in addition that, for Simpson, the Holy Spirit was the means by which Christ carried out His ministry. The second quote adds the nuance that the Holy Spirit now *indwelt* Christ—a relationship which was substantially different from that prior to His baptism. The Holy Spirit was now in union with Christ, though He remained an entity distinct from Christ.

Simpson explained the difference in this new relationship with the Spirit by contrasting it with Christ's previous state. Simpson acknowledged that "there is no doubt that in some sense the Lord Jesus had the Presence of the Holy Spirit" with him at His birth as well as in His early years.[43] Simpson particularly stressed the fact that the Holy Spirit was the agent of the divine conception of Christ: "Christ therefore was born in His divine and human Person through the Holy Ghost."[44] Moreover, Simpson mentioned that the Holy Spirit would certainly be present in Christ's developing years. However, he asserted:

> There came a day when in some new and . . . higher sense the Holy Spirit, like a dove, descended and abode upon [Jesus]. From that time, there were two personalities connected with the life and work of our Lord.[45]

Hence Simpson saw Christ's experience of the baptism of the Holy Spirit as effecting a profound change in Christ's relationship with the Holy Spirit.

Simpson drew two parallels between Christ's experience and that of believers. The first pertains to the ministry of the Spirit in a believer's life prior to being baptized by the Spirit. Since Christ was born through the agency of the Holy Spirit, Simpson said this parallels the regenerating work of the Holy Spirit in the believer at the time of conversion. He notes:

> Just as Jesus was born of the Spirit, so we, the disciples of Jesus, must also be born of the Holy Ghost; for "except a man be born from above he cannot enter the kingdom of God" [John 3:3].[46]

> From the very bosom of the Holy Ghost, as from a heavenly mother, has our new spirit been born—just as literally as Jesus Christ Himself was born of the eternal Spirit in the bosom of Mary.[47]

The manner in which Simpson uses this analogy suggests that he is aware of the tremendous difference which exists between the incarnation of the Son of God and the spiritual regeneration of a Christian.[48] The point of Simpson's comparison was the role of the Holy Spirit in the "birth" of each.

Simpson's second parallel between Christ's experience and that of believers flows also from Christ's baptism with the Spirit. Simpson points out that this experience brings both the power of God and the indwelling personal presence of the Holy Spirit. Speaking of the former dimension, Simpson wrote:

> If our Lord did not venture to begin His public ministry until He had been baptized with power from on high, and if He attributed all His work to the power and anointing of the Holy Ghost, what folly and presumption it must be for us to try to serve [God] by our own strength, resources, gifts and wisdom.[49]

Since Jesus did not begin His public ministry until after His experience at the Jordan, Simpson held that believers, too, should follow this pattern.

The other feature of Jesus' baptism by John that Simpson found significant was the subsequent personal indwelling of the Spirit in His life. The descent of the dove-like Spirit marked the time when the Spirit came to actually indwell Christ.[50]

Simpson considered the personal reception of the Spirit to be a cardinal part of the believer's experience also. He commented:

> Is it applying the parallel too rigidly to say that just as [Jesus] was born of the Spirit and yet afterwards was baptized of the Spirit in the sense of a direct personal union and indwelling of the Holy Ghost, so likewise His people should not only experience a new birth through the grace and power of the Holy Ghost, but should yield themselves, as [Jesus] did in His baptism, for the indwelling and abiding of the Comforter in the very same sense to which the Spirit came to Him.[51]

Elsewhere, Simpson referred to this parallel experience in the believer's life when he wrote:

> So there comes a time when the believer joins his hand with the Holy Ghost, and there is added to his new heart and his Christian experience the mighty, stupendous fact of God Himself and the personal indwelling of the Holy Ghost.[52]

> There comes a time when a new personality is added to ours and we go forth to life's conflicts and duties no longer alone, but in union with Him who has come to be our very life and all-sufficiency.[53]

Thus Simpson shows the union of the Holy Spirit with the believer and His subsequent indwelling presence in the believer's life to be both specific and normative.

Summary

Recapitulating our discussions thus far, Simpson saw Christ's earthly life, particularly with respect to the ministry of the Holy

Spirit, as a normative pattern for the Christian. The baptism of the Holy Spirit, beginning His personal union with the believer, brings power to the Christian's life and ministry. And this experience *follows* regeneration by the Spirit.

End Notes

1. A. E. Thompson, *The Life of A. B. Simpson* (New York: Christian Alliance Publishing Co., 1920). Thompson makes this statement concerning Simpson's writing: "In the ministry of the printed page, A. B. Simpson's plan was similar to John Wesley's, namely, 'Cheaper, shorter, plainer books' " (page 270).

2. John S. Sawin, "The Fourfold Gospel," *The Birth of A Vision: Essays on the Ministry and Thought of Albert B. Simpson,* David F. Hartzfeld and Charles Nienkirchen, eds. (Beaverlodge, AB: Buena Book Services, 1986) 279. Simpson freely admits that the majority of his writings were not always thoroughly edited for written communication and "begs [readers] to remember that these chapters are the substance of his weekly pulpit ministrations amid the pressure of a life of almost overwhelming work and care" [*The Holy Spirit or Power From on High,* vol. II (New York: Christian Alliance Publishing Co., 1896) 3].

3. Sawin, "Fourfold Gospel" (see note 2 above) 279

4. An inherent danger in the study of Simpson is the tendency of some writers to simply lump Simpson into the "Holiness- Keswick- Reformed-Deeper Life" theological bracket and thus have preconceived ideas on what Simpson meant by such terms as "sanctification" or "second blessing." An accurate analysis of his own writing spares us from such an inaccurate conclusion. Simpson wrote an article, "Phases and Phrases of the Deeper Life" [*Living Truths* (Oct 1902)] in which he attempts to evaluate the popular use of terms in "Deeper Life" teaching. He cites terms that he uses differently and proceeds to give them his own definitions.

5. Indeed, there is indication that this is the case for Simpson's view of healing, as suggested in the thesis of Ray W. Schenk ["A Study in the New Testament Basis for the Teaching of Dr. Albert B. Simpson on Divine Healing (Master's thesis, Wheaton Col, 1968)].

6. Simpson, "The Work of the Christian and Missionary Alliance," *The Alliance Weekly* (13 May 1916) 107. This article was originally published in 1893.

7. "... the sanctification and deliverance from self and sin of all who thoroughly yield themselves to God, through the indwelling of the Holy Spirit and the Lord Jesus Christ as their all-sufficient life. At the same time we guard this precious truth from all fanaticism. We repudiate every idea of self-perfection, personal infallibility, or such a state of self-sufficiency and sinlessness as would make us independent for an instant of the constant keeping of the Holy Spirit. It is not a self-sustaining, self-sufficient, or self-dependent state, but an absolute dependence every moment upon the Lord Jesus Christ. Self is accounted nothing, and Christ is all in all. The Christian life that it recognizes and emphasizes is not a self-life, but a Christ-life, ever abiding in Him, and utterly dependent on Him" [Simpson, "Work of C&MA" (see note 6 above) 107].

8. Simpson, "The Baptism with the Spirit," *The Christian Alliance and Missionary Weekly* (30 Sep 1892) 210

9. Simpson, *Walking in the Spirit* (New York: Christian Alliance Publishing Co., 1889) 9-10. Speaking of Christ's baptism in the Jordan, Simpson writes, "And so there is in the believer's life a similar experience, when the soul truly converted to God yields itself to His control and becomes the temple of the Almighty Spirit, who henceforth dwells in it, and walks in it, giving it not only a new nature received in regeneration, but Himself, a Divine Guest, a Presence, to dwell in that nature as its controlling Guide and almighty Strength" (page 10). In another section he mentions the power that works in and through a believer as a result of the baptism of the Holy Spirit (see page 104).

10. Simpson, "The Holy Spirit," *The Word, the Work and the World* (Apr 1885) 116. In a section subheaded "The Work of the Holy Spirit," Simpson says, "There are two stages which we must not fail to mark. The one is the Spirit's work in us, the other is the Spirit's personal coming to abide within us" (page 116). Simpson employed the analogy of building a house and later occupying the building. "There is as great a difference between the Holy Spirit's work in regenerating a soul—building the house—and His [subsequent] coming to reside in, abide in, and control in our inmost spirit and our whole life and being."

11. Simpson, "The Spirit-Filled Life," *The Alliance Weekly* (13 Jul 1918). In a section entitled "The Holy Spirit in Relation to Our Deeper Christian Life," Simpson writes, "It is one thing to build a house; it is another thing to live in it and make it your home. The former takes place when the Holy Spirit creates us anew; the latter when He enters our inmost being, and we become the temple of the Holy Ghost. ... Beloved, have you thus received the Holy

Ghost as a personal Presence?" (page 226). In addition he continues to show that the effects of the indwelling Holy Spirit are, among others, power for service and holy living.

12. The following articles, working forward sequentially from 1906, contain views which are similar to Simpson's theology in 1906:

> Simpson, "The Ministry of the Spirit," *Living Truths* (Aug 1907)
> Simpson, "Tarry," *Living Truths* (Sep 1907)
> Simpson, "The Spirit-Filled Life," *The Christian and Missionary Alliance Weekly* (16 Nov 1907)
> Simpson, "The Holy Ghost," *The Christian and Missionary Alliance Weekly* (24 Apr 1909)
> Simpson, "How to Enter In," *The Alliance Weekly* (27 Apr 1912)
> Simpson, "The Residue of the Spirit," *The Alliance Weekly* (5 Oct 1912)

13. We attain an additional indication of the value of the 1906 document as a guide when we view it against a statement adopted by the 1927 General Council of the C&MA. In a section dealing with "Christ our Sanctifier," the 1927 statement reads: "The second point of divine contact whereby sanctification is received is the work of the Spirit. The identification of the believer with Christ in death and resurrection is the historical side of holiness; the transformation of the believer in character and conduct through the baptism of the Holy Spirit is the experiential side of holiness. The one is apprehension; the other is appropriation. After the vision of victory comes the realization of victory. Now it is through the presence and power of the Holy Spirit that the vision of victory is transformed into realization. It is through the incoming of the Holy Spirit that the revelation of the indwelling Christ breaks with comforting cheer upon our despairing hearts, and it is through the Holy Spirit that we are enabled to die unto sin and live unto God" [see C. H. Crisman and W. M. Turnbull, *The Message of the Christian and Missionary Alliance* (New York: Christian Alliance Publishing Co., 1927) 11].

14. Simpson editorial, *The Alliance Weekly* (1 Mar 1913) 22. Simpson writes, "The related doctrine of the second work of grace, a spiritual crisis after conversion followed by entire consecration and the Baptism of the Holy Spirit, is also becoming obsolete even in evangelical circles." [See also Simpson, "Spiritual Sanity," *Living Truths* (Apr 1907) 191-193.]

15. This issue will be examined thoroughly in chapter 11. In an editorial [*The Christian and Missionary Alliance* (12 June 1909) 78], Simpson asserts that while he does not deny the validity of the gift of tongues, he is opposed to the view that this gift is for all and is the initial evidence of the baptism of

the Holy Spirit. [See also Simpson editorial, *The Christian and Missionary Alliance Weekly* (30 Apr 1910) 78.]

16. Gerald E. McGraw, "The Doctrine of Sanctification in the Published Writings of Albert Benjamin Simpson" (diss., New York U, 1986) 285-290. McGraw catalogues the reticence of later Alliance writers, such as Turner, Lee and Stoesz, to use this term because of the "Pentecostal" theological connotations. Likewise E. G. Wilson, in tracing the subtle changes in Alliance teaching on sanctification and the Holy Spirit, claims Pentecostal phobia as a reason for the gradual shift to more "Baptistic" doctrinal concepts in these areas [see Ernest Gerald Wilson, "The Christian and Missionary Alliance: Developments and Modifications of its Original Objectives" (diss., New York U., 1984) 374-377].

17. Simpson editorial, *The Christian and Missionary Alliance Weekly* (30 Dec 1905)

18. Simpson editorial, *The Christian and Missionary Alliance Weekly* (31 Mar 1906) 125

19. The document allows for breadth of opinion in such areas as "church government, the subject and modes of baptism, and the doctrines known as Calvinism and Arminianism" (see Appendix 2 for the complete text).

20. Simpson editorial (see note 18 above) 125

21. Simpson editorial, *The Christian and Missionary Alliance Weekly* (19 May 1906). Simpson again called for free discussion on the various contentious topics, along with the exercise of tolerance toward those who differed.

22. Sawin, "Fourfold Gospel" (see note 2 above) 21

23. Sawin, (see note 2 above) 24. Sawin was archivist at the C&MA National Office, then located in Nyack, NY, and devoted much of his time to collecting written records and memorabilia related to Simpson and the C&MA.

    The only paper from the 1906 Conference still preserved is George P. Pardington's presentation on sanctification. The text appears in the July, 1906, issue of *Living Truths* (pages 397-403). In the paper, Pardington devotes most of his thought to the nature of sanctification. The Holy Spirit is mentioned as the agent of transformation in the Christian's life (page 398). Pardington does not, however, discuss or use the term "baptism of the Holy Spirit." In a subsequent editorial in *The Christian and Missionary Alliance Weekly* (2 June 1906) 329, Simpson indicates that the Conference enthusiastically received Pardington's paper and called for its publication.

24. Simpson editorial (see note 23 above) 329

25. It was not until the 1965 General Council of The Christian and Missionary Alliance that an official Statement of Faith was adopted. The wording and content of the article on sanctification are somewhat different from that of the 1906 working paper. Article 7 of the C&MA Statement of Faith reads:

> It is the will of God that each believer should be filled with the Holy Spirit and be sanctified wholly, being separated from sin and the world and fully dedicated to the will of God, thereby receiving power for holy living and effective service. This is both a crisis and a progressive experience wrought in the life of the believer subsequent to conversion.

At least part of the delay in the formation of a Statement of Faith was the reluctance of North American pastors and members to view the Alliance as a church denomination. Membership in the Alliance was open to those affirming the basic tenets of Christian doctrine, along with the Alliance distinctives of Christ as Savior, Sanctifier, Healer and Coming King. Samuel J. Stoesz chronicles the progress of the Alliance from an interdenominational society to a denomination. In Stoesz's estimation, the chief factor for this change was the establishment of indigenous churches overseas through the C&MA's global missionary endeavors [Stoesz, *Understanding My Church* (Camp Hill, PA: Christian Publications, 1960) 119-143].

26. Simpson, *Walking in Spirit* (see note 9 above) 52

27. Simpson, *Walking in Spirit* (see note 9 above) 53

28. Simpson, *Echoes of the New Creation* (New York: Christian Alliance Publishing Co., 1903) 44

29. Simpson, "Christ: Our Model, Motive and Motive Power," *Living Truths* (May 1903) 249-252

30. Simpson, "Christ: Our Model" (see note 29 above) 249

31. Simpson, "Christ: Our Model" (see note 29 above) 249

32. Simpson, "Christ: Our Model" (see note 29 above) 250

33. Simpson, *Christ in the Bible*, vol. IX (Matthew through Luke) (New York: Christian Alliance Publishing Co., 1889) 39

34. Simpson, *Holy Spirit*, vol. II (see note 2 above) 19. Simpson expresses a similar statement in "Christ, Our Model" (see note 29 above) 250.

35. This does not necessarily imply that Simpson maintained a *kenosis* view of the Incarnation. There is not enough information in his writing to establish his precise view.

36. Simpson, *Christ in Bible,* vol. IX (Matthew through Luke) (see note 33 above) 40

37. Simpson, "The Holy Spirit and the Gospel," *The Christian and Missionary Alliance* (4 Mar 1905) 133

38. Simpson's two major works on the Holy Spirit, *The Holy Spirit, or Power from on High,* vols. I and II (see note 2 above), and *Walking in the Spirit* (see note 9 above) have key sections devoted to Jesus' baptism in the Jordan River. See particularly *The Holy Spirit,* vol. II, pages 3-36 and 49-196. Volume II is a collection of sermons preached by Simpson on this topic from May, 1895, until April, 1896. Simpson also explores this subject in his *Christ in the Bible* series. Note in particular vol. IX (Matthew through Luke) 34-46; vol. XIII (Matthew) (New York: Christian Alliance Publishing Co., 1904) 40-52; and vol. XIV (Mark) (New York: Christian Alliance Publishing Co., 1910) 26-39. Moreover, Simpson frequently alludes to this theme in his other writings, particularly in reference to the believer's baptism with the Holy Spirit. See for example references in the following articles:

    > Simpson, "Christ, Model, Motive" (see note 29 above)
    > Simpson, "The Baptism of the Holy Spirit, a Crisis or an Evolution?" *Living Truths* (Dec 1905)
    > Simpson, "The Holy Ghost," *The Christian and Missionary Alliance Weekly* (24 Apr 1909)
    > Simpson, "Holy Spirit and Gospel" (see note 37 above)

39. Simpson, *Holy Spirit,* vol. II (see note 2 above) 14. Simpson similarly states in *Christ in Bible* vol. IX (Matthew through Luke) (see note 33 above) 48, "Christ had no sin of His own to bury, but He had the sin of the world, and His baptism, therefore, was the assuming of the responsibility of human guilt and going down in a figure of death on account of it, and then coming forth in baptism again in a figure of resurrection. As he did so, John expressed the deep significance of this on the following day by pointing Jesus out and saying, 'Behold the Lamb of God that beareth the sin of the world.' "

    In *Christ in Bible,* vol. IX (Matthew through Luke) (see note 33 above) 35, Simpson says, "[Jesus] identified Himself with sinful men, and in symbol went down with them to the death which they deserved. . . . His baptism had been a rehearsal of the cross and a type of the great atonement which He was afterwards to accomplish on Calvary."

40. See chapter 5 of this book: "The Precise Nature of the Baptism."

41. Simpson, *Christ in Bible,* vol. IX (Matthew through Luke) (see note 33 above) 38

42. Simpson, *Christ in Bible,* vol. IX (Matthew through Luke) (see note 33 above) 40-41

43. Simpson, "Holy Spirit and Gospel" (see note 37 above) 133

44. Simpson, "Holy Spirit and Gospel" (see note 37 above) 133

45. Simpson, "Holy Spirit and Gospel" (see note 37 above) 133

46. Simpson, *Holy Spirit,* vol. II (see note 2 above) 13

47. Simpson, *Walking in Spirit* (see note 9 above) 9

48. That Simpson means this to be an analogy may be discerned by observing the context in which Simpson makes these statements. In each case he is commenting on the ministry of the Holy Spirit prior to the baptism of the Holy Spirit. In *Holy Spirit,* vol. II (see note 2 above) 13 and "Holy Spirit and Gospel" (see note 37 above) 133 are two other instances in Simpson's writings where this figure is apparent.

49. Simpson, "Holy Spirit and Gospel" (see note 37 above) 133

50. Simpson saw that this event was much more than merely a confirmation by the Father that Christ was His Son.

51. Simpson, "Holy Spirit and Gospel" (see note 37 above) 133

52. Simpson, *Holy Spirit,* vol. II (see note 2 above) 15

53. Simpson, "Baptism of Spirit, Crisis or Evolution?" (see note 38 above) 711

Chapter 4

The Baptism of the Holy Spirit in the Writings of A. B. Simpson, Part 2: Christ, *Our Sanctifier*

This is my wonderful story—
  Christ to my heart has come;
Jesus, the King of glory,
  Finds in my heart a home.

I am so glad I received Him,
  Jesus, my heart's dear King;
I who so often have grieved Him,
  All to His feet would bring.

Now in His bosom confiding,
  This my glad song shall be:
I am in Jesus abiding,
  Jesus abides in me.

  Christ in me,
  Christ in me,
Christ in me—Oh, wonderful story;
  Christ in me,
  Christ in me,
Christ in me, the hope of glory.

—Albert B. Simpson hymn

In the preceding chapter we delved into the significance of the life of Christ as Simpson taught it in his writings. In this chapter we want to focus on the sanctifying *work* of Christ as Simpson understood and taught it.

As we have seen, the working paper presented by the Simpson-chaired committee at the 1906 Conference for Prayer and Counsel Respecting Uniformity in the Testimony and Teaching of the Alliance reveals Simpson's conviction that the baptism of the Holy Spirit occurs within the general framework of what he calls "sanctification."[1] Having ascertained the implications for the baptism of the Holy Spirit that Simpson draws from the life of Christ, we now want to explore the relationship of the baptism of the Holy Spirit to sanctification.

"Be Holy"

In his writings Simpson is very emphatic: "God's Word requires that all His people should be holy in heart and life."[2] He cites numerous verses from the New and Old Testaments to substantiate this assertion.[3] He also believed the Scriptures to be specific as to the measure of holiness God requires:

> "Be ye holy, for I am holy" [Leviticus 11:44-45; 1 Peter 1:16]. God is our standard, and as His children we must be like Him. No lower standard will pass. We must not aim to be as good as some people. . . . It is God who is our pattern. "Be ye therefore perfect, even as your Father which is in heaven is perfect" [Matthew 5:48].[4]

Elsewhere he wrote:

> The holiness to which we are called, and into which we are introduced, is not the restoration of Adamic perfection, or the recovery of the nature we lost by the Fall. It is a higher holiness, even the very nature of God Himself, and the indwelling of Jesus Christ, the Second Adam, to whose

perfect likeness we shall be restored through the work of redemption.[5]

Simpson declared that the believer is faced with a dilemma. On the one hand he may choose to ignore this scriptural injunction and "explain away its plainest and most emphatic teachings, . . ." declaring that "God does not actually mean [holiness, perfection] or require it."[6] On the other hand, if Christians take these injunctions seriously then they will soon realize that they cannot obey them, for they possess "no power to produce them."[7]

Simpson asserts that this calling by God would be meaningless if man were left to his own efforts. Simpson points out, however, that the divine provision for this call has always been part of God's eternal plan.[8] Simpson cites two Old Testament prophecies, recorded in Jeremiah 31 and Ezekiel 36, which he saw as attesting to God's plan.

Sanctification and the New Covenant of Jeremiah 31 and Ezekiel 36

Simpson sets the background to his exploration of the new covenant by pointing out that the Old Testament shows repeatedly man's impotence to follow God in his own strength. Both Jeremiah and Ezekiel were speaking from situations in which Israel and Judah had failed to follow God. Within that context the prophets spoke of hope for the future.

Simpson highlighted several features contained in these prophecies. Contrasting Jeremiah's announced new covenant (31:31-34) with the old Mosaic covenant, Simpson saw its method of delivery as the distinguishing difference:

> The distinguishing feature of this new covenant which Jeremiah announced lies in the fact that God promises to write His law "upon our hearts," and to "put it in our inward parts." The old covenant gave light and law, but it did not give power and disposition to obey it. But the new covenant

writes it in our inmost being; makes it part of our very nature; incorporates it into our will; our choice; our desires; our very intuitions, so that it becomes second nature to us, our spontaneous desire, and our deepest life.[9]

The new covenant thus grants the ability to obey the requirements of the Scriptures. Simpson explains the dynamics of how this is achieved:

This is the work of the Holy Ghost. This is the meaning of sanctification. This is the great purpose of Christ's redemption and His indwelling in the heart of the believer through the Spirit. It is God who undertakes to keep this covenant . . . and grants the power of divine grace to keep [us] from sin, and to lead us into righteousness and holiness.[10]

Simpson saw that it was God Himself who imparted the ability to follow the divine injunctions. This provision is brought about as a result of Christ's work in redemption and the application of it by the Spirit in the life of the believer. We will examine both of these aspects in greater detail in subsequent sections of this chapter.

Ezekiel's "Three Very Distinct Stages"

Simpson made similar comments when discussing Ezekiel 36:25-28. He proposed that these verses outlined "three very distinct stages in the promised blessing."[11] Referring to verse 25, he wrote:

The first [stage] includes forgiveness and conversion; that is the sprinkling of clean water, . . . the forgiveness of sins, the taking away of the hard and stony heart, and the giving of the heart of flesh, the work of justification and regeneration.[12]

Elsewhere Simpson describes this first stage in Ezekiel 36 in these words:

"I will sprinkle clean water upon you" [36:25]. That is forgiveness; old sins are blotted out. "A new heart also will I give you "; that is regeneration.[13]

But Simpson recognized limits to this first stage. In another article he says, "The new heart makes you want to do right, but it does not give you the power to do right."[14] And what produces the enabling power? He declares:

It is the indwelling of the Holy Spirit and the incoming of His cleansing and sanctifying power in the heart of the believer. "I will put my Spirit within you, and cause you to walk in my statutes, and ye shall keep my judgments, and do them [36:27]." This is something different from the new spirit. It is God Himself coming to dwell in the new spirit by His Holy Spirit, and bringing a constraining and efficient power that causes the soul to walk in holiness and enables him to keep His commandments.[15]

In another place, Simpson provided a graphic illustration of God's provision to give this "power to do right":

Could we put on canvas the picture it would be something like this; first, we would paint the natural heart black and sinful; then, second, in the centre of this black heart we would place a little white heart, denoting the regenerated spirit, the new heart that comes at conversion, but which is still in the midst of darkness and sin, and has to maintain a painful and often unequal struggle with the surrounding and encompassing evil.

In the third place, we would paint a ray of heavenly light, or a living coal of celestial fire, which we would put in the centre of this new heart; and from it the effulgent rays of life and light would reach out into all the darkness round about, filling the new heart and the old, until the darkness and sin are crowded out, and God Himself possesses the whole being, enabled [sic] it to think and feel, to trust and love, to obey and persevere, even as Christ Himself would walk.[16]

The third stage, in the view of Simpson, involves the outflow of the indwelling Spirit in the believer's life and circumstances.[17] Simpson used the pastoral images—"you will live in the land, . . . I will call for the grain and make it plentiful, . . . I will increase the fruit of the trees and the crops of the field" [36:28-30]—to depict these various blessings.[18]

These three stages form a familiar pattern in Simpson's writing. Simpson saw regeneration followed by a distinct second stage—the indwelling of the Spirit—which has tangible ramifications in the life of the believer. The third stage is an abundantly fruitful Christian life. In this threefold imagery we see shades of Section II.b of the 1906 working paper.

The exciting fulfillment of these Old Testament prophecies was viewed by Simpson as part of the New Testament message. Examining the Holy Spirit in Hebrews, Simpson remarked:

> The ancient covenant, so gloriously revealed to Jeremiah, is three times repeated in the Epistle to the Hebrews; and it must, therefore, be entitled to the greatest significance and weight. It is, indeed, the very essence of the Gospel. It breathes the spirit of the New Dispensation.[19]

Simpson proceeded to explore these verses, making comments on the passages in Hebrews similar to those he made on Jeremiah 31 and Ezekiel 36.[20] Simpson remarked similarly when commenting on Paul's reference to Jeremiah 31 in Second Corinthians 6:16—"I will live with them and walk among them, and I will be their God, and they will be my people"—asserting, "This is the deepest truth concerning sanctification."[21]

Other New Testament verses that allude to Christ's indwelling also show the fulfillment of these two Old Testament prophecies (see, for example, Colossians 1:29, Galatians 2:20, 2 Corinthians

5:17). Furthermore, Simpson viewed the Day of Pentecost as particularly significant in the fulfillment of these Old Testament prophecies. He suggested that in God's sovereign plan, the outpouring of the Holy Spirit on the believers occurred on the day in the Jewish calendar that marks the giving of the Mosaic law. The Old Testament followers of God repeatedly had failed to obey the law. Now the Holy Spirit came to write the law "on tablets of human hearts" (2 Corinthians 3:3) and to impart to the surrendered believer an enabling to follow God's will and Word.[22]

In Simpson's mind, therefore, God has provided through the indwelling Holy Spirit the means for believers to follow His calling to a holy life.

We now inquire as to the precise nature of this divine provision for sanctification.

Sanctification and the Work of Christ

The means by which the benefits of this new covenant were secured was seen by Simpson to be Christ's work in the atonement. Simpson often mentioned the work of Christ for the justification of the believer.[23] However, within the atonement, Simpson also believed that part of Christ's work related particularly to sanctification. Speaking of the source of sanctification in *The Fourfold Gospel,* Simpson wrote:

> The heart and soul of the whole matter is seeing that Jesus is Himself our sanctification. . . . He has purchased [sanctification] for us. It is part of the fruit of Calvary. "By one offering He hath perfected forever them that are sanctified." "By the which will we are sanctified through the offering of the body of Jesus Christ once for all" [Hebrews 10:14, 10].[24]

In still other references Simpson comments:

> Christ fills the deeper need of sanctification. He has

provided for this in His atonement and in the resources of His grace. It is all wrapped up in Him and must be received as a free and perfect gift through Him alone.[25]

> Our sanctification has been purchased for us through the redemption of Christ. . . . Our sanctification, therefore, as well as our justification, was included in the finished work of Christ, and it is a free gift of His grace to every ransomed soul that accepts it in accordance with His Word and will.[26]

These citations show that Simpson saw sanctification as not only included in Christ's work of atonement but distinct from justification, to be received specifically and separately. On that observation we shall expand later.

Digressing momentarily, we need to clarify a very important issue arising from Simpson's formulations on sanctification. The issue concerns whether Simpson believed that Christ's work was of one piece or whether he subscribed to the "second work of grace" viewpoint. Many have categorized Simpson as holding to the latter position. Such a conclusion seems to be supported by the presence of terminology such as that found in the 1906 working paper:

> A definite second blessing, distinct in nature, though not necessarily far removed in time from the experience of conversion.

A careful examination of the broad scope of Simpson's writings, however, and the explicit statements which we have noted in the previous several pages clearly indicate that this is not the case. We must understand Simpson's use of terminology.

Simpson held that salvation and all of its attendant benefits are found in the one work of Christ upon the cross. All spiritual blessings flow from this one work of the atonement. But Simpson would assert that within this one work by Christ are many distinct provisions. It is possible for a believer not to have experienced all the provisions provided through Christ's one act of redemption. For

Simpson, Christ's provisions were not real, not effective, until consciously appropriated. Thus provision for sanctification is "distinct in nature" and "a definite second blessing" from other provisions and blessings such as justification.

Returning to our examination, we find that there are many citations in Simpson's writings testifying to this provision of Christ for sanctification. Unfortunately, his comments on these verses tend to be brief and cited only as support. Nevertheless, a recurring theme runs through these various references. Speaking of the believer's identification with Christ, Simpson stressed that the "old man . . . was crucified with Him" [Romans 6:6] and "it is our privilege to lay off the nature of self and sin and put on the very nature and life of Christ Himself" [1 Corinthians 1:30].[27] Simpson saw in Galatians 1:3, 4 that Christ died not only to deliver us from "the evil of the present in all of its forms" but also "from the evil of our own sinful hearts. Sanctification, therefore, is the purchase of Christ's blood and part of our great redemption."[28] Citing Romans 8:3, 4 and Second Corinthians 5:21, Simpson postulated:

> These passages undoubtedly teach that the death of Jesus Christ was God's provision for our sanctification, . . . and that He bore on the cross of Calvary not only our guilt . . . but our sinful nature with all the roots and springs of corruption which we inherited from a fallen race. It is our privilege, therefore, to reckon not only that our past life of sin was expiated on the cross, but that the principle of sin and the whole sinful man was crucified when Jesus died.[29]

The key thought here is that Christ's finished work broke the power of sin. This is a provision that only Christ can make. Accordingly, these citations indicate that Simpson maintained that believers needed to be aware of Christ's provision for sanctification and to appropriate it.

Perhaps Simpson's most lucid presentation concerning Christ's atonement and sanctification is found in his book, *The Cross of Christ*. There he makes an extensive reference to Walter Marshall's

Gospel Mystery of Sanctification.[30] In context, Simpson asserts, "The resurrection of Jesus Christ is the efficient cause of our sanctification."[31] He continues, "I cannot better express this great truth than by quoting the following paragraphs from an old and little known volume that is worthy of permanent and wide circulation, Marshall's *Gospel Mystery of Sanctification.*"[32] Unfortunately, Simpson simply quoted, adding no comments. But his remark, "I cannot better express this great truth," indicates that the sections quoted accurately represent his own view. Simpson's quotation from Marshall is very extensive; hence, we will highlight here only its salient points.[33] Marshall writes:

> The end of Christ's incarnation, death and resurrection was to prepare and form a holy nature and frame for us in Himself, to be communicated to us by union and fellowship with Him; and not to enable us to produce in ourselves the first original of such a holy nature by our own endeavors.[34]

Referring to the incarnation, Marshall indicates that Christ, being the Second Adam, was far superior to Adam, for "man was really joined to God by close, inseparable union of the divine and human nature in one person—Christ."[35] Christ lived out His life in full dependence on God's enabling, and it is His life that is communicated to the believer. Through His death "He prepared a freedom for us from our whole natural condition" so that the old self is destroyed not by what we do, but "by our partaking of the freedom from it, and death unto it, that is already wrought for us by the death of Christ."[36] Moreover, through His resurrection, Christ "took possession of spiritual life for us" and "by union with Christ, we partake of that spiritual life that He took possession of . . . and [are] thereby enabled to bring forth fruits from it."[37]

Christ's incarnation and atoning work, as Marshall sets them forth, together with the believer's union with Christ, are at the heart of Simpson's teaching as well. Marshall and Simpson held that both the penalty and the power of sin were effectively dealt with in the atonement. Our next section amplifies the nature of that provision.

Sanctification Explained

A statement in the 1906 working paper affirms, "Sanctification [is] . . . *a distinct gift* [emphasis added] of God's grace to every open and surrendered soul." As we have already noted, Simpson saw Christ's work in the atonement as providing this "distinct gift of God's grace." We now want to understand from his writings what he meant by the words, "to every open and surrendered soul."

The definition of terms is vital to an accurate understanding of Simpson's perception of the nature of sanctification. His use of the word "sanctification" contained nuances other than those usually associated with the word, a fact which he freely admitted.[38] In the article "Phases and Phrases in the Deeper Life," written in 1902, Simpson discussed at length all the various terms used in his day to describe the "Deeper Life." He asserted that "sanctification" was the process of entering the Deeper Life. In his writings, therefore, he uses *sanctification* as "an experiential, behavioral, moral term rather than a forensic, theoretical, positional term."[39]

Simpson is very emphatic that sanctification is not regeneration (see Appendix 4). Regeneration, he says, is "the breath of God breathing life into man."[40] Remarking on Jesus' statement to Nicodemus, "No one can enter the kingdom of God unless he is born of water and the Spirit" (John 3:5), Simpson writes:

> The Holy Ghost creates in us a new life and a new set of spiritual senses altogether, through which we discern, understand, and enter into the life of God and the spiritual realm.[41]

In another place Simpson says of this new birth: "[The heart is] disposed to serve God and follow righteousness."[42] Frequently he uses the image of a just-constructed, yet tenantless building to depict this new state.[43] Sanctification, on the other hand, says Simpson, "is the deeper work which follows justification, and deals directly with the inherent state of the heart."[44]

Simpson is also vigorous in his declaration that sanctification is not achieved by "any efforts or struggles of our own."[45] Such an accomplishment would prove impossible because of the power of the sin nature.[46] Moreover, it would be a denial of the provision that God had graciously extended to believers.[47]

Simpson's most frequent definition of sanctification stresses the experiential implication that he finds in the word's etymology:

> Sanctification has three meanings in the Bible; to be separated from things that are unholy; to be dedicated to God by the choice of our will and heart, and then to be filled with the Spirit of the life of God. . . . There is first the negative side, the things we are separated from; the positive side, the things we are saved to, then the filling of the vessel that has thus been given to God by the Holy Spirit and the indwelling Christ.[48]

Each of these constituent elements warrants more detailed investigation. The *first,* negative in nature, is the idea of separation from. To explain this concept Simpson sometimes refers to the Genesis account of creation, where God "separated" light from darkness (1:3) and the water above the "expanse" from the water below it (1:7). Simpson points out that separation did not annihilate either element but marked a definite demarcation between them.[49] He says:

> [Separation] is not the extinction of evil. It is the putting off, the laying aside of evil by detaching ourselves from it and placing an impassable gulf between us and it. . . . We are to be in the attitude of negation and resistance with our whole beings saying no! We need not annihilate the evil or resist it in our own strength but simply, by a definite act of the will, separate ourselves from it, hand it over to God and renounce it utterly.[50]

This voluntary choice, Simpson told his constituents, is to be exercised against "the whole evil self and sinful nature" as well as the "world."[51] This action, he adds, is first a crisis, a decisive expression to God of separation from the old life, and then also progressive, for God will continue to reveal new expressions of "your old sinful self and evil working of your fallen nature."[52] The principle lying behind this injunction is that "God will not put His hand on the evil until you authorize Him with your glad consent."[53]

Simpson repeatedly stresses the believer's responsibility to express willingness, all the while knowing it is only God who can put the old nature to death.[54]

The *second* constituent element of sanctification, positive in nature, is the act of dedication. Actually, this element is implied in one aspect of separation: God separated the nation Israel *to* Himself. Simpson saw this as involving Israel volitionally, as the people responded to God's call.[55] He was of the opinion that this positive aspect of separation—separation to God—as well as the negative aspects are illustrative of what the believer's response to God should be. Referring to Paul's appeal in Romans 12:1, Simpson writes:

> We offer ourselves to God for His absolute ownership, that He may possess us as His peculiar property, prepare us for His purpose and work out in us all His holy and perfect will.[56]

Simpson describes this act as "a voluntary surrender or self-offering," and as "clay yielding itself to the potter's hand."[57] Simpson also referred to the Old Testament tabernacle and the various articles that were "set apart to holy use."[58] Again, this action is both an initial decision and a progressive response to God.[59]

The *third* and final aspect of sanctification in Simpson's writings is to fill with. He outlines the background of this concept in the following quotation:

> The literal translation of the old Hebrew word to consecrate is "to fill the hand." It suggests the deepest truth in connection with sanctification, viz., that Christ Himself

must be the substance and supply of our spiritual life and fills us with His own Spirit and holiness.[60]

Simpson continues this thought, stating, "We bring to Him but an empty hand . . . and He fills it. We are a capacity; He is the supply."[61] Union with Christ, then, is the source of sanctification. "We are sanctified by the indwelling life and power of the Holy Spirit in us and filling our spirit, soul and body with the life of Jesus Christ."[62]

Before we proceed to Simpson's view of union with Christ, a brief summary of His concepts of sanctification is in order. Simpson defines sanctification as a believer's obedient response to God and the appropriation of God's divine resources to live a holy life. The result is not so much a crystallized state as a new relationship which effects changes in the believer's life. As Simpson himself states:

> There is a moment in which we actually enter into personal union with Jesus and receive the baptism of the Holy Ghost. In that moment we are fully accepted, and are fully sanctified up to all the light we have. But as the light grows deeper and clearer [God] leads us farther down, and farther on, at once revealing and healing every secret thing that is contrary to His perfect will, as we are able to bear it, and bringing us into perfect conformity to the very nature and life of Christ.[63]

The Indwelling Christ

At the heart of Simpson's account of sanctification is his concept of union with Christ. Simpson had no doubt that union with Christ provides the effectual power to overcome the inherent sin nature. We have already seen this in point II.2.c of the 1906 working paper.[64] The nature of this union was not simply forensic in Simpson's mind, though this aspect was not neglected. A. E. Thompson in his Simpson biography points this out:

Nor would [Simpson] give ground to those teachers who make the terms of intimate union used in the New Testament mere figures. "This is not a beautiful figure of speech, but it is a real visitation of God. I wonder if we know what this means. . . . Christ is not to be an outside influence which moves on our emotions and feelings and elevates us into a sublime idea of God, but the real presence of Christ has come within us to remain, and He brings with Him all His resources of help and love and mighty power."[65]

Thompson argues in a chapter entitled, "Simpson: A Pauline Mystic," that Simpson was committed to both the historical facts of Christ's life—"the Christ picture presented to the mind by the Gospel history"—and also the internal experience of Christ, the mystical supra-rational experience of the living Jesus.[66] Hence, Simpson, while not denying the historical space/time dimension of Christianity, clearly sought and emphasized the existential reality of Christ in the consecrated believer's life.[67] To him the reality of Christ's presence was the source of holy living.

Simpson often chose Romans 7 and 8 to explicate the nature of the Christ's indwelling. He held that Romans 7:14-26 depicted a regenerated Christian who is "given a heart disposed to serving God and following righteousness," yet finds that this new nature is in a losing battle "with the surviving element of the flesh."[68] Self-effort is ineffectual in this fight. Simpson intimated that the effectual ability is revealed in Romans 8:2-11.[69] He wrote:

A supernatural holiness becomes a fact of our lives, for sanctification is not our own personal virtues, graces or attainments, but it is the life of Christ manifested in us . . . as the inworking and outworking of Christ's own life in us.[70]

On another occasion, Simpson critiqued Thomas à Kempis' *The Imitation of Christ*:

It is Christ Himself who comes to imitate Himself in us

and reproduce His own life in the lives of His followers. This is the mystery of the Gospel. This is the secret of the Lord. This is the power that sanctifies, that fills, that keeps the consecrated heart. This is the only way that we can be like Christ.[71]

Simpson suggested that this "mystery of the new life" and "great mystical truth" was something "Paul delighted in unfolding to the saints of the apostolic church."[72] As support, Simpson frequently cited Paul's reference in Colossians 1:27 to "this mystery, which is Christ in you, the hope of glory."[73] On Galatians 2:20 Simpson suggested that it was "in dying to his own life and taking Christ instead" that Paul entered into union with the crucified Christ.[74] Simpson suggests that Paul's later reference to his travail "until Christ be formed in you" (Galatians 4:19) relates to a regenerated person who has not known the "birth of Christ in his soul."[75] Additionally he comments, "This is not a character to be formed, but a Person coming to live in you."[76]

Simpson also believed "this conception of the deeper spiritual life runs all through the more profound teachings of our Lord Himself."[77] The parable of the vine and the branches shows that "the true Christian life . . . is just living out the Christ-life as He lives within."[78] He held Christ's message to the Laodicean church (Revelation 3:14-22) to reflect the state of "modern Christianity," particularly the failure of many Christians to have Christ indwelling their lives.[79]

Though Simpson has much to say about the indwelling of Christ, he does not neglect to discuss the importance of the historical reality and implications of Jesus' ascension.[80] For Simpson, Christ, after His ascension, was clearly at the right hand of the Father, yet He is present intimately in the lives of believers. Communion with Christ and continual dependence on Christ are the ensuing responsibilities of the believer. Conformity to Christ is achieved through the application of Christ's righteousness by the Spirit in a believer's life. Simpson, therefore, held that discussion on sanctification could not remain in the abstract sphere but must become relational.

The Holy Spirit: The Agent of Union with Christ

The manner in which Christ's presence is manifested to believers is through the presence of the Holy Spirit. Just prior to Pentecost, Jesus Christ ascended to heaven. In His place, He sent His promised Holy Spirit upon the church. Simpson therefore saw this as the age of the Holy Spirit, and the Spirit's principal ministry in this age is the completion of Christ's work.[81] Consequently, Simpson described the Holy Spirit as "the administrator on earth of all the work of redemption."[82] He declares:

> [The Holy Spirit] is the Executive of the divine Trinity, the supreme Guide and Overseer of the church, and the sovereign Dispenser of all the gifts of the Ascended Christ. Every grace that the Saviour has purchased and the Father is ready to bestow in His name must come through the hands of the Holy Ghost. As the Father committed all things to the Son, so the Son has committed all things to the Spirit, and it is through Him that we must receive the blessings which Christ died to purchase and lives to bestow.[83]

With respect to sanctification, Simpson pays particular attention to the Spirit's work of bringing about union with Christ, "making Jesus real to us, to give us a conception of Him, and the witness of His personal union with us."[84] He describes how this is so:

> [The Holy Spirit] is the Spirit of Christ. He resided in [Christ's] bosom during the three and a half years of His earthly ministry, and now He comes to us softened, coloured and humanized by the heart of Jesus, and really brings to us the Master Himself in all that was really essential to His character and ministry. In a sense therefore the presence of the Spirit is the presence of Christ. As Jesus never did anything without the Holy Spirit, so the Holy Spirit never does anything without Jesus. It is His supreme delight

to make Christ real to us and take of the things that are His and show them unto us.[85]

Simpson's comments, which we surveyed in the previous section on the indwelling Christ, must be seen in the light of this understanding of the Spirit's work. The Holy Spirit is the agent of Christ's presence, making Christ, in an interior manner, just as real now to believers as He once was, in an exterior manner, to the apostles. But His presence cannot be precisely explained:

> It is impossible for us to analyze, dissect or trace by any biological and psychological process the method of this divine mystery. This is all we can distinctly formulate— somewhere down in the depths of our subconscious being, God through the Spirit takes up His abode. His actual personal presence is hidden from our consciousness, just as the hidden spring of that artesian well is far out of sight in the bowels of the earth. All we are conscious of is the manifestations of His presence from time to time in various influences, operations, emotions, and effects in our spirit and life. The Holy Spirit is just as truly in us when He makes no sign as when the fountains of joy are overflowing, or the waters of peace are softly refreshing our weary and troubled hearts.[86]

Besides testifying to Christ's presence, the Spirit is also the agent of transformation in the Christian life. Simpson writes:

> It is [the Spirit's] especial work to unite us to Christ and transfer to us from the Lord Jesus all the qualities and graces of His nature and enable us to relive them in our actual experience. He is the great Artist that transfers the divine picture to the living tablets of our lives, so that "we beholding as in a glass the glory of the Lord, are transformed into the same image from glory to glory even as by the Spirit of the Lord" (II. Cor. iii:18).[87]

It is difficult to gather from Simpson's writings precisely how this process takes place. It appears he believed that the Holy Spirit's ongoing ministry is to reveal sin and expressions of the self-life in believers, principally through the illumination of the Scriptures.[88] Once aware of some issue of sin, the believer must realize that he or she cannot change by his or her own strength. At this point the believer prays and asks for grace. The glorified humanity of Christ becomes the source and the Holy Spirit the agent of transformation. The import of this process is embodied in this quotation:

> Jesus is not only the Pattern, but the Source of our life, and it is the business of the Holy Spirit, day by day, and moment by moment, to transfer [Jesus'] qualities into our life. Do we need patience? We just draw it from Him through the Holy Spirit. Do we need power? We take a deeper draught of His fullness, and He becomes our power. Do we need love? We draw a little nearer to Christ the Loving One, and through the Holy Spirit, His love is shed abroad in our hearts.[89]

Before we move on, we should note that Simpson was careful to point out the dangers of being preoccupied with any one Person of the Trinity. Though he emphasized the work of the Holy Spirit in discussing the baptism with the Holy Spirit and the Person of Christ in his focus on a believer's union with Christ, he asserts that believers are "the temple of the Triune God":[90]

> There is a subtle danger that in our theological conception of the glorious Trinity we sometimes make three Gods instead of one. While there are three Persons in the God-head, yet there is one divine presence which the Holy Spirit brings to the heart and that is the presence of the Lord Jesus who is to us the Living Word and the one eternal Revelation of the Father.[91]

Simpson, therefore, although he gives great attention to the individual Persons of the Godhead, does not neglect the importance of God's essential unity.

Summary

At this point, we need to recapitulate the major elements of Simpson's teaching on Christ, our Sanctifier, which we have discovered through our exploration of his writings. Simpson held that Christ's earthly life was a model for believers regarding dependence both on the Father and the ministry of the Holy Spirit. The phrase "Christ, *our Sanctifier*" alludes to the fact that it is Jesus Himself, through His work of atonement, who provides not only forgiveness from sins but also power over sin. Christ's work fulfilled the Old Testament promises (Jeremiah 31 and Ezekiel 36) which declared God would supply the means to live a holy life.

Sanctification is most commonly used by Simpson in an experiential sense, not to describe a state of being. He applies the term to believers who have recognized their personal inability to follow God and have therefore appropriated the New Covenant resources offered by God in Christ. The "indwelling of Christ," in Simpson's terminology, refers to the fact that Christ's character and presence are painted on the life of the believer. Christ Himself is the source of new life and His presence provides the ability to live a holy life. The Holy Spirit applies the provisions of Christ's atonement to the believer. He brings the very presence of Christ into the believer's life and experience.

From examining the broader scope of Simpson's writings we have outlined what Simpson meant by statements II.2.a, c and d in the working document presented to the 1906 Conference for Prayer and Counsel Respecting Uniformity in the Testimony and Teaching of the Alliance. It is now time to move to section II.2.b—the issue of the baptism of the Holy Spirit.

End Notes

1. *Sanctification* is in quotes to signify Simpson's distinctive use of the term.

2. A. B. Simpson, *Walking in the Spirit* (New York: Christian Alliance Publishing Co., 1889) 54

3. Following are a selected presentation of these various references:

   Simpson, *Walking in the Spirit* (see note 2 above) 54, citing Heb. 12:4; Rev. 21:27; 22:12; Isa. 33:15-17; Psa. 24:3-4; 1 Pet. 1:16; Mat. 5:48; 1 John 2:1; 3:6.
   Simpson, "Misapprehensions Respecting Sanctification," *The Christian Alliance* (Apr 1888) 54, has a similar list.
   Simpson, *Christ in the Bible*, vol. XXIII (Peter, John, Jude) (New York: Christian Alliance Publishing Co., 1920) 29, 56. In this last mentioned, Simpson writes, "It is an obligation. . . . We have no right to call ourselves [God's] children if we continue to live in sin. . . . There are not two classes of Christians between which you may choose; there are no options here. Every child of God is called to be holy" (page 56).

4. Simpson, *Christ in Bible,* vol. XXIII (Peter, John, Jude) (see note 3 above) 56

5. Simpson, *Walking in Spirit* (see note 2 above) 53

6. Simpson, *Walking in Spirit* (see note 2 above) 55

7. Simpson, *Walking in Spirit* (see note 2 above) 55

8. Simpson, *Walking in Spirit* (see note 2 above) 53
   Simpson, "Misapprehensions" (see note 3 above) 54
   Simpson, *Christ in Bible,* vol. XXIII (Peter, John, Jude) (see note 3 above) 56
   Simpson, "Phases and Phrases of the Deeper Life," *Living Truths* (Oct 1902) 181

9. Simpson, *The Holy Spirit, or Power from on High,* vol. I (New York: Christian Alliance Publishing Co., 1895) 227

10. Simpson, *Holy Spirit,* vol. I (see note 9 above) 227-228

11. Simpson, *Holy Spirit,* vol. I (see note 9 above) 240

12. Simpson, *Holy Spirit,* vol. I (see note 9 above) 240

13. Simpson, *The Fourfold Gospel* (New York: Word, Work and World Publishing Co., 1887) 40

14. Simpson, "Phases and Phrases" (see note 8 above) 182

15. Simpson, *Holy Spirit,* vol. I (see note 9 above) 240. In *Fourfold Gospel* (see note 13 above), Simpson makes a similar comment on this text in Ezk. 36: "Our whole being will be prompted by the springing life of God within. It is God manifest in flesh again. This is the only true consummation of sanctification. Thus only can man enter completely into the life of holiness" (page 40).

16. Simpson, *Holy Spirit,* vol. I (see note 9 above) 240-241

17. Simpson, *Holy Spirit,* vol. I (see note 9 above) 241

18. Simpson, *Holy Spirit,* vol. I (see note 9 above) 241-242

19. Simpson, *The Holy Spirit, or Power from on High,* vol. II (New York: Christian Alliance Publishing Co., 1896) 206. Simpson refers to Heb. 8:8-10 and 10:15-17.

20. Simpson, *Holy Spirit,* vol. II (see note 19 above) 205-208

21. Simpson, *Christ in the Bible,* vol. XVIII (1 & 2 Corinthians) (New York: Christian Alliance Publishing Co., 1904) 81

22. Simpson, *Christ in the Bible,* vol. XVI (Acts) (New York: Christian Alliance Publishing Co., 1902) 31

23. See comments Simpson makes in the 1906 document (Appendix 2) under "Christ, Our Savior." Numerous references appear in Simpson's writings on the nature of Christ's atonement. He saw Christ's death as substitutionary, taking the penalty of sin that rightfully belonged to individuals [see, for example, *Fourfold Gospel* (see note 13 above) 12-20, esp. 17]. In *A Larger Christian Life* (New York: Christian Alliance Publishing Co., 1890) 42, Simpson comments on Rom. 3:21-24, discussing Christ's "vicarious sacrifice for sin." Furthermore, Christ's death was a "ransom" for the redemption of believers and a "satisfaction," or "propitiation," of the righteous wrath of God [*Echoes of the New Creation,* (New York: Christian Alliance Publishing Co., 1903) 45]. The resurrection of Christ sealed His atoning work, and His ascension to the right hand of the Father marked the beginning of His priestly work on man's behalf [*Fourfold Gospel* (see note 13 above) 17, and *The Cross of Christ* (New York: Christian Alliance Publishing Co., 1912) 85-87]. Simpson indicates that salvation is available to those who receive Christ and place their faith in His finished work. Although Simpson was raised and trained in a Presbyterian Calvinist theological milieu, his writings on Christ's saving work seldom reveal his views on such areas as predestination and election. Simpson seems to suggest that salvation is available to anyone who

willingly receives it. "Salvation," he says, "is possible to him who believes." [*A Larger Christian Life* 5; *Fourfold Gospel* 22-23; *Christ in the Bible*, vol. XI (Romans) (New York: Christian Alliance Publishing Co., 1894) 90-93, 114-117]. In Christ the believer is redeemed from sin, reconciled to God and declared justified in the divine presence.

24. Simpson, *Fourfold Gospel* (see note 13 above) 37

25. Simpson, *Larger Christian Life* (see note 23 above) 43

26. Simpson, *Walking in Spirit* (see note 2 above) 53

27. Simpson, *Cross of Christ* (see note 23 above) 27

28. Simpson, *Christ in the Bible*, vol. XIX (Galatians, Ephesians) (New York: Christian Alliance Publishing Co., 1904) 20

29. Simpson, *Echoes* (see note 23 above) 13-14. Simpson continues, "It is our privilege, therefore, to lay [the sin principle within us] over upon [Christ], to reckon it crucified with Him, to refuse to recognize it any longer as having a right to control us, to repudiate it, lay it off, and take our new life from His resurrection and reckon ourselves alive unto God through Jesus Christ." Simpson cites also Heb. 2:11 and John 17:19 in support of what he writes. [See also Simpson, *Wholly Sanctified* (New York: Christian Alliance Publishing Co., 1890) 110.]

30. In chapter 2, we noted the influence this book by Walter Marshall had on Simpson's life. Little has been written on *The Gospel Mystery of Sanctification*. It is known that Marshall completed the book in 1860, purposing "to teach you how you may attain to that practice and manner of life which we call holiness, righteousness or godliness, obedience, true religion; and which God requires" (page 7).

31. Simpson, *Cross of Christ* (see note 23 above) 90

32. Simpson, *Cross of Christ* (see note 23 above) 90

33. A complete copy of this lengthy citation from Marshall's *Gospel Mystery of Sanctification* is included in Appendix 3.

34. Simpson, *Cross of Christ* (see note 23 above) 24. Simpson does not indicate the page or pages in the *Gospel Mystery of Sanctification* from which he quotes.

35. Simpson, *Cross of Christ* (see note 23 above) 91

36. Simpson, *Cross of Christ* (see note 23 above) 92. It is interesting to note that Marshall also uses Rom. 8:3-4 to support this section of his comments, as did Simpson. We do not know to what extent Marshall may have influenced

Simpson in this regard.

37. Simpson, *Cross of Christ* (see note 23 above) 93

38. Gerald E. McGraw, "The Doctrine of Sanctification in the Published Writings of A. B. Simpson" (diss., New York U, 1986) 282. McGraw writes, "Since disagreements frequently arise over terminology, Simpson was wary of controversial terms. He believed sanctification's fervent advocates proved its worst foes by insistence on some theory. Extremes frighten the needy. . . . Despite his own preferences, Simpson refused to quarrel over terms. He taught unity on the 'essentials' but moderation, flexibility, and compatibility on lesser points." Simpson did not quibble over terms. Lee makes similar observations in his thesis [see Mark W. Lee, "The Biblical View of the Doctrine of the Holy Spirit in the Writings of A. B. Simpson" (Master's thesis, Wheaton Col, 1952) 23-24].

39. McGraw (see note 38 above) 282. See also his pages 277-278.

40. Simpson, *Holy Spirit,* vol. I (see note 9 above) 31

41. Simpson, *Holy Spirit,* vol. II (see note 19 above) 50

42. Simpson, *The Old Faith and the New Gospels* (New York: Christian Alliance Publishing Co., 1911) 54

43. Simpson, *Fourfold Gospel* (see note 13 above) 28. Simpson, "What is the Difference between Sanctification and Regeneration?" *The Christian Alliance* (Mar 1888). These are but two sources where Simpson uses the analogy.

44. Simpson, Correspondence Bible School, *Bible Commentary,* (2nd year, no. 11) 15

45. Simpson, *Christ in Bible,* vol. XI (Romans) (see note 23 above) 133

46. Simpson, *Fourfold Gospel* (see note 13 above) 30, 32

47. Simpson, *Christ in Bible,* vol. XIX (Galatians, Ephesians) (see note 28 above) 19

48. Simpson, "Phases and Phrases" (see note 8 above) 180. Similar definitions are found, for example, in *Fourfold Gospel* (see note 13 above) 33-34 and *Wholly Sanctified* (see note 29 above) 15.

49. Simpson, *Wholly Sanctified* (see note 29 above) 15

50. Simpson, *Wholly Sanctified* (see note 29 above) 16-17

51. Simpson, *Wholly Sanctified* (see note 29 above) 17-18

52. Simpson, *Wholly Sanctified* (see note 29 above) 18

53. Simpson, *Wholly Sanctified* (see note 29 above) 19

54. Simpson, *Wholly Sanctified* (see note 29 above) 19

55. Simpson, *Wholly Sanctified* (see note 29 above) 16. Simpson alludes to the Davidic covenant of 2 Sam. 7:8, 14 and refers to this quote when discussing 2 Cor. 6:17-7:1.

56. Simpson, *Wholly Sanctified* (see note 29 above) 19
Simpson editorial, *The Christian and Missionary Alliance Weekly* (Nov 1899) 390

57. Simpson, *Wholly Sanctified* (see note 29 above) 20-21

58. Simpson, *Fourfold Gospel* (see note 13 above) 35

59. Simpson, *Wholly Sanctified* (see note 29 above) 20-21. Simpson says this action of setting apart presupposes a confidence in God's goodness and provision. This awareness should deepen as believers mature in their relationship with God.

60. Simpson, *Wholly Sanctified* (see note 29 above) 21

61. Simpson, *Wholly Sanctified* (see note 29 above) 22

62. Simpson, *Christ in Bible,* vol. XI (Romans) (see note 23 above) 133

63. Simpson, *Holy Spirit,* vol. II (see note 19 above) 229-230

64. Section II.2.c of the 1906 working paper reads: "The indwelling of Christ in the heart of the consecrated believer *as a distinct experience.*"

65. A. E. Thompson, *The Life of A. B. Simpson* (New York: Christian Alliance Publishing Co., 1920) 181. Thompson does not indicate the source of the quote.

66. Thompson (see note 65 above) 172

67. George P. Pardington, *The Crisis of the Deeper Life* (Harrisburg, PA: Christian Publications, n.d.) 97-100
Henry Wilson, *The Internal Christ* (New York: Christian Alliance Publishing Co., 1902). George Pardington, a teacher at the C&MA Missionary Training Institute, and Henry Wilson, associate pastor of the Gospel Tabernacle in New York City—both men close associates of Simpson—make much the same emphasis in their writings. Pardington devotes an entire chapter to union with Christ. Wilson captures the same truth, suggesting there are basically three views of how believers relate Christ to their lives: imitation, inspiration and incarnation. The former two, he says, prove inadequate, for they offer no

effectual power. Only the last is the true nature of Christ's presence in a believer's life (page 12). Wilson also chronicles the shallowness of views which limit Christ to the "Historic Christ" or the "Theological Christ" or the "Ceremonial Christ" (page 36). He writes, "To these and similar cries we have one answer: 'Yes, yes, yes, but *more!*' "He continues: " 'We in Christ and Christ in us,' another phrase we use much, will become indeed a fact and a fact of such vital force that all agonizing and straining after and for things and blessings will pass away in the steady quiet absorption of Deity into our being. . . . [This is] no mystery to the yielded soul, but much mystery and much misery to those who have not yet learned the A, B, C of real surrender to God" (pages 42, 44). One must not suppose from these words that Wilson was a pantheist. He purposely mentions in the context of this quote that he is not speaking of pantheism. Rather, he is trying to explain the glories of the indwelling Christ. (See also note 70 below, where Simpson makes similar statements.)

68. Simpson, *The Old Faith* (see note 42 above) 53-54

69. Simpson, *The Old Faith* (see note 42 above) 54. Note also the use of this Romans text in a similar manner in Marshall's *Gospel Mystery of Sanctification* (see Appendix 3).

70. Simpson, *Present Truth* (New York: Christian Alliance Publishing Co., 1897) 39

71. Thompson (see note 65 above) 180. Thompson does not identify the source of this quote.

72. Simpson, *Christ in Bible,* vol. XIX (Galatians, Ephesians) (see note 28 above) 120
    Simpson, *The Old Faith* (see note 42 above) 55

73. Simpson, *Christ in Bible,* vol. XIX (Galatians, Ephesians) (see note 28 above) 120
    Simpson, *The Christ Life* (London: Morgan and Scott, 1911) 49. These are just two of many citations.

74. Simpson, *Christ Life* (see note 73 above) 49

75. Simpson, *Christ Life* (see note 73 above) 46

76. Simpson, *Christ Life* (see note 73 above) 47. Simpson makes similar comments on Eph. 3:14-19 and 2 Cor. 5:17. Compare:

    Simpson, *Christ in Bible,* vol. XIX (Galatians, Ephesians) (see note 28 above) 120.
    Simpson, *Christ Life* (see note 73 above) 28. Simpson discounts the argument

that 2 Cor. 13:5 attests to the indwelling of Christ in all believers. He writes, "The apostle has just been speaking of a test that he proposes to have whether the Corinthians are walking in the complete will of God or not." [Simpson, "The Baptism of the Holy Spirit, a Crisis or an Evolution?" *Living Truths* (Dec 1905) 707]. Simpson claims the same word is used in 1 Cor. 9:27 to refer to a race where "Paul has no idea of being lost at all, but simply losing the great reward of the victor." Hence, the passage in 2 Cor. 13:5 simply means "that if Christ is not in them, they are disapproved; they are not living up to the high standard of Christian life which they should" [707].

77. Simpson, *The Old Faith* (see note 42 above) 55

78. Simpson, *The Old Faith* (see note 42 above) 55

79. Simpson, *Christ Life* (see note 73 above) 50

80. Simpson, *The Christ of the Forty Days* (New York: Christian Alliance Publishing Co., 1890) 83-92. Simpson regarded Christ's ascension as prerequisite to the sending of the gift of the Holy Spirit. His ascension displayed the "seal of God upon the finished work of redemption and the final token of His full acceptance of Christ's great sacrifice." The ascension was "the beginning of His work of intercession as our great High Priest." It "was a prerequisite necessary to His assumption of His kingly place on the mediatorial throne."

81. Simpson, *Holy Spirit*, vol. II (see note 19 above) 11. Simpson suggested that there have been three eras in the working of the Holy Spirit. Each era, or "dispensation," was marked by differences in the way the Holy Spirit manifested Himself. (Simpson uses the term "dispensation" to mean a time period which has definite parameters and marks a distinct manner in which the Holy Spirit worked. This term should not be confused with John Nelson Darby's "dispensationalism." Simpson never espoused this view of God's work, which gained widespread influence within North American Fundamentalism.)

The first era was that of the Old Testament. During that time, the Holy Spirit was (1) "given to special individuals to fit them for service" [11]. He was (2) *with* people and *upon* people rather than *in* people [12]. Further, (3) "the Holy Ghost was not resident upon the earth, but visited it from time to time as occasion required" [12].

The second era, says Simpson, occurred during the earthly life of Christ. That was a transitional time. The relationship of the Holy Spirit to Christ during His ministry on earth was the paradigm for the third era.

The third era, as a result, is basically the universalization of the relationship of the second era. The Holy Spirit is now available to all believers, coming to "dwell in us and to unite us personally with God." Simpson goes on to explain that He comes "to be in us not only a Spirit of power and preparation for service, but a Spirit of life, holiness and fellowship with the Divine Being" [12].

82. Simpson, "The Ministry of the Spirit," *Living Truths* (Aug 1907) 438

83. Simpson, "Ministry of Spirit" (see note 82 above) 438-439

84. Simpson, *Christ in Bible,* vol. XIX (Galatians, Ephesians) (see note 28 above) 124

85. Simpson, "Ministry of Spirit" (see note 82 above) 439. Simpson makes a similar statement elsewhere when he writes, "The Holy Spirit is the Spirit that once dwelt in Christ, and He brings to us a spiritual Christ with a new touch and a higher form of manifestation than when He walked the earth of old and touched the bodies of men with His living hands" [Simpson, *Christ in Bible,* vol. XIX (Galatians, Ephesians) (see note 28 above) 124].

86. Simpson, *When the Comforter Came* (New York: Christian Alliance Publishing Co., 1911) Day 7 (there are no page numbers in this book; instead, each section is assigned a day of the month). Simpson uses other figures as well to express "this extraordinary relationship" [see Simpson, *Christ in Bible,* vol. XIX (Galatians, Ephesians) (see note 28 above) 121].

87. Simpson, "Ministry of Spirit" (see note 82 above) 439

88. Simpson, *Larger Christian Life* (see note 23 above) 70-79
    Simpson, *Holy Spirit,* vol. I (see note 9 above) 47

89. Thompson (see note 65 above) 243. The source from Simpson's writings is not given. But Simpson makes similar statements elsewhere [see, for example, *Walking in Spirit* (see note 2 above) 55].

90. Compare Simpson's *Christ in Bible,* vol. XVIII (1 & 2 Corinthians) (see note 21 above) 82, and "The Spirit-Filled Life," *The Alliance Weekly* (13 July 1918) 226. The latter article contains an extensive section dealing with the Holy Spirit's relationship to the Godhead.

91. Simpson, *When Comforter Came* (see note 86 above) Day 1

Chapter 5

The Baptism of the Holy Spirit in the Writings of A. B. Simpson, Part 3: The Precise Nature of the Baptism

In chapter 4 we looked at a seminal statement Simpson and a handful of his close associates presented to the 1906 Conference for Prayer and Counsel Respecting Uniformity in the Testimony and Teaching of the Alliance. We focused on part II.2, Christ our Sanctifier, and particularly II.2.b. There Simpson recognizes the baptism of the Holy Spirit

> . . . *as a distinct experience,* not merely for power for service, but for the personal holiness and victory over the world and sin [emphasis in the original document].

We saw that this position coincided with other statements made by Simpson well prior to 1906 and well after 1906. Thus we have every reason to conclude that, respecting sanctification and the baptism of the Holy Spirit, the document presented to that 1906 conference of Alliance workers fairly expresses Simpson's settled views.

And so we come to the key phrase of our inquiry: "The baptism of the Holy Spirit." We want to examine the precise nature of the baptism of the Holy Spirit as Simpson understood it. As in chapter 4, we will be exploring the broader scope of Simpson's writings, using this 1906 statement as our interpretive key. By so doing, we should be able to clarify Simpson's understanding of the term.

The Relationship between Sanctification, the Indwelling Christ and the Baptism of the Holy Spirit

Our previous investigation of the 1906 document suggested a relationship between sanctification, the indwelling Christ and the baptism of the Holy Spirit. It is time now to crystalize that relationship as Simpson understood it.

First, each of the three terms expresses an aspect of what Simpson viewed as God's provision for holy living.[1] He makes that evident in comments like these:

> The indwelling of Christ and the indwelling of the Spirit represent different sides of the same experience.[2]

> [This experience is] variously described in the New Testament as "the baptism of the Holy Ghost," "abiding in Christ and He in us" and such promises as John 14:23 ["We will come unto him, and make our abode with him"].[3]

Simpson also suggests this interrelationship between the terms in his article, "Phases and Phrases of the Deeper Life," where he attempts to cut his way through all the terminology prevalent in his time. Specifically mentioning these three terms, Simpson stresses that they are all part of God's provision for holy living.[4]

Second, these phrases do have their own distinctive meaning, each being a "phase" of the larger provision. Simpson depicts sanctification as the experiential "separated from, dedicated to, and filled with." To Simpson, the indwelling of Christ is the presence of Christ in the believer's life, the source for holy living. The indwelling of the Holy Spirit begins with the baptism of the Holy Spirit, the initiatory event that brings to the surrendered believer the effectual ability to appropriate God's provisions as promised in Jeremiah 31 and Ezekiel 36.

It is to the baptism of the Holy Spirit that our investigation now turns.

The Nature of the Baptism of the Holy Spirit

In response to a reader's inquiry in 1892 as to the meaning of the baptism of the Holy Spirit, Simpson replied that it involved "the coming of the Holy Ghost personally to abide in the heart forever."[5] In 1902 Simpson wrote that it was "a definite experience in which we receive the Spirit Himself."[6] In 1907, in an article written after the 1906 Conference, Simpson states that the baptism of the Holy Spirit "marks the moment when the Spirit comes to dwell within the converted heart, and henceforth it becomes the temple of the Holy Ghost."[7] In this sense, "there is, therefore, one baptism with the Spirit once for all, and from that time, the Holy Ghost Himself is our indwelling life."[8]

In connection with the nature of this baptism, Simpson asks, "Is it some special experience subjective to ourselves, involving a marked change of character and feeling? Or is it something more?"[9] He replies:

> It seems to be clearly taught both by the experience of our Lord Himself and by all the references to the subject in the New Testament writings, that we are to regard the baptism of the Spirit as a baptism with the Spirit. It is not that Christ baptizes us with some special feeling, gift, or blessing, but rather that Christ baptizes us with the Spirit Himself. The baptism is simply the receiving of the Person—the personal Holy Ghost.[10]

A number of elements of Simpson's teaching on the baptism of the Holy Spirit emerge from this quote. First, Simpson emphasized that the focus must not be so much on the experience as on the reception of a Person. Second, Jesus is the Baptizer. Since He was anointed with the Spirit by the Father and has ascended into heaven, He now baptizes believers with the Spirit.[11] Accordingly, the Spirit is always related to the person of Christ. Third, Simpson held that the more specific usage of the term is baptism *with* the Spirit rather than baptism *of* the Spirit. Simpson, however, frequently uses *of* to depict this initial reception of the Spirit.[12]

As a consequence of this baptism, the Spirit "henceforth becomes united to our life, and in communion with Him we are divinely enabled for every Christian experience and every spiritual ministry."[13] Paralleling Christ's union with the Spirit at His baptism, Simpson writes:

> This is exactly what occurs when we receive the Holy Ghost. We become personally united to the Lord through the Holy Spirit, and we go forth into our future life, no longer alone, but leaning upon our Beloved [Christ], and drawing our sufficiency and strength for everything from His constant presence and abiding life. It is not power we receive, but Him, and He administers the power as He reigns upon the throne of our hearts and administers the government of our life.[14]

Thus, in relational terms, the baptism of the Holy Spirit brings the personal presence of Christ, who is able to provide the means to follow God. The Spirit is the agent of transferring the ability of Christ into the believer's life.

No Longer Alone

The believer is, as this citation mentions, no longer "alone." Simpson elsewhere expands on what he meant by this terminology:

> There comes a time when a new personality is added to ours and we go forth to life's conflicts and duties no longer alone, but in union with Him who has come to be our very life and all-sufficiency.[15]

Rather than to struggle in his or her own resources, the believer has the enabling presence of Christ to meet "life's conflicts and duties." At the heart of Simpson's view of this matter was his argument that God was profoundly personal. He would meet people decisively at significant points in their spiritual journey.[16] God was a God who "broke into" people's lives. He had done this in the Old Testament and Simpson argues that this pattern continued into the New Testament. A person was not simply converted by repentance and regeneration and then set on life's journey. God wanted His people to open themselves to His mighty presence.[17]

Christianity was a relational religion between the Creator and His people. Simpson argued that such a profound relationship did not simply attend regeneration. It occurred when people opened every part of their beings to God. God, in turn, came into their lives in a new, deeper and more profound manner.[18] This, argued Simpson, was the issue that undergirded any discussion of the baptism of the Holy Spirit.

In summary, then, we see that sanctification is the necessary response of the believer to God's gracious provision. The indwelling of Christ is the means by which a believer can live a holy life. The baptism of the Spirit comes the *moment a person experientially enters into this full provision of God.*

The Baptism of the Holy Spirit and Conversion

Simpson's teaching on the baptism of the Holy Spirit is more easily understood when we examine his understanding of the Spirit's role in the conversion process. Simpson held that the Holy Spirit turned sinners' hearts toward God, convicting them of their sin, and, as they repented and received Christ as their Savior, spiritually regenerating them.[19] At the instant of regeneration, Simpson saw the Holy Spirit as *with* the believer.[20] Although present with and acting upon believers at their conversion, the Spirit does not "automatically" indwell them. Simpson writes:

> Is it then true that the Holy Spirit is not residing in the Christian until after this new experience [of the baptism of the Holy Spirit]? The answer to this question is found in

two prepositions used by our Lord in John xiv. 17: "He dwelleth with you and shall be in you." The Holy Spirit is *with* the converted Christian as He was with God's people in the Old Testament dispensation, but only in the entire surrender and definite act of faith do we receive Him in all His fulness. Then he becomes resident *in* us [Simpson's emphases].[21]

As the 1906 document implies, Simpson was adamant that the baptism of the Spirit was a "distinct blessing." The aforementioned quote states that the believer must volitionally ask for the Spirit. Compare his words, ". . . in the entire surrender and definite act of faith do we receive Him in all His fulness." The implication is that a believer must apprehend the provision of God and then appropriate it, just as in asking for salvation.

Simpson makes much of the subtle change in the prepositions *with* and *in,* as the preceding quote attests. For Simpson, this change in prepositions described the difference between the experience of believers who had, and believers who had not, received the baptism of the Spirit. For those who had not, their experience was essentially that of an Old Testament believer. They were struggling to follow God in their own strength. However, those who had received the baptism of the Spirit through "entire surrender and [a] definite act of faith" received the Spirit "in all His fulness."

Critics often have charged Simpson with asserting that a person may be a Christian and not actually have the Holy Spirit, or that he or she may somehow have "part" of the Spirit. Indeed, a reading of some of Simpson's statements appears to assert this very fact. His statements on the indwelling of the Spirit, however, must be understood within the framework of his call to appropriate God's provision for holy living. In his concern that people truly experience a vital new relationship with God, he saw in Christ's words in passages such as John 14:17 that the terms *with* and *in* described differences of experience. As the quotation above declares, "Only in the entire surrender and definite act of faith do we receive [the Holy Spirit] in all His fulness. Then He becomes resident in us."

Simpson is quite explicit in his writings that the normative pattern in the New Testament was that believers should immediately receive the baptism of the Holy Spirit once they had been converted. Referring to Acts 2:38-39, Simpson writes:

> There is every reason to believe that on the day of Pentecost and in the Apostolic church, [the two works, conversion and the baptism of the Holy Spirit,] were contemporaneous or close together in the actual experience of believers. The difference is one in the nature of things rather than in the order of time. The early Christians were expected to pass quickly into the baptism of the Holy Ghost and the fulness of their life in Christ. When Paul came to Ephesus and found believers, his first question was, "Have ye received the Holy Ghost since ye believed?" And when he found they had not he immediately led them on to this deeper and fuller blessing.[22]

The baptism of the Spirit follows repentance sequentially, but there need be no time delay. Hence Simpson's comment, "The difference is one in the nature of things rather than in the order of time." While acknowledging that the baptism of the Holy Spirit may be contemporaneous with repentance, Simpson continually stressed the distinctiveness of this work. Elsewhere he writes:

> We are willing, however, to concede that the baptism of the Holy Ghost may be received at the very same time a soul is converted. We have known a sinner to be converted, sanctified, and saved all within a single hour, and yet each experience was different in its nature and was received in proper order and by a definite faith for that particular blessing.[23]

Again, the reception of the Holy Spirit is shown to be a gift specifically asked for and explicitly received.

Scriptural Support Simpson Found for His View

Simpson was keenly aware of those passages usually cited by others to prove the automatic, nonvolitional possession of the Spirit's fullness by all believers from conversion onward. Many in Simpson's day held that, once saved or converted, all a person needed to do was to grow in grace. In his article, "The Baptism of the Holy Spirit, A Crisis or an Evolution?" Simpson takes on this challenge to his view.[24] He begins with Romans 8:9-10—"[their] favorite passage and the strongest argument which they present."[25] The core sentence in the passage is this: "If anyone does not have the Spirit of Christ, he does not belong to Christ." While admitting that "at first glance this seems to be a very convincing argument," Simpson suggests that the verse should be reexplored.[26] He argues, first, that "it is possible for a truly converted soul to be in the flesh and not in the Spirit," as verses such as First Corinthians 3:1, 3 clearly show. Consequently, Romans 8:9-10 is not speaking of all Christians, "but of those who are no longer in the flesh, and have received the Spirit of God and have become spiritual simply through the Holy Spirit."[27] As for the phrase "he does not belong to Christ," Simpson argues, "[It] does not mean necessarily that such an one is not a Christian, but rather that he has not surrendered to Christ in such a sense that he belongs to Him."[28] He mentions "the two classes of Christians that we find everywhere today"[29] and stresses, "All things are not ours until we are all the Lord's."[30]

Responding to Peter's quoted exhortation found in Acts 2:38-39, to "Repent . . . [and] you will receive the gift of the Holy Spirit," Simpson writes that he does not question God's intention to give the Holy Spirit to all believers as one of the provisions of His grace, but this does not mean that all the promises of God "are received at the same moment."[31] He likens salvation to the entering of the vestibule of a house, asserting that the various rooms of God's provision are not all entered immediately.[32]

Peter's statement that "God has given [the Holy Spirit] to those who obey him" (Acts 5:32) was also used in objection to a subsequent baptism of the Spirit. Simpson, however, sees the statement as actually supporting his position. Obedience, in his view, implies a full following after God. He goes on:

> It cannot be denied that multitudes of Christians are not obedient Christians. They have not surrendered to the will of God. They have not given up the world and sin.[33]

A Further Objection Answered

In the *Living Truths* article Simpson cites still a further objection to his views:

> A very strong text used by our friends is I. Corinthians iii. 16: "Know ye not that we are the temple of God and that the Spirit of God dwelleth in you? If any man defile the temple of God, him shall God destroy, for the temple of God is holy, which temple ye are." . . . It is enough to say that there were evidently two classes of Christians in the church at Corinth, and the apostle alternately addresses these two classes. Speaking to the one class he says, "In everything ye are enriched so that ye come not behind in any gift, waiting for the coming of our Lord Jesus Christ" [1:5-7].
>
> And yet, in the next breath he says, "There is evil among you [3:3]. Ye do wrong and defraud, and that your brethren. Ye are carnal and walk as men" [6:8].[34]

Simpson countered this argument by referring his opponents to Second Corinthians 6:16-18: "What agreement is there between the temple of God and idols? . . . 'Come out from them / and be separate / says the Lord.' " Separation from the world is the prerequisite to being the temple of God.[35]

The final Scripture Simpson mentions as cited by those who argued that the baptism of the Spirit comes at conversion was First Corinthians 12:13: "For we were all baptized by one Spirit into one body." Simpson maintains that this verse deals with believers being united with the Church, the body of Christ.[36] The preposition *into,* the Greek *en,* is best rendered "by," in Simpson's view, for it is through the Spirit that Christians are united to the Body of Christ.[37]

Simpson declared that the last phrase—"we have all been made to drink into one Spirit"—refers to "the individual reception of the Holy Spirit."[38] He elaborates:

> Some one has finely illustrated this by the figure of the bottle in the sea, and the sea in the bottle. It is possible for the bottle to be in the sea and the sea not to be in the bottle. It is possible for us to be in the Spirit and in Christ by the faith that saves us and yet not have the Spirit in us by the faith that sanctifies us.[39]

This quotation once again points to the separation Simpson makes between initial penitent confession of sins and entering the full provision of God by a specific appropriation of God's sanctifying blessing.

Besides critiquing some of the arguments used against his contentions, Simpson also offers his own arguments in support of his position. "The strongest proof we know," he says, "is derived from the experience of the Master Himself, our glorious Forerunner."[40] This dimension of Simpson's teaching has already been explored in chapter 3. Simpson saw in Christ the paradigm of a two-step conversion experience. Moreover, in chapter 4 we have already delineated Simpson's understanding of the Jeremiah 31 and Ezekiel 36 passages. "Respecting the coming of the Holy Ghost," Simpson says "[these passages] clearly distinguish it from conversion."[41]

Simpson also cites the experience of the disciples before and after Pentecost. He maintains that "they were undoubtedly saved" prior to Pentecost.[42] Yet at Pentecost "there came to them an entirely new experience," giving them not only power for ministry but power for personal holiness. "The men were as changed as their ministry."[43]

Very Clear Conditions

Simpson says, "The promise of Christ to His disciples that the Comforter should come was accompanied with very clear conditions and definitions."[44] As we earlier noted, the Holy Spirit was said to be *with* the disciples and soon would be *in* them[45] (John 14:17). Simpson pointed out that Christ "identifies the coming of the Comforter with His own indwelling. 'At that day ye shall know that I am in the Father and ye in me and I in you.' "[46] At the same time, Simpson reminds his readers, "His coming to abide is connected with a spirit of devotion and obedience."[47] To support his statement, he directs them to John 14:21 and 23: "Whoever has my commands and obeys them, he is the one who loves me. . . . If anyone loves me, he will obey my teaching." Simpson writes further:

> Christ's indwelling is here connected with a spirit of love and obedience. Who will say that the men and women who are loving and living for the world and trying to have barely enough religion to save them from the flames of hell, are fit subjects for such an experience? Is it not a degradation of such a glorious promise to make such an application of it?[48]

Clearly the twin themes of separation and complete dedication to God, distinct from regeneration, appear once again as foundational to Simpson's perception of the dynamics of the full working of the Spirit in a believer's life.

Simpson saw Galatians 4:19 as indicative of Paul's concern that the Galatian Christians move into the full salvation God had for them. Paul calls the Galatians his "dear children" and says he is "again in the pains of childbirth until Christ is formed" in them. They already have been converted, Simpson is sure, but Paul "is travailing in birth for another blessing: that Christ may be formed in them."[49]

Simpson alludes to the "types which we find in ancient Israel that foreshadow this deeper life."[50] In his writings Simpson makes recurring mention of a number of images. Israel's exodus from Egypt "typified our conversion," but when "they entered the land of promise and crossed the Jordan, they set forth our coming into the 'rest' which remaineth for the people of God [Hebrews 4:9]." He draws a similar analogy from God's cloud of fire that directed Israel through the desert. After the tabernacle was completed "and solemnly handed over to God, . . . then that mystic cloud came down and no longer led them from the sky or the mount, but took up its abode in the very bosom of the tabernacle."[51]

Simpson argues that "the experiences of the saints of God, both in the Scriptures and in modern Christian life, involves [sic] this deeper blessing."[52] He cites Jacob, Job, Isaiah, Joshua and Paul as scriptural examples.[53] He mentions the "Moravian saints" and John Wesley, who "became changed and filled with the Holy Spirit."[54] He says this same experience has been "multiplied in scores and hundreds of saintly lives in these last days."[55] He goes on:

> While no experience in itself is a sufficient foundation for Christian doctrine, but backed by such an array of Scripture as we have endeavored to present, we see . . . in these lives . . . eloquent appeals to us to-day, saying, "I beseech you therefore by the mercies of God that ye present your bodies a living sacrifice" [Romans 12:1]. . . . "Tarry ye till ye be endued with power from on high" [Acts 1:4]. "Abide in me and I in you" [John 15:4].[56]

Water Baptism and the Baptism of the Holy Spirit

Simpson suggests that water baptism depicts the essential nature of the baptism of the Holy Spirit.[57] As we noted in chapter 1, Simpson came to see that water baptism was "much more than the rite of initiation into the Christian church, much more than the sign and seal of a hereditary conviction on the part of parents for their children."[58] To him it was

. . . *the* symbol of personal, intelligent, voluntary and profoundly earnest surrender of our lives to God in self crucifixion, and the act of dying with Christ . . . and entering into a new world of life through the resurrection of Jesus Christ.[59]

Adult believers' baptism, therefore, best expresses complete commitment to God and, like Christ's baptism, provides the opportune time and stepping stone for the baptism of the Holy Spirit.

From this awareness, Simpson saw that there was

. . . but one baptism, for the water and the Spirit were each but part of a greater whole, and both were linked in the divine appointment, the one as the sign and the other as the divine reality of a great crisis by which we passed through death into resurrection life and became united through the Holy Ghost henceforth to the living God as the Source and Power of our new and heavenly life.[60]

Water baptism should mark the crisis of dedication to God which Simpson so frequently points out as the precursor to the incoming of the Holy Spirit. It is unclear from his writings whether he held that one needed to be baptized in water in order to receive the indwelling Holy Spirit. More likely, his point would be that the *significance* of water baptism is separation from sin and dedication to God.

We have now surveyed in Simpson's writings the various areas pertaining directly to the baptism of the Holy Spirit. In the rest of this chapter we will examine the dynamics of receiving the baptism of the Holy Spirit.

The Problem of Deficient Conversions

Simpson was well aware of the inherent dangers in mass evangelism. Paul wrote to the Ephesians, "Having believed, you were marked in [Christ] with a seal, the promised Holy Spirit, who is a deposit guaranteeing our inheritance until the redemption of those who are God's possession—to the praise of his glory" (1:13-14). Commenting on those verses, Simpson says:

> We are told it was after they believed, probably just after that they received the Holy Spirit. This [seal of the Holy Spirit] should immediately follow the experience of conversion. Indeed, there is no assurance that we can keep our conversion without the sealing of the Holy Ghost. That is the great lack in the religious teaching today. Men and women are hurried into a profession of religion under a superficial excitement, and it is little wonder if they fall away. Every disciple ought to be led on to the baptism of the Spirit.[61]

The result of these superficial conversions, in Simpson's view, was a lowered standard of Christianity. Salvation was portrayed merely as escape from punishment, with little stress given to God's irrevocable call to holy living.[62] Simpson suggested that the condition of the Ephesian disciples cited in Acts 19 was "representative of a great majority of professing Christians today."[63] He comments further:

> They have accepted the ministry of repentance. They have experienced, to some extent, conversion. They have begun to "quit their meanness" and change the course of their life. But they do not know Christ as a personal and abiding presence. They have not received the Holy Ghost.[64]

To Simpson the true gospel message was not just the forgiveness of sins, but "the Holy Ghost filling the hearts of saved men and changing them supernaturally, sanctifying them from the power of evil and keeping them for that great day."[65]

The question arises once again as to whether Simpson believed people could be saved and not have the Spirit dwelling in them. In attempting a response, we must remember that Simpson always made his statements in the context of a believer's entering into God's full provision for holy living. Simpson's writings compared these deficient conversions to Israel's wanderings in the Sinai desert prior to the full blessings of Canaan.[66] Simpson attributes people's failure to enter the "land of Promise" to "ignorance, unbelief or disobedience."[67] We find this diagnostic analysis recurring again and again in Simpson's writings. Pointedly he urges his readers to move into full salvation. He wants them to apprehend and appropriate the provision of the Holy Spirit. He wants them to be aware of, and obediently move into, their full inheritance as Christians.

The Place of the Will in the Spiritual Life

Our exploration of Simpson's thought as expressed in his writings has revealed that believers have specific volitional responsibilities in the dynamics of their spiritual lives. Simpson describes the human will as "the real engine and helm of character, life, and action" and as "that which gives impulse, power, and direction to the whole mind and life."[68] The will is the part of a person that must respond to God. Simpson asserts that a believer's responsibility in the divine order is to recognize volitionally, and submit to, the declared will of God. God, in Simpson's view, respected personhood. He would not circumvent the human will. Simpson comments on this matter:

> While we recognize the sovereign power of the Holy
> Ghost, visiting the heart at His pleasure and working according to His will upon the objects of His grace, yet God
> has ordained certain laws of operation and cooperation in
> connection with the application of redemption. And He
> Himself most delicately recognizes His own laws and
> respects the freedom of the human will; not forcing His
> blessings upon unwilling hearts, but knocking at the door
> of our heart, waiting to be recognized and claimed, and then
> working in the soul as we heartily cooperate, hear, and obey.
> There is, therefore, a very solemn and responsible part for
> every man in cooperating with the Holy Spirit.[69]

The statement, "waiting to be recognized and claimed," is vital to this matter of the will. A believer must in a sense "will" or "permit" God to work. Simpson acknowledged the danger of exalting the human will, and stated that even in the submission to God's working, believers need His effectual grace.[70] Simpson's point, therefore, is that believers must volitionally respond to God, acknowledging His declared will, particularly in matters involving the Spirit's work in their lives.

Receiving the Gift of the Holy Spirit

The previous discussions in this chapter serve as the foundation for this next important matter. In an editorial published in 1893, Simpson poses the question, "How shall we receive the Holy Ghost?"[71] By way of response he asks, "How shall we receive anything from God?" Then he proceeds to outline the answer.

The first element, Simpson asserts, must be an awareness or apprehension of God's promised provision.[72] We must be aware of what God has intended for us. We must also know that it is fruitless to try to follow God by means of our own human resources.

The second element is appropriating faith.[73] Simpson defined this simply as "believing that [God] gives what He promises."[74] The implicit understanding here is that God gives when we ask; therefore, we must ask for the gift of the Holy Spirit.[75] Simpson stresses that this act of faith is not "works" on our part, but just a response to God's gracious invitation.[76]

Simpson emphasizes in his writing that we do not have to make ourselves perfect in order to receive the Holy Spirit. He writes:

> You don't need to wait until you are faultless and sinless to receive the Holy Ghost. There is a kind of teaching about sanctification, telling people they must get sanctified and all right themselves, and then the Holy Ghost will come. If you can get ready for the Holy Ghost without Him you can get along without Him afterwards.[77]

The final element is to believe the Spirit has come as promised and to begin to acknowledge His presence.

Prior to moving to chapter 6, we need to recall that this discussion about receiving the Spirit falls within the broader context of sanctification. As we noted in the previous chapter, Simpson understood sanctification to be (1) separation *from* unholy things, (2) separation *to* God by the conscious choice of our will and heart, after which comes (3) the baptism of the Holy Spirit and the indwelling life of God:

> There is first the negative side, the things we are separated from; the positive side, things we are saved to, then the filling of the vessel that has thus been given to God by the Holy Spirit and the indwelling of Christ.[78]

Part of the experience of sanctification is to be "filled with." Through the baptism of the Spirit, the life of God comes fully into the believer's experience. Thus once more we see from Simpson's view an inseparable link between the baptism of the Spirit and sanctification.

In summary, the baptism of the Spirit in Simpson's view had two aspects. On the human side, believers were responsible to recognize God's provision for holy living and respond by separating themselves from the unholy, giving themselves totally to God and appropriating His blessing by faith. From the divine side, God made provision for all believers in the atoning work of Christ on the cross. He imparts His provision for sanctification to those who meet His conditions.

An illustration may further our understanding. A coin has two sides. Both sides are equally important and together comprise the coin. If either side of the coin is missing, the coin is really not a coin. Simpson saw God's provision in Christ for the believer as a two-sided coin. There was the objective side: believers were justified—put in right standing with God. They were placed "in" Christ. They had the Spirit "with" them. At the same time, there was the other, experiential side of the coin. The objective facts must be translated into experiential realities. For that to happen, the Christian had definite responsibilities. This other side of the "coin" did not simply "happen." It demanded specific choices. It demanded obedience. If believers did not respond appropriately, their Christian lives would be deficient. They would be saved, but they would be living a half-salvation.

Simpson's burning passion was to communicate the need for experience, the need for believers to respond to God. Simpson saw in what he called "the baptism of the Holy Spirit" the fulfillment of that appropriate response.

End Notes

1. John S. Sawin concurs with this assessment [see "The Fourfold Gospel," *The Birth of A Vision,* David F. Hartzfeld and Charles Nienkirchen, eds. (Beaverlodge, AB: Buena Book Services, 1986)]. So do Mark W. Lee ["The Biblical View of the Doctrine of the Holy Spirit in the Writings of A. B. Simpson" (Master's thesis, Wheaton Col, 1952) 24-32] and Gerald E. McGraw ["The Doctrine of Sanctification in the Published Writings of Albert Benjamin Simpson" (diss., New York U, 1986) 292].

2. A. B. Simpson editorial, *The Christian and Missionary Alliance Weekly* (Nov 1899) 380. In context Simpson writes: "It means to be filled with or baptized with the Spirit and carries along with it the idea of the indwelling of Christ in our hearts. Jesus dwells within us and becomes the power and substance of our new life. The indwelling of Christ and the indwelling of the Spirit represent different sides of the same experience. The Spirit-filled life therefore is the Christ-filled life. When Christ fills our life with Himself, it is then meet for the Master's use and prepared unto every good work [2 Timothy 2:21]."

3. Simpson, *Christ in the Bible,* vol. XVIII (1 & 2 Corinthians) (New York: Christian Alliance Publishing Co., 1904) 81

4. Simpson, "Phases and Phrases of the Deeper Life," *Living Truths* (Oct 1902)

5. Simpson, "The Baptism with the Spirit," *The Christian Alliance and Missionary Weekly* (30 Sep 1892) 120

6. Simpson, "Phases and Phrases" (see note 4 above) 181

7. Simpson, "The Ministry of the Spirit," *Living Truths* (Aug 1907) 440

8. Simpson, *The Holy Spirit, or Power from on High,* vol. II (New York: Christian Alliance Publishing Co., 1895) 23

9. Simpson, "Baptism, and the Baptism of the Holy Spirit," *The Christian and Missionary Alliance Weekly* (17 May 1902) 296

10. Simpson, "Baptism, and Baptism" (see note 9 above) 296

11. Refer, for example, to Simpson, *Holy Spirit,* vol. II (see note 8 above) 21-25.

12. This is evident in the 1906 document. Simpson was flexible in the use of this term. Later in this investigation it will be demonstrated that he also used "baptism" of the Spirit to describe subsequent fillings of the Spirit after the initial reception of the Spirit. McGraw (see note 1 above) 553-555 has shown that the later Simpson articles tend to avoid "new baptism" terminology, although Simpson was certainly open to repeated fillings.

13. Simpson, "Baptism, and Baptism" (see note 9 above) 296

14. Simpson, "Baptism, and Baptism" (see note 9 above) 296

15. Simpson, "The Baptism of the Holy Spirit, a Crisis or an Evolution?" *Living Truths* (Dec 1905) 710. This quotation was already cited in chapter 3 in the section dealing with the Holy Spirit's relationship to Christ.

16. Simpson succinctly argues this point in his article "The Crisis of the Deeper Life," *Living Truths* (Sep 1906) 520-526.

17. Simpson, "Crisis of Deeper Life" (see note 16 above) 521

18. Simpson, "Crisis of Deeper Life" (see note 16 above) 521

19. Referring to John 1:12 and 3:5-7, Simpson sees regeneration as the impartation of new life and spiritual senses "through which we discern, understand and enter into the life of God, and the spiritual realm" [*Holy Spirit,* vol. II (see note 8 above) 50]. Elsewhere in the same volume he cites Titus 3:5 and describes regeneration as the "quickening of the soul that is dead in sin, and bringing it into the life of God" (see page 197).

20. See, for example, Simpson's discussion in *The Holy Spirit, or Power from on High,* vol. I (New York: Christian Alliance Publishing Co., 1895) 67-69. This matter was discussed in chapter 4 in relation to Simpson's use of Jeremiah 31 and Ezekiel 36.

21. Simpson, "Some Aspects of the Holy Spirit," *Living Truths* (Jul 1905) 389

22. Simpson, "The Crisis of the Deeper Life," *Living Truths* (Sep 1906) 523. Similar comments on the immediate nature of the baptism of the Holy Spirit

are found in Simpson's *Christ in the Bible*, vol. XI (Romans) (New York: Christian Alliance Publishing Co., 1894) 115; in *Christ in the Bible*, vol. XIX (Galatians, Ephesians) (New York: Christian Alliance Publishing Co., 1904) 77; and in his editorial, *Living Truths* (Mar 1906) 130.

23. Simpson, "Baptism, Crisis or Evolution?" (see note 15 above) 708

24. Simpson, "Baptism, Crisis or Evolution?" (see note 15 above) 708. The full title of this article—"The Baptism of the Holy Spirit, a Crisis or an Evolution?"—is indicative of one of Simpson's major contentions regarding the work of the Spirit. He suggests in his writings that Christians had been adversely affected in their understanding of the work of the Spirit by several trends in the society of the day. Foremost was the rising theory of evolution, which tended to rule out the supernatural and to focus on secondary causality [see, for example, Simpson's *The Old Faith and the New Gospels* (New York: Christian Alliance Publishing Co., 1911) 9-19]. His "Crisis of Deeper Life" article (see note 16 above) 520-521 is in the same vein. Simpson asserts that Christians need to maintain a worldview that sees God as supernaturally involved in their lives. It is by this inflow of the life of God that they are sustained. Thus believers need to recognize the Spirit. Salvation is not a germ of life, implanted in a person, that gradually unfolds; rather, it is a series of recreative divine acts within the person. Receiving the Spirit initiates this life of dependence on God.

25. Simpson, "Baptism, Crisis or Evolution?" (see note 15 above) 705

26. Simpson, "Baptism, Crisis or Evolution?" (see note 15 above) 705

27. Simpson, "Baptism, Crisis or Evolution?" (see note 15 above) 706

28. Simpson, "Baptism, Crisis or Evolution?" (see note 15 above) 706

29. Simpson, "Baptism, Crisis or Evolution?" (see note 15 above) 706

30. Simpson, "Baptism, Crisis or Evolution?" (see note 15 above) 706

31. Simpson, "Baptism, Crisis or Evolution?" (see note 15 above) 708

32. Simpson, "Baptism, Crisis or Evolution?" (see note 15 above) 708

33. Simpson, "Baptism, Crisis or Evolution?" (see note 15 above) 708

34. Simpson, "Baptism, Crisis or Evolution?" (see note 15 above) 708

35. Simpson, "Baptism, Crisis or Evolution?" (see note 15 above) 710

36. Simpson, "Baptism, Crisis or Evolution?" (see note 15 above) 711. Simpson makes similar statements in *Holy Spirit*, vol. II (see note 8 above) 119-121.

37. Simpson, "Baptism, Crisis or Evolution?" (see note 15 above) 711

38. Simpson, "Baptism, Crisis or Evolution?" (see note 15 above) 711

39. Simpson, "Baptism, Crisis or Evolution?" (see note 15 above) 711. Once again, this illustration must be understood within the context of a believer's entering God's provision for sanctification. Simpson's comments on preceding pages reiterate this concern.

40. Simpson, "Baptism, Crisis or Evolution?" (see note 15 above) 711

41. Simpson, "Baptism, Crisis or Evolution?" (see note 15 above) 711

42. Simpson, "Baptism, Crisis or Evolution?" (see note 15 above) 711

43. Simpson, "Baptism, Crisis or Evolution?" (see note 15 above) 711. Elsewhere Simpson discusses the tremendous change in the apostles' characters, particularly their holiness and their resolution and boldness in proclaiming the gospel [see, for example, *Holy Spirit,* vol. II (see note 8 above) 77]. In *A Larger Christian Life* (New York: Christian Alliance Publishing Co., 1890), Simpson declares, "All that God requires in each of us is an opportunity to show what He can do and to prove over and over again that 'where sin abounded, grace did much more abound' [Simpson's paraphrase of Romans 5:20]" (page 101). Simpson goes on to explore the various ways in which God extends His grace in the transformation of believers (pages 100-104).

44. Simpson, *Larger Christian Life* (see note 43 above) 101

45. Simpson, *Larger Christian Life* (see note 43 above) 101

46. Simpson, *Larger Christian Life* (see note 43 above) 101

47. Simpson, *Larger Christian Life* (see note 43 above) 101

48. Simpson handles the "sealing of the Holy Spirit" (Ephesians 1:13-14) in a similar manner: "We first yield ourselves, and then we believe and receive the Holy Ghost by a definite act of committal and faith; then His work begins" [*Holy Spirit,* vol. II (see note 8 above) 129].

49. Simpson, "Baptism, Crisis or Evolution?" (see note 15 above) 712

50. Simpson, "Baptism, Crisis or Evolution?" (see note 15 above) 711

51. Simpson, "Baptism, Crisis or Evolution?" (see note 15 above) 712. See also Simpson's "Ministry of Spirit" (see note 7 above) 440. We previously noted Simpson's analogy of the builder, who having completed the house now comes to live in it.

52. Simpson, "Baptism, Crisis or Evolution?" (see note 15 above) 714

53. Simpson, "Baptism, Crisis or Evolution?" (see note 15 above) 714. Simpson writes: "Jacob came to his Peniel and through a divine transformation came forth no longer Jacob but Israel, a prince with God. Job dies to his self-life and came out with a new experience and blessing. Isaiah saw himself unclean and received the touch of fire that sanctified and sent him forth to his glorious service. Joshua, notwithstanding all the victories of the wilderness, had to meet the angel of the Lord and die to his own leadership before he could bring Israel into the land."

54. Simpson, "Baptism, Crisis or Evolution?" (see note 15 above) 714. In *Walking in the Spirit* (New York: Christian Alliance Publishing Co., 1889), Simpson refers to George Whitfield and Charles Finney (see pages 104-107).

55. Simpson, "Baptism, Crisis or Evolution?" (see note 15 above) 714

56. Simpson, "Baptism, Crisis or Evolution?" (see note 15 above) 715

57. Simpson most fully explicates these views in "Baptism, and Baptism" (see note 8 above).

58. Simpson, "Baptism, and Baptism" (see note 8 above) 286. In this article Simpson chronicles how his views on water baptism had changed over the course of his life. In our chapter 1 we looked at a lengthy excerpt from this article, in which Simpson describes the profound impact this discovery had upon his theological formulations. Simpson never rejected the fact that baptism was an ordinance significant for salvation. But he also came to see that baptism also pictured death to the old life and resurrection to new life—matters which Paul details in Romans 6. Ironically, as a student at Knox College, a Presbyterian school in Toronto, Simpson had won first prize in an essay competition for defending the practice of infant baptism. However, during his Presbyterian ministry in New York, his views changed. For more details see pages 286-287 of his article.

59. Simpson, "Baptism, and Baptism" (see note 8 above) 286

60. Simpson, "Baptism, and Baptism" (see note 8 above) 286

61. Simpson, *Christ in Bible,* vol. XIX (Galatians, Ephesians) (see note 22 above) 77

62. Simpson, *Christ in Bible,* vol. XI (Romans) (see note 22 above) 115

63. Simpson, *Christ in the Bible,* vol. XVI (Acts) (New York: Christian Alliance Publishing Co., 1902) 122

64. Simpson, *Christ in Bible,* vol. XVI (Acts) (see note 63 above) 122

65. Simpson, *Christ in the Bible*, vol. XIV (Mark) (New York: Christian Alliance Publishing Co., 1910) 29-30

66. For examples, see Simpson's *Christ in Bible*, vol. XI (Romans) (see note 22 above) 115, and his editorial (see note 22 above) 131.

67. Simpson editorial (see note 22 above) 131

68. Simpson, "The Place of the Will in the Spiritual Life," *The Christian Alliance and Missionary Weekly* (11 Mar 1892) 169

69. Simpson, *Christ in Bible*, vol. XIX (Galatians, Ephesians) (see note 22 above) 137

70. Simpson, "Place of the Will" (see note 68 above) 169

71. Simpson, "Receive Ye the Holy Ghost," *The Christian Alliance and Missionary Weekly* (17 Nov 1893) 305

72. Simpson, "The Holy Spirit," *The Word, the Work and the World* (Apr 1885) 115-117
    Simpson editorial (see note 22 above) 131
    Simpson, "Tarry," *Living Truths* (Sep 1907) 504
    Simpson, *Walking in Spirit* (see note 54 above) 138-140

73. Simpson editorial (see note 22 above) 131

74. Simpson, "Receive Ye Holy Ghost" (see note 71 above) 305

75. Simpson, "Receive Ye Holy Ghost" (see note 71 above) 305

76. Simpson, "Holy Spirit" (see note 72 above) 118

77. Simpson, *Christ in Bible*, vol. XVI (Acts) (see note 63 above) 33

78. We referred to this quotation in chapter 4 in the section dealing with sanctification [see Simpson, "Phases and Phrases" (see note 4 above) 180]. Similar definitions of sanctification are found in Simpson's *The Fourfold Gospel* (New York: Christian Alliance Publishing Co., 1887) 33-34, and in his *Wholly Sanctified*, legacy edition (Harrisburg, PA: Christian Publications, 1982—originally published 1890) 15.

The Baptism of the Holy Spirit in the Writings of A. B. Simpson, Part 4: *After the Baptism, What?*

Come, blessed, holy, heavenly Dove,
Spirit of Light and Life and Love,
  Revive our souls we pray!
Come with the power of Pentecost,
Come as the sevenfold Holy Ghost,
  And fill our hearts today.

Spirit of Life, the dead awake,
The slumbering sinner's fetters break,
  And set the captive free!
Speak with the gospel's ancient power,
And let us all this sacred hour
  Thy great salvation see.

Celestial Dove of peace and rest,
Hide us 'neath Thy brooding breast,
  Thine overshadowing wing!
Bid all our doubts and cares to cease,
And keep our hearts in perfect peace
  And everlasting spring.

Refrain:
Come with the power of Pentecost,
Come as the sevenfold Holy Ghost;

Come, save us to the uttermost
And fill our hearts today.

—A. B. Simpson hymn

The Results of the Spirit's Indwelling

We now want to see what Simpson says concerning the results of the baptism of the Holy Spirit. In the latter part of this chapter we will also explore what he says about the subsequent process of spiritual growth once a person has been baptized with the Holy Spirit. We turn again to the statement Simpson and his close associates presented to the 1906 Conference for Prayer and Counsel Respecting Uniformity in the Testimony and Teaching of the Alliance. Under subheading II.2, "Christ, our Sanctifier," note the five explicit statements:

a. a definite second blessing, *distinct in nature,* though not necessarily far removed in time, from the experience of conversion;

b. the baptism of the Holy Spirit as *a distinct experience,* not merely for power for service, but for personal holiness and victory over the world and sin;

c. the indwelling of Christ in the heart of the consecrated believer *as a distinct experience;*

d. sanctification by faith *as a distinct gift* of God's grace to every open and surrendered soul;

e. growth in grace and the deeper filling of the Holy Spirit *as distinct from,* and the result of, the definite experience of sanctification.

What are the results of the baptism of the Holy Spirit? The 1906 document is specific:

- power for service (II.2.b)
- personal holiness (II.2.b)
- victory over the world and sin (II.2.b)
- the indwelling of Christ (II.2.c)
- sanctification (II.2.d)
- growth in grace (II.2.e)
- the deeper filling of the Holy Spirit (II.2.e)

These results fall within two broad categories. In the terminology of II.2.b, one is power for service and the other is victorious Christian living. We want to reverse the order and first explore what Simpson has to say about personal holiness and a life of victory over the world and sin.

Personal Holiness and Spiritual Victory

Our previous investigations have shown that the prophetic announcements of Jeremiah 31 and Ezekiel 36, along with the paradigm of Christ's life, constitute the promise and provision of God for holy living. Moreover, the Holy Spirit's principal task, in Simpson's view, is to apply Christ's righteousness to the believer's life, thereby enabling the believer to be conformed to Christ's image. This latter idea needs elaboration.

We have already noted that in Simpson's perspective, part of Christ's atoning work was to break the power of sin. Simpson frequently explains this provision by referring to the two "laws" in Romans 8:2, "the law of the Spirit" and "the law of sin and death." Of the latter he writes:

> It is that principle in our fallen nature which operates with the power and uniformity of a law and leads us to sin and death. We are unable to resist this law through the mere force of our human will.[1]

As a result of the work of the Holy Spirit, the domination of this "law of sin and death" can be superseded.

Simpson describes "the law of the Spirit" thus:

> We put the natural law under its opposite, viz.: the spiritual life of Christ Jesus. That is the life of Jesus Christ brought into our hearts by the Holy Spirit, and operating there as a new law of Divine strength and vitality, and counteracting, overcoming and lifting us above the old law of sin and death.[2]

The role of the Holy Spirit is to impart "the nature and life of Jesus to us."[3] Simpson sees in the Spirit-baptized believer "a consciousness of complete helplessness" and a continual "taking from [Christ] moment by moment and breath by breath His very life and strength for everything."[4]

This impartation of Christ's righteousness to overcome the power of the sin nature Simpson compares to overcoming the law of gravity.[5] Just as he was able to lift his hand by a force superior to the law of gravity, so the indwelling power of Christ "counteracts the power of sin in my fallen nature."[6] "This is not so much the expulsion of sin," he says, as it is the operation of a stronger force which overcomes the power of the old sin nature.[7]

Simpson goes on to say the Holy Spirit produces in the believer "a spirit of obedience." Simpson takes this to mean a new delight to follow the will of God as that will is declared in the Scriptures.[8] Simpson sees this desire as part of the fulfillment of God's promises of the new covenant made back in Jeremiah 31 and Ezekiel 36.

It is the Holy Spirit, Simpson declares, who "enables us to mortify the deeds of the body."[9] He says elsewhere:

> Many Christians try to do this disagreeable work themselves, and they are going through a continual crucifixion, but they can never accomplish the work permanently. This is the work of the Holy Spirit.[10]

Although it is the Holy Spirit who enables the believer to put to death the deeds of the old nature, Simpson holds that the believer must cooperate in this work.[11] Thus personal holiness, as a result of the baptism of the Spirit, consists in realizing the means God has provided for holy living and responsibly acting in obedience to God.[12]

Power for Service

The tone of the wording in the 1906 statement—"not merely power for service"—appears to carry the undercurrent of reaction. This was indeed the case, for Simpson and his C&MA associates were reacting against the rather utilitarian "power for ministry" focus that was beginning to be featured in teaching on the Holy Spirit at that time. In a magazine editorial just before the conference, Simpson writes:

> It is a common and most paralyzing view that the Holy Spirit is simply an enduement of power for service and has no direct connection with our personal character and holiness.[13]

Simpson emphasized that what believers did flowed from their inner character. Referring to Acts 1:8—"You will receive power when the Holy Spirit comes on you"—Simpson observed that Christ's provision of power was

> . . . power to be, rather than to say and do. Our service and testimony will be the outcome of our life and experience. . . . Nothing is so strong as the influence of a consistent, supernatural and holy character.[14]

Simpson also pointed out the importance of recognizing the personhood of the Holy Spirit. "It is not abstract power under your control, but [He] is a Person."[15] Therefore, "it is not our power, but His, and [it is] received from Him moment by moment."[16] Simpson stressed that this power was for God's purposes, not ours. Referring to Jesus' Great Commission (Matthew 28:18-20), he observes:

> Power is not given to us, but to Christ, and we are constantly to recognize His living and perpetual presence, and to count upon His direct working. If, therefore, we would have this power, we must be personally united to Him and have Him as an abiding presence. God does not want to glorify us and to show the world our importance, but He wants to glorify His Son Jesus Christ, and hold up His power and glory.[17]

In another passage in the same book Simpson says:

> It is the power of the Holy Spirit. He is the agent who reveals Christ and manifests His mighty working; therefore, the power is directly connected with the Spirit personally.[18]

Consequently, Simpson emphasizes that all discussions on power for service must be understood from within a relational framework. A person does not "use" the power of the Spirit. Rather, the Christian allows the indwelling Holy Spirit to use him or her to accomplish God's purposes.

These cautions notwithstanding, Simpson stresses that believers are living in the new era of the Spirit. The Spirit who indwelt Christ now indwells believers and empowers them to serve God. Concerning Jesus' comments about driving out demons by the Spirit of God (Matthew 12:28), Simpson observes:

> It is the Holy Ghost who casts out demons in us and this same Holy Ghost is to remain in us and to perpetuate the kingdom of God in the church through the dispensation.
>
> It is a very wonderful truth that it is the same Spirit who wrought in Christ, that He has [been] given to the church to perform her works of love and power.
>
> This was what the Master meant when He said, "He that believeth on Me, the works that I do shall he do also; and

greater works than these shall he do; because I go unto the Father" [John 14:12]. The Holy Ghost in us is the same Holy Ghost that wrought in Christ.[19]

Simpson understood the "kingdom of God" referred to here to be God's rule in the world.[20] Therefore Simpson viewed the power of the Spirit to be principally for equipping believers to spread the gospel and to serve in the church.[21]

Simpson believed that the power of the Holy Spirit was made evident through the spiritual gifts He gave for the purpose of equipping the church. A spiritual gift was a "power communicated to the believer through the Holy Ghost for some special ministry."[22] Simpson continues:

> Every disciple of Christ ought to have some special manifestation of the Holy Ghost and some gift for Christian service (I Cor. 12:7). . . . There is no place for idlers and drones, and there is no excuse for the fruitless Christian. God has power and work for all who yield themselves to Him for His service and glory.[23]

In this regard, Simpson particularly stressed that a Spirit-filled man or woman "is but an instrument . . . [whom] the divine Presence uses . . . for . . . the exercise of the ministry in which God holds the power."[24] For this reason, "no man . . . can call these works his works or these gifts his gifts or this power his power."[25]

Simpson saw no separation between the apostolic era and the present day. In his view, all the spiritual gifts continue to be available, including the miraculous.[26] He asserts:

> The age of miracles is not past. The Word of God never indicated a hint of such a fact. . . . We are in the age of miracles, the age of Christ, the age that lies between the two advents. . . . Every generation needs a living Christ and every new community needs these "signs following" to confirm the Word. . . . Until Christ returns, the world will never

cease to need the touch of His power and presence. "God also bearing them witness, both with signs and wonders and gifts of the Holy Ghost, according to his own will" (Hebrews 2:4).[27]

Simpson held that these manifestations of the Spirit's power—"signs and wonders"—authenticated the gospel and were a normative part of this present church age. Moreover, he believed that as the return of Christ drew closer, there would be increasing outpourings of the Spirit and increasing supernatural manifestations of God's power for the final global spread of the gospel.[28] This expectation was a common one during Simpson's day and was generally referred to as the "latter rain," a phrase taken from the King James Version of Zechariah 10:1.[29] Furthermore, Simpson believed he was actually living in the period just prior to Christ's second advent. He comments:

> The Holy Ghost is preparing for Christ's return by the spiritual enrobing of his children. . . . There is a marked movement in all sections of the Christian world for an entire consecration to Christ. . . . This is the very time that the Bridegroom is near at hand.[30]

In Simpson's view believers should expect and seek this "enrobing" as a normative element of the final days.

It is evident from his writings that Simpson believed the empowering for service occurs when one who is born again initially receives the baptism of the Spirit.[31] But it is also clear that Simpson believed there may be subsequent "enduements" for ministry which impart increased power and effectiveness.[32] This brings us to our second major consideration in this chapter.

The Spiritual Journey of the Believer after the Baptism

Despite all the attention Simpson gives to the initial baptism of the Spirit, he is very explicit that this action merely completes a believer's initial salvation experience. As section II.2.e of the 1906 document attests, Simpson believed Christians are called to "growth in grace and the deeper filling of the Holy Spirit *as distinct from* and the result of the definite experience of sanctification."

We want then to explore in Simpson's writings his thoughts concerning the various aspects of this statement.

Subsequent "Crisis" Experiences

Simpson observed that many believers had a truncated work of the Spirit in their lives. "There is no doubt that a great multitude of Christians have received the Holy Ghost," he writes, "but comparatively few have entered into the fullness of their inheritance."[33]

Simpson saw several reasons for this problem. One was the failure of people to give God control of some remaining aspect of their lives. Simpson says:

> It is possible to have the Spirit actually indwelling and yet not fully know or use all His attributes and resources. It is possible to have the Holy Spirit, but to confine Him to some isolated chamber of our being and not open to Him all our faculties, powers and interests. The Holy Spirit comes to fill every channel of our manifold being and every department of our diversified life, and He is grieved and disappointed when we keep back any part of our life from His control.[34]

Once Christians come to a crisis of yieldedness on the disputed point, the Spirit fills them in a deeper and fuller way.

Simpson cited other reasons for a less-than-full ministry of the Spirit: ignorance as to what the Spirit is prepared to do, and theological systems that prejudice people's thinking on the nature of the Spirit's working.[35] Simpson figuratively compared the resultant condition to that of the widow in Second Kings 4:1-7. These believers had "the Holy Ghost confined to a little pot of oil and hidden away on the shelf of a cabinet."[36] For reasons like this, Simpson postulated that people often experience a deeper work of the Spirit at some point after their initial baptism with the Holy Spirit.

Besides these kinds of new openings to the Spirit's work, Simpson also suggests that Christians may from time to time spontaneously experience a deeper working of God in their lives. He refers to the times in the Acts when the Spirit came upon those who had already been baptized with the Spirit. These instances were a "higher manifestation" of God's power, in which God clothed these Christians "with power from on high for special ministry in the kingdom."[37]

Simpson uses various phrases for this experience. Sometimes he uses the term "fullness."[38] He even uses "baptism of the Spirit" to describe it,[39] not employing the term in the technical sense of receiving the Spirit, but in the figurative sense of a believer's being "immersed" in the Spirit.[40] Whatever the term, the effect of this experience is a greater dependency upon and openness to the work of the Spirit.[41] From the divine perspective, there is an "intensification" of the Spirit's work in the individual.[42]

Simpson saw that God prepared people for these experiences. Part of the Spirit's ministry was to prod believers gently, exposing areas of need which would serve to motivate them to seek a greater work of God in their lives. This perception of need could arise through the exigencies of life, a sense of ineffectiveness in service for God or through the illumination of the Scriptures.[43] Whatever the cause, this sense of longing resulted in an intense desire for God.

Simpson described this seeking for God's "fullness" as being similar to the disciples' "waiting" prior to the day of Pentecost.[44] Simpson intimates that the "lessons learned" by the disciples as they waited can and need to be learned by believers still.[45] He suggests that the process of seeking God accomplishes a number of objectives:

- It taught the disciples "to cease from themselves," knowing their own utter helplessness and wretchedness
- It gave time to allow God to search their hearts and for them "to make full room and right of way in their hearts for His indwelling and outworking"

- It served to "deepen the hunger and the longing, which were necessary for them to appreciate the blessing"[46]

Simpson hesitated to specify when a believer should cease tarrying, holding that each individual's situation was unique. He asserted that believers would know when God had met them.[47]

Simpson also indicated in his writings that believers may have numerous "Pentecosts"—outpourings of the Spirit—in their spiritual journey.[48] Simpson refers to the disciples' subsequent fillings with the Spirit—for example, Acts 4:31—as indicative of these periodic outpourings of God's Spirit.[49] According to Neinkirchen, Simpson considered the season of Pentecost in the liturgical year a "most appropriate time for seeking 'a deeper filling, a mightier baptism' of the Holy Spirit through a personal reenactment of the apostles' waiting for the first Pentecost."[50]

The Filling of the Spirit

While not denigrating the "more marked experiences" of the Holy Spirit's working, Simpson at the same time emphasized the absolute necessity of the "continual receiving, breath by breath and moment by moment" of the Holy Spirit. This he considered "needful for . . . spiritual steadfastness and healthfulness."[51] Simpson says both have "their necessary place in the spiritual economy."[52] For this latter aspect, Simpson uses the term "filling."

Simpson employs *filling* to denote the continuous daily relationship of the believer with the Holy Spirit. He explains:

> To be filled with the Spirit means to be filled in every department, capacity and power of our being. Human nature is complex and possessed of many sides and capacities.[53]

Speaking of this process of the Spirit's entering all aspects of a believer's nature, Simpson writes:

He leads us to things in our life not yet surrendered, avenues of our being, capacities of our nature that have not yet been yielded to Him and possessed by Him; and as the new light is given and the heart yields to it in prompt surrender and obedience, He comes more and more fully into every part of our life till there is nothing that is not yielded to Him and used by Him to the glory of God.[54]

Clearly Simpson saw the Spirit's infilling not only as a crisis but also as a progressive experience of increasing dependence upon God and corresponding response in the areas God pointed out. Ephesians 5:18 is the key verse cited by Simpson to demonstrate the nature of this dependence: "Be filled with the Spirit." Simpson affirmed that this verse highlighted the importance of a continuous attitude of submission, the yielding of one's being to God and the relying upon the resources granted by God.[55]

Walking in the Spirit

Closely tied to the idea of being filled with the Spirit is Simpson's emphasis on walking in the Spirit. Referring to the importance of both conditions, Simpson observes:

[Life in the Spirit] is not merely a momentary act, but a life-long experience. The life of holiness is really a life in the Spirit, and in this life the Holy Ghost nurtures, teaches, guides and develops our spiritual experience just as fully as we will let Him, ever leading us on to "the measure of the stature of the fulness of Christ" [Ephesians 4:13]. . . . It is here that so many of God's children come short. They receive the baptism of the Spirit, but they do not "follow on to know the Lord." They do not walk in the Spirit and they are not filled with the Spirit.[56]

Thus Spirit-filled believers, in Simpson's view, had a moral responsibility to allow the Holy Spirit to "nurture, teach, guide" them and, in His ways, to "develop [their] spiritual experience."

Foremost of these responsibilities was the discipline of abiding. Simpson often referred to the parable of the vine and the branches (John 15) to develop this concept. Abiding, for Simpson, was "to maintain the habit of dependence upon the Holy Ghost for our entire life—spirit, soul, and body."[57] If this abiding was disrupted, the inflow of the Spirit was severed, the believer was rendered powerless and spiritual growth was accordingly truncated.[58]

Part of the practice of abiding, for Simpson, involved his developing the awareness of God's presence, continually communing with God and discerning His prompting.[59] He emphasized obedience. "If we would walk in the Spirit," he would say, "we must obey Him when He speaks. We must remember that the first part of obedience is to listen."[60]

In Simpson's opinion, listening to God had to be cultivated. It did not come naturally. He wrote several articles on what might be termed "contemplative prayer."[61] More than once he recounts his personal pilgrimage in the discipline of listening to God. He recalls his difficulties and the help he received in developing a listening attitude.[62]

Simpson believed God speaks to His children in a variety of ways. The Bible is primary and preeminent, but it is not the only way.[63] Impressions from God, God's "gentle whisper" [1 Kings 19:12], dreams and visions are but a few of the channels of His communication.[64]

To overlook this strand of "contemplative spirituality" in Simpson's teaching is to miss an important element in his presentation of the work of the Spirit in the believer. Since Simpson held a relational view of the working of the Spirit, he believed quite naturally that in a Christian's prayer life God would be speaking. The enduement with the Holy Spirit's resources was accordingly dependent upon the believer's awareness of what God desired to do in his or her life.

Walking in the Spirit also involved specific acts of obedience on the believer's behalf. Although Simpson emphasizes that progressive holiness is achieved through divine grace and not works, he asks:

Is there then nothing for us to do but to just lie passive in His hands while He works in us? Oh yes, there is much for us to do.[65]

Among the "much" for the Christian to do, Simpson mentions especially the need for the believer to continue to reckon himself or herself dead to sin and the need to "keep in step with our blessed Companion"—walking in the Spirit. "We must follow as He leads the way."[66]

Simpson often used the image of Israel's conquest of Canaan to depict progressive Christian growth. God brings numerous battles into the life of the "Christian soldier," who by God's grace is able to triumph over the forces that oppose him or her.[67] These opposing forces are temptations and trials that God permits in the believer's life.[68] They serve to expose sinful areas yet remaining to be dealt with. They also are opportunities for the believer to prove God's sufficiency in every area of need.[69] God's primary manner of revealing sin, however, is through the Holy Spirit's illumination of the Scriptures.[70]

Summary

In this chapter and the previous one, we have investigated certain statements in the document that Simpson presented at the 1906 Conference for Prayer and Counsel Respecting Uniformity in the Testimony and Teaching of the Alliance. From the broad scope of Simpson's writings we have attempted to amplify and clarify those same statements.

Simpson's writings make it certain that what he had to say on the baptism of the Holy Spirit must be understood within the framework of his doctrine of sanctification. Simpson held that the baptism of the Holy Spirit marked the distinct reception of the Holy Spirit into a believer's life subsequent to conversion. The Spirit's indwelling, therefore, was not something that happened automatically at regeneration. The Spirit must be distinctly asked for and appropriated. At the same time, Simpson believed the Holy Spirit to be "with" every regenerated person. Only at a point of "appropriating faith," however, did the Spirit actually take up residence "in" the believer. How much of the Spirit one has is not the important issue. The distinction is between experiencing or not experiencing the fullness of God's provision for the Christian life.

The indwelling Holy Spirit is the believer's means of union with Christ, who is the all-sufficient Resource for holy living. Following the paradigm of Christ's life, the baptism of the Spirit marks a new relationship with the Spirit and a new empowering for service.

Once baptized by the Holy Spirit, the believer's dependence on God increases and he or she continues to be "filled with the Spirit" (Ephesians 5:18). This process will be marked by periodic "anointings," or refillings, of the Spirit. In this entire process, the believer is deemed accountable to respond to God in obedience and to cultivate an increasing consciousness of His presence.

End Notes

1. A. B. Simpson, *Christ in the Bible,* vol. XI (Romans) (New York: Christian Alliance Publishing Co., 1894) 174

2. Simpson, *Christ in Bible,* vol. XI (Romans) (see note 1 above) 174-175

3. Simpson, "The Spirit-Filled Life," *The Christian and Missionary Alliance Weekly* (16 Nov 1907) 108

4. Simpson editorial, *The Christian and Missionary Alliance Weekly* (21 Jul 1906) (page number illegible)

5. For example, see Simpson, *Christ in Bible,* vol. XI (Romans) (see note 1 above) 175, and Simpson, "The Spirit-Filled Life," *The Alliance Weekly* (13 Jul 1918) 226.

6. Simpson, *Christ in Bible,* vol. XI (Romans) (see note 1 above) 175

7. Simpson, *Christ in Bible,* vol. XI (Romans) (see note 1 above) 175

8. Simpson, "Spirit-Filled Life" (see note 3 above) 108

9. Simpson, "Spirit-Filled Life" (see note 3 above) 108

10. Simpson, *Christ in Bible,* vol. XI (Romans) (see note 1 above) 179. He makes

similar comments in Simpson, *The Holy Spirit, or Power from on High,* vol. I (New York, Christian Alliance Publishing Co., 1895) 40-41.

11. Although Simpson emphasizes that progressive holiness is achieved through divine grace and not works, he asks, "Is there then nothing for us to do but just lie passive in [God's] hands while He works in us?" Simpson's reply: "Oh, yes, there is much for us to do" [Simpson, *The Holy Spirit, or Power from on High,* vol. II (New York: Christian Alliance Publishing Co., 1896) 140]. An extensive catalog of these responsibilities is not possible in this confined study, But the most important are: (1) continuing to reckon ourselves dead to sin, and (2) "walking in the Spirit. . . . We must keep in step with our blessed Companion, we must follow as He leads the way" (page 140). Simpson often used the image of Israel's conquest of Canaan to depict progressive Christian growth. God brings numerous battles into the life of the "Christian soldier." These may be temptations and trials that God allows to enter the life of the believer. They serve to expose latent sin in the believer's life, but they also demonstrate God's sufficient grace to enable the believer to triumph [see, for example, Simpson, *A Larger Christian Life* (New York: Christian Alliance Publishing Co., 1890) 85-86, 89-90]. God's primary manner of revealing sin, however, is through the Holy Spirit's illumination of the Scriptures [see, Simpson, *Holy Spirit,* vol. I (see note 10 above) 47].

12. Some comment should be made on Simpson's view of man's sin nature. A broad survey of Simpson's writings indicates that he certainly was aware that his teaching might lead people to think a believer could live a sinless life. B. B. Warfield explores these tendencies in *Perfectionism,* vol. 2 (Philadelphia: Presbyterian and Reformed Publishing Co., 1971) 597-660. The extent of Warfield's examination of Simpson's writings appears to have been the reading of his single brief tract "Himself" (Harrisburg, PA: Christian Publications, n.d.).

Simpson's writings suggest, first, that he held the sin nature to never be removed from a believer [see, for example, Simpson, *Wholly Sanctified* (New York: Christian Alliance Publishing Co., 1882) 86-87; Simpson, "Failure and Sin After Sanctification," *The Christian Alliance* (Mar 1888); Simpson, "Sanctification," *The Word, Work and World* (Jun 1885) 173; Simpson, "The Work of the Christian and Missionary Alliance," *The Alliance Weekly* (13 May 1916) 107].

Second, although the power of sin may be broken, a believer will continually be tempted to sin (*Wholly Sanctified* 86-87). Third, Simpson defines *sin* as "wilful disobedience against God." Moreover, a believer needs continual cleansing as a result of his or her involvement in the world (again, see *Wholly Sanctified* 86-87).

Fourth, Simpson places supreme emphasis on the believer's need to continuously "abide" in Christ. Without such moment-by-moment contact, the believer is powerless to resist the sin nature (*Wholly Sanctified* 97). "The life God gives us is not a self-contained endowment but a link of dependence, and every part of our being must continually draw its replenishment and nurture from our living Head." In his *Echoes of the New Creation* (New York: Christian Alliance Publishing Co., 1903) 51, Simpson makes reference to 1 John 3:6—"No one who lives in [Christ] keeps on sinning." Simpson says, "There is no account here of our perfection, but it is only as we cling to [Christ] and draw our life each moment from Him that we are kept from sin."

Fifth, Simpson disclaimed both the "eradication" and "suppression" views of sanctification (see 1906 document II.2.e in Appendix 2). In an editorial in *The Christian and Missionary Alliance Weekly* (Jun 1899) 8, Simpson writes: "The Alliance teaching on [sanctification] is neither Wesleyan nor an echo of the excellent teaching given at Keswick. While speaking in greatest appreciation of all who endeavor to hold up the true Scriptural standard of Christian life, yet we believe that the view of the teachers and workers in the Christian Alliance regarding personal holiness is what we might term the 'Christ Life.' There is always a little danger of seeing our experience more than seeing the source of that experience, the Lord Jesus. We have been led to rise above all our experiences and recognize our new and resurrection life as wholly in Him. We need to maintain an attitude of constant dependence and abiding so that our holiness is dependent every moment on our union and communion with Him." For more specific disclaimers of the "eradicationist" and "suppressionist" viewpoints, see Simpson editorial, *The Christian and Missionary Alliance Weekly* (9 Dec 1905), and Simpson, "Misapprehensions Respecting Sanctification," *The Christian and Missionary Alliance Weekly* (31 Mar 1906).

13. Simpson editorial, *Living Truths* (Mar 1906) 130. Such a sense came out in some of Simpson's contemporaries. In the next chapter we will explore their teaching.

14. Simpson, *Holy Spirit*, vol. II (see note 11 above) 79-80

15. Simpson, *Holy Spirit*, vol. II (see note 11 above) 78

16. Simpson, *Holy Spirit*, vol. II (see note 11 above) 78

17. Simpson, *Walking in the Spirit* (New York: Christian Alliance Publishing Co., 1889) 100

18. Simpson, *Walking in Spirit* (see note 17 above) 110

19. Simpson, *Holy Spirit*, vol. II (see note 11 above) 19. Paraphrasing Jesus'

teaching (Matt. 12:28), Simpson elsewhere wrote: "It was as if He had said, 'If I perform My miracles and accomplish My work by virtue of My own inherent power and deity and then withdraw from the world after My resurrection and ascension, it might be said that I had taken the power with Me, but if on the other hand, these ministries and miracles are accomplished not by My own inherent power, but by the Spirit that dwells in Me and is afterwards to dwell in you and perpetuate My ministry, then indeed the kingdom of God is come nigh to you. The gifts and powers of the kingdom are not withdrawn by My return to heaven, but they continue permanently through all the future generations of the Christian age, and the Holy Ghost still carries on My work just as truly as I have begun to carry it on during My earthly ministry' " [see Simpson, "The Holy Spirit and the Gospel," *The Christian and Missionary Alliance Weekly* (4 Mar 1905) 133].

20. For example, see Simpson, "The Holy Ghost," *The Christian and Missionary Alliance Weekly* (24 Apr 1909) 62; Simpson, *Holy Spirit,* vol. II (see note 11 above) 79-82; Simpson, "Gifts and Graces," *The Christian and Missionary Alliance Weekly* (29 Jun 1907) 303; Simpson, *The Gospel of Healing* (New York: The Word, Work and World Publishing Co., 1886) 40-42.

21. Simpson, *Gospel of Healing* (see note 20 above) 40-42. In addition, see Simpson, *Walking in Spirit* (see note 18 above) 109.

22. To explore Simpson's views on the "gifts" passages such as 1 Corinthians 12-14, see, for example, Simpson, "The Supernatural Gifts and Ministries of the Church," *The Christian and Missionary Alliance Weekly* (Jan 1898), and Simpson, "Gifts and Graces" (see note 20 above).

23. Simpson, "Gifts and Graces" (see note 20 above) 302

24. Simpson, "Supernatural Gifts" (see note 22 above) 54

25. Simpson, "Supernatural Gifts" (see note 22 above) 54

26. Simpson, *Christ in the Bible,* vol. XVI (Acts) (New York: Christian Alliance Publishing Co., 1902) 126
Simpson, "The Ministry of the Spirit," *Living Truths* (Aug 1907) 444
Simpson, "Spiritual Sanity," *Living Truths* (Apr 1907) 191

27. Simpson, *Gospel of Healing* (see note 20 above) 43-45

28. Simpson, *Holy Spirit,* vol. II (see note 11 above) 281-282
Simpson, *Christ in Bible,* vol. XVI (Acts) (see note 26 above) 19-22, 41
Simpson, "What is Meant by the Latter Rain?" *The Christian and Missionary Alliance Weekly* (19 Oct 1907) 38

29. Simpson wrote "What is Meant by the Latter Rain?" (see note 28 above) on

this subject. Simpson defined the latter rain as the coming of the Spirit upon believers, "clothing us with power from on high for special ministry in the kingdom" (page 39). "Along with this we are justified in expecting the manifestation of God's miraculous power not only in many extraordinary healings, but in such a manner as to reflect no personal glory on the instruments and compel an unbelieving world to recognize the authority of God's Word and the majesty of the name of Jesus." Simpson also anticipated an unprecedented sending forth of missionaries and increasing revival "to fall upon heathen lands" (page 40). Donald W. Dayton [*Theological Roots of Pentecostalism* (Grand Rapids, MI: Zondervan, 1986) 11, 22-23, 26-28, 33 footnote 44, 88, 143, 145] explores this contemporary movement in Simpson's day.

30. Simpson, *Holy Spirit*, vol. II (see note 11 above) 281-282

31. Simpson, *Holy Spirit*, vol. II (see note 11 above) 281-282. Again Simpson points to the example of Christ's baptism [see Simpson, *Christ in the Bible*, vol. XIV (Mark) (New York: Christian Alliance Publishing Co., 1910) 85, and Simpson, "Spirit-Filled Life" (see note 3 above) 227].

32. For example, "Latter Rain?" (see note 28 above) 38-40, and Simpson, *Larger Christian Life* (see note 11 above) 44-47, 59-68, 111-113.

33. Simpson, "Tarry," *Living Truths* (Sep 1907) 505

34. Simpson, "Ministry of Spirit" (see note 26 above) 441

35. See, for example, Simpson, *Gospel of Healing* (see note 20 above) 40-43; Simpson, *The Christ of the Forty Days* (New York: Christian Alliance Publishing Co., 1890) 40-48; Simpson, *The Cross of Christ* (New York: Christian Alliance Publishing Co., 1912) 133-134.

36. Simpson, *Holy Spirit*, vol. II (see note 11 above) 92

37. Simpson, "Latter Rain?" (see note 28 above) 39

38. Simpson uses the term, for example, in "Tarry" (see note 33 above) 505

39. See, for example, Simpson, *When the Comforter Came* (New York: Christian Alliance Publishing Co., 1911) Day 7; Simpson, "Tarry" (see note 33 above) 505; Simpson, *Walking in Spirit* (see note 17 above) 140.

40. Simpson is careful to point this out in "Tarry" (see note 33 above) 505, and in "Latter Rain?" 39.

41. Simpson, "Tarry" (see note 33 above) 505
    Simpson, "Latter Rain?" (see note 28 above) 38

42. Simpson, "Latter Rain?" (see note 28 above) 38. This intensification may include an "enduement" or a "clothing with power" for special ministry.

43. Simpson, *Holy Spirit,* vol. II (see note 11 above) 92, 217-224.

44. Simpson, *Holy Spirit,* vol. II (see note 11 above) 67-69. Simpson suggests that Luke 24:49 and Acts 1:4 and 2:1 refer to this waiting for the fullness of the Holy Spirit.

45. Simpson certainly acknowledged the differences between the waiting, or "tarrying," prior to Pentecost and that practiced by believers today. Among the differences: (1) the Holy Spirit had not yet been given then, and (2) God's plan to use the historically significant day of Pentecost necessitated an interlude [Simpson, *Holy Spirit,* vol. II (see note 11 above) 67-68, and Simpson, *Christ in Bible,* vol. XVI (Acts) (see note 26 above) 24].

46. Simpson, *Holy Spirit,* vol. II (see note 11 above) 69-72
Simpson, *Christ in Bible,* vol. XVI (Acts) (see note 26 above) 23-24

47. Simpson, "Tarry" (see note 33 above) 504
Simpson, *Holy Spirit,* vol. II (see note 11 above) 90

48. For example, see Simpson, *Christ in Bible,* vol. XVI (Acts) (see note 26 above) 41.

49. Simpson, *Christ in Bible,* vol XVI (Acts) (see note 26 above) 41-43. See also Simpson, *Larger Christian Life* (see note 11 above) 46.

50. Charles Neinkirchen, "A. B. Simpson: Forerunner and Critic of the Pentecostal Movement," *The Birth of a Vision,* David F. Hartzfeld and Charles Neinkirchen, eds. (Beaverlodge, AB: Buena Book Services, 1986) 131 alludes to this suggestion of Simpson found in *Cross of Christ* (see note 35 above) 131.

51. Simpson, *Larger Christian Life* (see note 11 Above) 46

52. Simpson, *Larger Christian Life* (see note 11 Above) 46

53. Simpson, "Filled with the Spirit," *The Christian and Missionary Alliance Weekly* (26 Nov 1904) 401

54. Simpson, "Some Aspects of the Holy Spirit," *Living Truths* (Jul 1905) 390

55. Simpson, "Filled with Spirit" (see note 53 above) 413
Simpson, "Some Aspects" (see note 54 above) 390-391
Simpson, "The Holy Ghost" *The Christian and Missionary Alliance Weekly* (24 Apr 1909)
Simpson, "Spirit-Filled Life" (see note 3 above) 227

Simpson, *Holy Spirit,* vol. II (see note 11 above) 97-98

56. Simpson, "Ministry of Spirit" (see note 26 above) 440

57. Simpson, *Walking in Spirit* (see note 17 above) 14

58. Perhaps Simpson's fullest explication of this theme is in *The Christ Life* (London: Morgan & Scott, 1888).

59. Simpson, *Walking in Spirit* (see note 17 above) 14-17

60. Simpson, *Walking in Spirit* (see note 17 above) 16

61. Simpson referred to this subject, for example, in *Holy Spirit,* vol. I (see note 10 above) 160-162, in "The Secret of Prayer," *Living Truths* (4 Mar 1904), and in *Walking in Spirit* (see note 17 above) 39-42. "Contemplative prayer," Simpson says, "denotes the kind of prayer in which the mind does not function discursively but is arrested in a simple attention and one-pointedness" [J. Neville Ward, "Contemplation," *The Westminster Dictionary of Christian Spirituality,* Gordon S. Wakefield, ed. (Philadelphia: Westminster Press, 1983) 95].

62. Simpson, "The Power of Stillness," *The Christian and Missionary Alliance Weekly* (Oct 1909) 37
    Simpson, *Holy Spirit,* vol. I (see note 10 above) 202-204
    A. E. Thompson, *The Life of A. B. Simpson* (New York: Christian Alliance Publishing Co., 1920) 181-182
    Dwayne Ratzlaff explores this area in his essay "An Old Medieval Message: A Turning Point in the Life of A. B. Simpson," *Birth of a Vision* (see note 50 above) 165-194. Simpson's own writings on prayer and contemplation show that he was influenced by the work of Madame Guyon, Francois Fenelon and Miguel de Molinos (see "The Power of Stillness," page 37). Simpson refers to a book entitled *True Peace,* a compilation of writings by Guyon, Fenelon and Molinos on prayer and contemplation. In an editorial in *Living Truths* (Jul 1906), Simpson highly recommends the help Guyon gives in these areas. He writes, "We are certain our thoughtful and spiritually minded readers will take great delight in reading the striking paper in this number quoted from the invaluable writings of Madame Guyon. It is well for us to remember in this material age that conversion is much more than turning from sin to righteousness and that its deepest essence lies in turning from the outward to the inward, from the human to the divine, from all things to God."

63. See, for example, discussions in Simpson, *Walking in Spirit* (see note 17 above) 139-142.

64. See, for example, Simpson, *Walking in Spirit* (see note 17 above) 40, 43, 120. Simpson warns that it takes considerable time to accurately discern these promptings of the Spirit. He stresses that they must always be tested against the Scriptures [see, for example, Simpson, "Some Aspects" (see note 54 above) 391-392]. Also, Simpson printed an article, "Deceptive Leadings," by M. M. Anderson in *The Christian and Missionary Alliance Weekly* (11 Apr 1908) 25-27 and (18 Apr 1908) 40-42, which offers principles in discerning God's voice amidst error.

65. Simpson, *Holy Spirit*, vol. II (see note 11 above) 140

66. Simpson, *Holy Spirit*, vol. II (see note 11 above) 140

67. See, for example, Simpson, *Larger Christian Life* (see note 11 above) 85.

68. Simpson, *Larger Christian Life* (see note 11 above) 85

69. Simpson, *Larger Christian Life* (see note 11 above) 86

70. See, for example, Simpson, *Holy Spirit*, vol. I (see note 10 above) 47.

Chapter 7

The Baptism of the Holy Spirit in the Teachings of A. B. Simpson's Contemporaries, Part 1: Phoebe Palmer, Asa Mahan, Charles G. Finney, Dwight L. Moody

H aving thoroughly explored Simpson's own views on the baptism of the Holy Spirit, we want now to outline the positions set forth by those who were theologically and experientially closest to him among his contemporaries.[1]

As we noted in chapter 1, there were in Simpson's day three major theological positions regarding the baptism of the Holy Spirit: (1) the Methodist-Holiness group, (2) the so-called "Third Blessing" group and (3) the "Revivalistic Reformed"[2] group. We will amplify the views of each of these groups in this chapter and chapter 8, giving particular attention to the "Revivalistic Reformed" position, the group with which Simpson most closely aligned himself.[3]

In chapter 9 we will compare the views of Simpson with those of his contemporaries. To assist us in that task, we want to ask in this chapter a number of critical questions of each of the three groups:

- How do the proponents employ the term "baptism of the Holy Spirit"?
- How is the Spirit's relationship to the believer different after the "baptism"?
- How are sanctification and "power for service" related to

this experience?
- What are the conditions for receiving the baptism of the Holy Spirit?
- What texts or arguments do the proponents use to explicate their viewpoint?

Those questions will be the grid we use to undertake our investigation. The answers to these questions should assist us in highlighting the relevant elements of the teachings of each theological stream. Thus we have made much easier the task of comparing Simpson's views with these others.

The Methodist-Holiness View and Phoebe Palmer

The trends within American society noted in chapter 1 had a great impact on the Methodist-Holiness camp. Wesley's teaching on "entire sanctification" underwent significant modification in this milieu. In particular the rise of interest in the "restoration of Pentecost" during the 1850s prompted many within the Methodist sphere to use the book of Acts to present Wesley's teachings. The resulting teaching was what one writer has termed "Pentecostal sanctification," implying an attempt to use the day of Pentecost as a paradigm for "entire sanctification."[4] In this single event they endeavored to highlight the "perfect love" and "cleansing" motifs of classical Wesleyanism along with the emerging concern for "power for ministry."

Phoebe Palmer was one of the earliest in the Holiness movement to attempt this reformulation. Her book, *The Promise of the Father,* (1859) is an explication of the consequences for the church that result from the outpouring of the Holy Spirit.[5] Foremost was a call for the "recognition of the full baptism of the Holy Ghost as a grace to be experienced and enjoyed in the present life."[6] She calls this baptism "the distinguishing doctrine of Methodism."[7] This latter statement is indicative of the extent to which Palmer had assimilated the traditional Wesleyan view to the events depicted in the book of Acts. Accordingly she asserts that Acts 2 presents entire sanctification:

"Holiness unto the Lord," or, in other words, the full baptism of the Holy Spirit as received by the one hundred and twenty disciples on the day of Pentecost, is set forth as the absolute necessity of all believers of every name.[8]

In using the Pentecost paradigm, Palmer coalesces cleansing with empowering for service, declaring that "holiness is power"[9] and "purity and power are identical."[10] Elsewhere she declares, "Holiness possesses an almightiness of power that will raise any sinking church."[11] Palmer therefore virtually equates holiness with "power for service." The power the disciples received was holiness, and this constitutes the experience granted to believers today.

Palmer did not discuss in *The Promise of the Father* any difference in the nature of the Spirit's work prior to or after the baptism of the Holy Spirit. In fact, the emphasis of the book is on the change in a believer's experience, with little being mentioned of what actually transpires from the divine perspective.[12] Palmer asserts clearly, however, that this Pentecostal gift is attained by complete dedication to God and specific faith.[13]

A. M. Hills, a leader in the Methodist movement, and H. C. Morrison, a member of the Southern Holiness movement, reflect a more fully developed Methodist-Holiness view on the baptism of the Holy Spirit. Unlike Palmer, they both recognize that the accounts in the book of Acts distinguish between holiness and power for ministry. Hills believed that Pentecost brought "holiness and power,"[14] while Morrison declared "the baptism of the Holy Spirit purifies believers' hearts and empowers them for service."[15] Thus, both viewed the cleansing dimension as the negative side and the empowering dimension as the positive side of the same work of the Spirit.

An excellent articulation of the Holiness view is preserved in an 1885 statement issued at the First General Holiness Assembly in Chicago:

Entire Sanctification, more commonly designated as "sanctification," "holiness," "Christian perfection" or "perfect love," represents that second definite stage in Christian experience wherein, by the baptism with the Holy Spirit, administered by Jesus Christ and received instantaneously by faith, the justified believer is delivered from inbred sin and consequently is saved from all unholy tempers, cleansed from all moral defilement, made perfect in love and introduced into full and abiding fellowship with God.[16]

A later comment in this 1885 statement outlines the new power for service which also occurs as a consequence of the baptism. Several items are notable here. The baptism of the Holy Spirit produces entire sanctification, the classical formulation of Wesley's doctrine. This "baptism" is received by faith and produces instantaneous results in a believer's life. Note the implication of the phrase, "delivered from inbred sin." The extent of "entire sanctification" appears to be the termination of the sin nature in man. This is why opponents of the Holiness wing termed them "eradicationists."[17] Finally, this baptism is described, in the preceding quotation as the "second definite stage in Christian experience."

To recapitulate the Holiness viewpoint: (1) The term "baptism of the Holy Spirit" is used to describe a second definite work of grace, (2) Acts 2 is the principal proof text, (3) holiness and power are viewed as two aspects of the same experience and (4) the baptism is received by faith.

The "Third Blessing" View

The "Third Blessing" perspective on the baptism of the Holy Spirit was in actuality held by a sub-group within the Holiness wing of the American church.[18] This group was never a formal organization, but rather consisted of various individuals who altered the Holiness view of the baptism of the Spirit and added their own nuance. They saw that the synthesis between holiness and power reached in the Holiness camp was easily critiqued. Their empirical observations turned up many who claimed to be "entirely sanctified," yet they seemed to lack spiritual power and effectiveness in ministry.[19] Moreover, many within the Holiness camp had experiences in which they claimed to have received special power for service subsequent to entire sanctification.[20] As a result, the position was advanced that the second blessing was entire sanctification, followed by a subsequent third blessing which was the baptism of the Holy Spirit. Hence, the term "Third Blessing" was given to those holding this view of the Spirit's work.

Simon P. Jacob, president of the Southwestern Holiness Association, vigorously debated the "Pentecostal sanctification" position adopted by many Methodist people. He declared:

> If purity of heart and the Pentecostal baptism of the Holy Spirit are identical or inseparable experiences, then no one before Pentecost ever had a pure heart. But such is not the case. . . . Purity of heart was enjoyed both under the Mosaic and Patriarchal dispensations. In fact, all writers on holiness quoted from the Old Testament, both [for] doctrine and [to cite] witnesses [to] complete unity of heart. . . . All will concede that our Lord lived in perfect purity thirty years before He received the personal indwelling of the Holy Spirit. . . . Therefore such indwelling of the Holy Ghost, or the baptism of the Holy Ghost, and perfect heart purity are neither identical nor inseparably connected. . . . It follows, then, that one being cleansed from all sin (1 John 1:7) is not thereby necessarily baptized with the Holy Ghost.[21]

Notable in this quote is Jacob's refutation of Pentecostal sanctification by the appeal to classical Methodist writers who used Old Testament figures to depict entire sanctification. Moreover, Christ also is held to be in the entirely sanctified stage prior to His baptism. This quotation also seems to imply that the actual indwelling of the Holy Spirit accompanies the baptism of the Spirit. Unfortunately, Jacob did not elaborate on this point. In traditional Holiness understanding, believers receive the Spirit upon conversion; hence, perhaps Jacob's concept of "indwelling" relates to a qualitative difference in the nature of the Spirit's relation to believers.

The exponents of the Third Blessing view claimed that their interpretation accurately represented the logical ordering of events in God's plan. Believers were first purified and thereby were prepared for the "enrobing" with spiritual power. Asbury Lowrey, a Methodist leader advocating the Third Blessing view, expresses this thought when he argues:

> The work of the Holy Ghost, up to the point of entire sanctification, is renovating, the baptism is qualifying. The first purges and refines; the second empowers. The first works in, and restores the image of God in the heart; the second works out, and, touching society, hallows the world.[22]

Furthermore, Lowrey argues that the sanctified need to receive the baptism of the Spirit on the basis of Christ's example, who was "holy, harmless, undefiled, and separate from sinners [Hebrews 7:26] and yet He sought and received the baptism of the Spirit."[23] Like Jacob, Lowrey regards Christ as a Model; He was "entirely sanctified" prior to His baptism. As in the classical Holiness teaching, believers needed to appropriate each of these blessings specifically through faith.

Two other notable proponents of the Third Blessing view were Benjamin H. Irwin, founder of the Fire-Baptized Holiness Church, and R. C. Horner, an itinerant Canadian evangelist. While maintaining views similar to those cited previously, they also affirmed that physical manifestations demonstrate the coming of the Spirit upon a person.[24] In this respect, they were forerunners of some of the manifestation emphasis found in the more radical wings of the Pentecostal movement.

In summary, then, the Third Blessing view was similar to the Methodist-Holiness view with respect to the manner of obtaining the blessing. However, those who held to this position believed they corrected the Methodist-Holiness overemphasis on the purifying effect of the baptism and its neglect of the need for empowering for service. Moreover, the Third Blessing view emphasized the sequential and distinct nature of each blessing. Purification had to precede empowering.

The "Revivalistic Reformed" View

"Revivalistic Reformed" is a collective term used to describe a diverse group of people who emerged primarily in the Reformed-Calvinist wing of the church. One writer describes them as

> . . . Evangelicals . . . who restated orthodox doctrines with a particular reassertion of the need for an "overcoming" Christian life, and a reaffirmation of the importance of both the personhood and the ministry of the Holy Spirit.[25]

Those in this camp also categorically denied the radical eradication view of sanctification presented by the Methodist-Holiness groups.[26] Other than these common tenets, there existed a wide spectrum of views within this classification, particularly in their teaching of the baptism of the Holy Spirit.

Actually, there are five major segments of opinion within this group. Asa Mahan and Charles Finney led the first. They developed their views on the Spirit during the transition years of 1850 to 1870. The second was headed by American evangelist Dwight L. Moody and his associate, Reuben A. Torrey. Together they attained wide influence in the North American context. The third is identified with Adoniram J. Gordon—a person especially important to our investigation because both his activities and his theology paralleled Simpson's in many ways. The fourth segment was made up of Higher Life proponents. The fifth was comprised of those who embraced Keswick teaching. Although the last two were British in origin, both had a great influence in North America.

Asa Mahan (1800-1889)

Asa Mahan was a Congregationalist minister. His book, *The Baptism of the Holy Spirit*, published in 1870, was seminal in the rising interest in North America in the work of the Holy Spirit. Moreover, it was indicative of changes in the American milieu as a whole. In his early years, he had been a key proponent of Oberlin Perfectionism.[27] Influenced by many of the trends we outlined in chapter 1, Mahan's theological pilgrimage caused him to reformulate his position. *The Baptism of the Holy Spirit* was the result.

The book is significantly different from his 1839 *The Scripture Doctrine of Christian Perfection.*. For one thing, he made the book of Acts his principal exegetical foundation. For another, he viewed salvation history as divided into three major eras, the then current era being the "age of the Spirit." He emphasized such themes as "power," "the gifts of the Spirit" and the "evidence" of being baptized by the Holy Spirit. Perhaps the greatest shift was in his formulation of "holy living." Whereas his earlier work focused on the goal and nature of the "holy" life, his later book focused on the event in which this change took place. Hence, there is a shift from the content of holiness to the event or method whereby it is attained.[28]

Mahan retired to England in the early 1870s. While residing there he made a significant impact on many people who were part of the rising Keswick movement.[29] Though the Keswick movement did not adopt his more radical views, it certainly was influenced by his teaching.[30]

Mahan begins *The Baptism of the Holy Spirit* with an exhortation to recognize that the Holy Spirit is the divine agent for attaining godliness.[31] The Spirit's ministry is to reveal Christ's grace and glory and to produce Christ's righteousness in a person's life. Because the Spirit's ministry is so vital, Mahan poses the crucial question to Christians: "Have you received the Holy Spirit since you believed?" (Acts 19:2 KJV). In this respect Mahan puts forward two competing views regarding the reception of the Holy Spirit. Of the one view Mahan writes:

> "The promise of the Spirit" [Ephesians 1:13] is always fulfilled at the moment of conversion. What is subsequently to be expected is merely a continuation and gradual increase

of what was conferred.[32]

Of the other he postulates:

> "The Spirit falls upon," "comes upon," believers and the "sealing and earnest" of the Spirit are given, not in conversion, but "*after* we have believed." The Spirit, first of all, induces in [us as sinners] "repentance toward God, and faith toward our Lord Jesus Christ" [Acts 20:21]. "After ye believed" [Ephesians 1:13], that is, after conversion, "the Holy Ghost comes upon," "falls upon" and is poured out upon [us] and thus endues [us] "with power from on high" [Luke 24:49] for [our] life's mission and work. In His baptism of power, this "sealing and earnest of the Spirit" which is always given not in conversion but "*after* [we] believed," "the promise of the Spirit" is fulfilled.[33]

A Second Visitation

Although not discounting the Spirit's work in conversion, this later view identifies a subsequent event as the time when the Spirit "falls upon, comes upon" an individual. Mahan devotes the rest of his book to proving this second visitation of the Spirit. He asserts:

> Here, then, we have God's revealed method of attaining this ideal of the Christian character—that is, of rendering real, in our experience and life, His divinely developed and perfected pattern of the New Testament saint.[34]

Mahan marshals a number of proofs to support this position. First he points to the life of Christ, the paradigm for believers with respect to the Spirit-filled life. Suggesting that Christ knew the place the Spirit would have in the life of the Messiah ("The Spirit of the LORD will rest on [this Branch from the stump of Jesse]"—see Isaiah 11:1-3), Mahan asserts that Christ's baptism marked His conscious reception of the baptism of the Spirit.[35] Christ Himself was "dependent upon the indwelling, and influence, and baptism of the Holy Spirit, the same in all essential particulars as in us."[36] Hence, Mahan remarks, "in seeking, and obtaining, and acting under that baptism, Christ is our Exemplar in respect to the spiritual and divine life which is required of us."[37]

Mahan also appeals to the evidence of the New Testament Scriptures. He cites Acts 2 and Acts 19:1-6 to show that a person can be converted and not possess the Holy Spirit. Of these situations, Mahan notes

- that the believers in Acts were not qualified for service until after their reception of the Spirit
- received the Spirit as a result of a special baptism
- that when the Holy Spirit came there was such a change that the believers were "distinctly conscious" of it
- "the gift of the Holy Spirit does not ordinarily come to believers unsought or unexpected, but where and when they are seeking it and waiting for it"[38]

Mahan also refers to Jesus' parable about the man who solicits bread from his friend (Luke 11:5-13) and suggests that only those who seek and ask God for the Spirit obtain Him.[39]

An "Explicit Order of Progression"

In addition, Mahan cites what he sees in Ephesians 1:13 as an explicit order of progression: "hearing, then believing, then sealing."[40] In his opinion Ephesians 3:14-21 suggests the various stages of the Spirit's work of indwelling: "He may strengthen you with power through his Spirit, . . . Christ may dwell in your hearts through faith. . . . You, being rooted and established in love, . . . may be filled to the measure of all the fullness of God."[41]

Mahan also appealed to the experiences of believers throughout the history of the church. Among those he cites are Luther, the Scottish Covenanters, Fenelon, Madame Guyon, Wesley, Fletcher and Finney. All had significant changes wrought in their lives subsequent to conversion. Although these experiences varied in detail, Mahan points out that in each case the gospel was illuminated in a new way which radically transformed their lives.[42] He terms these experiences "a baptism with the Holy Spirit." Mahan also points out that in each case these experiences were preceded by "a state of fervent desire, earnest seeking, importunate prayer, and waiting expectancy."[43]

Having laid out the basis for this special work of the Spirit, Mahan sets out guidelines on how believers can experience this special baptism. First, they must settle in their own minds the issue of whether or not there is in fact a special baptism, lest they doubt. Second, they should dedicate themselves completely to God. Finally, they must ask for and rest in the assurance that Christ has promised the Spirit. They then should wait, in an attitude of seeking and openness to God, and in God's sovereign prerogative the Holy Spirit will bear witness to the baptism.[44]

In addition, Mahan outlines some cautions believers must exercise in seeking the baptism. The greatest is the avoidance of dogmatism regarding the manner in which the Holy Spirit will come upon them.[45] Oftentimes, Mahan believed, this witness was simply the calm inner assurance of the presence of God.

Believers will consciously know when they have received the Spirit. This awareness will be intensified by the effects wrought in their lives. Among these: (1) "natural powers are quickened and developed into unwonted activity and energy,"[46] (2) there is spiritual "power to endure and power to accomplish" the divine will,[47] (3) there is a conscious awareness of the Father and the Son[48] and (4) the Holy Spirit makes possible a purified and holy walk before God.[49]

Several features are notable in Mahan's formulations. He is emphatic that the Spirit is not received unless one asks for Him. He appeals to several passages in Ephesians and Acts in support of this view together with the witness of saints throughout history. The effect of this baptism is empowering for service and enabling to lead a holy life. It is important to note that the emphasis, however, is much more on the power that the Spirit brings. In contrast to

Mahan's earlier book, the discussions on holy living receive only one minor chapter in *The Baptism of the Holy Spirit.*

Charles G. Finney (1792-1875)

Like Asa Mahan, Charles Finney adopted the term "baptism of the Holy Spirit" in his later years. Cited in our chapter 1 as the principal leader of Oberlin "Perfectionism" and the development of revivalism in America, Finney adopted a more pneumatic view of the Christian life in his later years. His earlier writings placed great emphasis on a transformed ethical life as the sign of a true believer, in keeping with the American social idealism prevalent during his era.[50] In this understanding, Christ's atonement imparted the ability to live the sanctified life. Holiness was accomplished through exercising faith, which he defined as "yielding up all our powers and interests to Christ, in confidence, to be led, and sanctified and saved by Him."[51]

Later he came to see that Ezekiel 36 and Jeremiah 31 promised a new covenant in which God's Spirit would transform people. His later writings, therefore, concentrated on the work of the Spirit in imparting Christ's sanctification. He asserted that the baptism of the Holy Spirit (the initial reception of the Spirit, in his view), was the privilege of all believers though not all had received this special baptism.[52]

Christians must receive the baptism by faith which begins with "a perception of the truth." This act of consecration becomes complete only when a person has yielded his will to "the guidance, instruction, influences and government of the Holy Spirit."[53]

It is important at this juncture to reiterate Oberlin's presuppositions regarding the human will.[54] Impacted by Nathaniel Taylor's postulations, Finney believed that God's moral ordering for divine working required the consent of the human will to all that God provided or demanded. Hence, Finney believed that one needed to recognize and volitionally consent to this provision of the baptism of the Holy Spirit.[55]

The Enduement of Power (1871) was one of Finney's last works.

The central intent of the book was the exploration of God's provision to accomplish the Great Commission—power through the baptism of the Holy Spirit.[56] The reasons, support and procedure given for this special baptism were virtually identical with those of Mahan. We may postulate that developments within the American milieu contributed to this intensification in Finney's concern for "spiritual power."

Dwight L. Moody (1839-1899)

From the 1870s onward, D. L. Moody became the leading figure in the mass evangelism movement. Although known primarily as an evangelist, his writings reflect a concern for holy living and especially power for service. The role of the Spirit in these areas is representative of mainstream revivalist Protestantism in the late 1800s.

Moody's concern for holy living is reflected in his efforts in establishing the Northfield (Massachusetts) Conference.[57] Northfield became a key center for disseminating the new Revivalistic Reformed teachings in America.[58] Like so many teachers of his era, Moody believed that the majority of professing believers lived the frustrated existence depicted in Romans 7 instead of pressing into the victorious existence of Romans 8.[59] Moreover, he believed the decision to conquer sin was entirely up to the individual. "Whatever the sin is, make up your mind that you will gain victory over it" was his challenge.[60] Moody acknowledged, however, that only in the Holy Spirit's power could "daily, hourly, constant victory over the flesh and over sin" be attained.[61] Contrary to the Methodists, Moody believed that sanctification was not the product of an instantaneous event but was progressively worked out in the life of the believer. In his discussions on the work of the Spirit he was very cautious to avoid any implication that sanctification was the result of the baptism of the Holy Spirit.[62] Actually, his comments on the work of the Spirit in sanctification are vague. This attitude marked much of Moody's writing. Some suggest that it was the result of his desire to avoid theological controversy, thereby maintaining a broad ecclesiastical base for his evangelistic campaigns.[63]

But Moody was not reticent in his call for believers to be empowered by the Spirit. The "Pentecostal enduement for service" was a constant theme in his preaching and writing. Though he used the phrase "baptism of the Holy Spirit" occasionally, he preferred to avoid this more controversial term.[64] Moody's enthusiasm for Spirit power flowed from his own experience of "empowering" early in his ministry. In 1871 two women confronted Moody after hearing him preach and told him "he lacked what the apostles received on the day of Pentecost."[65] This sparked a period of intense searching by Moody, about which he testified:

> I began to cry out as I never did before. I really felt that I did not want to live if I could not have this power for service. . . . I was crying all the time that God would fill me with His Spirit.[66]

God met him, Moody later said, and his evangelistic preaching immediately began to have a dramatic new effectiveness.[67]

Moody's emphasis on power for service was also influenced, as we noted in chapter 1, by the milieu of his era. Moreover, the agenda of Moody's evangelistic ministry would certainly heighten both the concern and need of "effectual power."

Moody attempted to encapsule his teachings on the empowering work of the Spirit in *Secret Power* (1881). The central intent of the book is to illustrate the equipping God has provided for believers to make them effective in ministry. Moody used the phrase, "the Holy Spirit is in you and shall come upon you" to summarize his view.[68] "It is clearly taught in Scripture that every believer has the Holy Ghost dwelling in him," was his conviction.[69] At the same time there are many Christians who, though they have the Spirit, do not have Him "dwelling within them in power."[70] It is the privilege of all believers to experience their own personal Pentecost, yet few do. Moody equated such an existence with that of the believers in Acts 19 who did not understand the ministry of the

Spirit.[71] He asserted, "I firmly believe that the church has just laid this knowledge aside, mislaid it somewhere, and so Christians are without power."[72]

Moody based his convictions principally on the texts in Acts 2:1-12 and Acts 4:31. He asserted that Pentecost illustrated the Spirit's coming *upon* believers.[73] The immediate effect was bold witness. So also Acts 4:31 indicates the Spirit's again "coming upon" the disciples.[74] Moody therefore asserted that receiving the empowering of the Spirit is a crisis followed by an ongoing process. Moreover, though it is wrong to ask for the Spirit since He indwells at conversion, a believer can ask that He might come in mighty power.[75]

Moody outlined some conditions for receiving the empowering. First, he stressed the importance of dedication and submission to God. He writes:

> If a man isn't willing to do anything or everything for the Lord, I don't believe he will get the Spirit baptism. God can't trust him with power. But when a man is completely emptied of self and is ready to do anything or to go anywhere, then it is then that God fills him.[76]

Upon the complete dedication of his or her life to God, a believer should "tarry," or wait, for the outpouring of God's Spirit. Moody asserts that a believer will consciously know when the Spirit has come upon him or her.[77] Moreover, there will be far greater fruitfulness.

To summarize, then, Moody placed a pronounced emphasis on power when discussing the baptism of the Spirit. While every believer has the Spirit, all must seek for and receive a definite anointing of the Spirit. Although sanctification was important to Moody, he was careful to dissociate it from this crisis experience of the Spirit's "coming upon" a believer.

We will continue our survey of the Revivalistic Reformed viewpoint regarding the baptism of the Holy Spirit in Chapter 8.

Endnotes

1. The references throughout this study to Simpson's "contemporaries" are specifically to those of his era who were closest to him theologically and experientially.

2. The term "Revivalistic Reformed" is defined in chapter 1, page 22. Edith L. Waldvogel-Blumhoefer employs it to represent a group from within the Reformed tradition who called for an "overcoming" Christian life and reaffirmed the importance of both the personhood and ministry of the Holy Spirit [see "The Overcoming Life: A Study in the Reformed Evangelical Contribution to Pentecostalism" (diss., Harvard U, 1977)]. Men such as A. J. Gordon, R. A. Torrey, and D. L. Moody belonged to this group. Further discussion may be found on pages 151-159 of this chapter.

3. In chapter 1, we discussed how Simpson's views can be best categorized (see pages 16-23). Our conclusion: he most closely matches those who have been termed "Revivalistic Reformed." For an overview of this position, see chapter 1, page 22.

4. Donald W. Dayton, *The Theological Roots of Pentecostalism* (Grand Rapids, MI: Zondervan, 1986) 90. See also Dayton, "The Doctrine of the Baptism of the Holy Spirit: Its Emergence and Significance," *Wesleyan Theological Journal* (Spring, 1978) 114-121.

5. Part of the agenda of this Palmer book was an apologetic for the ministry of women, particularly in the area of preaching. Palmer used the Joel 2 quotation in Acts 2 and equated the ministry of "prophesying" with preaching.

6. Phoebe Palmer, *The Promise of the Father* (Boston: H. V. Degen, 1859) 55

7. Palmer, *Promise* (see note 6 above) 55

8. Palmer, *Four Years in the Old World* (New York: W. C. Palmer, Jr., 1870) 107

9. Palmer, *Four Years* (see note 8 above) 206

10. Palmer, *Pioneer Experiences; or the Gift of Power Received by Faith, Illustrated and Confirmed by the Testimonies of Eighty Living Ministers of Various Denominations* (New York: W. C. Palmer, Jr., 1868) vi, as quoted in Dayton, *Theological Roots* (see note 4 above) 94.

11. Palmer, *Four Years* (see note 8 above) 385, as quoted in Dayton, *Theological Roots* (see note 4 above) 94.

12. See Melvin E. Dieter, *The Holiness Revival of the 19th Century* (Metuchen, NJ: Scarecrow Press, 1980) 28-30 for a succinct overview of Palmer's teaching on the experience of "entire sanctification."

13. See, for example, Palmer, *Faith and Its Effects: Or, Fragments from My Portfolio* (New York: Published for the author at 200 Mulberry St., 1854) 52-55, as cited in Dieter (see note 12 above) 28.

14. A. M. Hills, *Holiness and Power for the Church and the Ministry* (Cincinnati: Revivalist Office, 1897)

15. H. C. Morrison, *The Baptism of the Holy Ghost* (Louisville: Pentecostal Herald, 1900) 31

16. S. B. Shaw, *Echoes of the General Holiness Assembly* (Chicago: S. B. Shaw, 1901) 29-30, as quoted in Robert Mapes Anderson, *Vision of the Disinherited: The Making of American Pentecostalism* (New York: Oxford U Press, 1979) 39.

17. There was a divergence of opinion within the holiness stream as to whether sanctification was truly instantaneous and complete or progressive and incomplete. See Anderson (see note 16 above) 43.

18. The "Third Blessing" view is included in this study in order to present a complete depiction of the various interpretations of the baptism of the Spirit contemporaneous with Simpson. Simpson's writings, however, do not appear to interact explicitly with this position. Nevertheless, the fact that he does not separate "sanctification" and "power" from his view of the baptism of the Spirit suggests the possibility that he may have been aware that other teachers were doing so.

19. Dayton, *Theological Roots* (see note 4 above) 95

20. Dayton, *Theological Roots* (see note 4 above) 95

21. S. P. Jacob, "Receiving the Holy Spirit," *Canadian Methodist and Holiness Era* (Sep 1893) 146, as quoted in Dayton, *Theological Roots* (see note 4 above) 98.

22. Asbury Lowrey, "Is the Baptism of the Holy Ghost a Third Blessing?" *Divine Life* (Sep 1879) 47

23. Lowrey (see note 22 above) 47

24. Dayton, *Theological Roots* (see note 4 above) 100

25. Waldvogel-Blumhoefer (see note 2 above) 1. This quote from Waldvogel-Blumhoefer is also mentioned in chapter 1.

26. For Simpson's view of the sin nature, see chapter 6, endnote 12.

27. Mahan was a close associate of Charles Finney. For a good summary of Oberlin Perfectionism see Timothy Smith, "The Doctrine of the Sanctifying Spirit: Charles Finney's Synthesis of Wesleyan and Covenant Theology," *Wesleyan Theological Journal* (Spring, 1978) 92-113.

28. Dayton, "Asa Mahan and the Development of American Holiness Theology," *Wesleyan Theological Journal* (Spring, 1974) 66

29. Dayton, "Asa Mahan" (see note 28 above) 66

30. In Andrew Murray, *The Spirit of Christ: Thoughts on the Indwelling of the Holy Spirit in the Believer and the Church* (London: James Nisbet and Co., 1888) 313-324, Asa Mahan is noted as a teacher who promulgated a more radical view of the Spirit. Murray remarks that while Mahan's Keswick sessions were well attended, few at the conference adopted his view that believers were not indwelt with the Spirit at conversion.

31. Asa Mahan, *The Baptism of the Holy Spirit* (New York: Palmer and Hughes, 1870) 5

32. Mahan (see note 31 above) 16

33. Mahan (see note 31 above) 16

34. Mahan (see note 31 above) 8

35. Mahan (see note 31 above) 17

36. Mahan (see note 31 above) 21

37. Mahan (see note 31 above) 21

38. Mahan (see note 31 above) 35-37

39. Mahan (see note 31 above) 22

40. Mahan (see note 31 above) 34. Mahan cites Paul's comment in Acts 19:2, emphasizing the words "after you believed."

41. Mahan (see note 31 above) 39

42. Mahan (see note 31 above) 109

43. Mahan (see note 31 above) 109

44. Mahan (see note 31 above) 122-125

45. Mahan (see note 31 above) 119

46. Mahan (see note 31 above) 50

47. Mahan (see note 31 above) 51

48. Mahan (see note 31 above) 136-152. Mahan devotes a lengthy section to the implications of this truth: namely, that a believer must learn to live his or her life listening to and communing with God.

49. Mahan expands on this thought in a chapter entitled "The Fountain Opened for Sin and for Uncleanness, or the Cleansing Power of the Spirit" [Mahan (see note 31 above) 186-206]. He asserts that salvation is "perfect and entire, wanting nothing," yet the provisions contained in it are not necessarily all experienced immediately. They become efficacious "when the soul, supremely desirous to be wholly free from the condemnation, power and inbeing of sin, sees in Christ a sovereign remedy for this death-plague, and comes to Him, and trusts in the virtue of His blood as the 'fountain opened for sin and for uncleanness' " (page 189). This fountain figuratively represents the provision of God which the believer is continually to ask to be applied to his life. Christ, hence, is the "all purifying, quickening, and life imparting" presence in a believer's life. Mahan asserts that at Pentecost the disciples became aware of this provision (pages 193-194). The key change was a clear apprehension of the all-sufficient provision of Christ.

50. Smith, "Sanctifying Christ" (see note 27 above) 100. Smith observes, "Oberlin's political radicalism was rooted in the central theme of the Old and New Testament Scriptures: the God of eternity had bound Himself in covenant with those who would be His people, making them morally responsible to Him and to one another to help His kingdom come, as Jesus put it, and His will be done, on earth as it is in heaven."

51. Charles G. Finney, *Lectures to Professing Christians* (New York: Publisher not stated, 1837) 213, as quoted in Smith, "Sanctifying Christ" (see note 27 above) 38.

52. Finney article, *Oberlin Evangelist* (28 Aug 1839) 147, as quoted in Smith, "Sanctifying Christ" (see note 27 above) 103.

53. Finney article, *Oberlin Evangelist* (14 Aug 1839) 137-138, as quoted in Smith, "Sanctifying Christ" (see note 27 above) 103.

54. For a more extensive survey of Taylor's postulations and their influence on Finney see chapter 1, endnote 26.

55. Smith, "Sanctifying Christ" (see note 27 above) 104

56. Finney, *The Enduement of Power*, included in Mahan (see note 31 above) 231.

57. George M. Marsden, *Fundamentalism and American Culture: The Shaping of Twentieth Century Evangelicalism, 1870-1925* (New York: Oxford U Press, 1980) 37

58. Among those who spoke at this conference center were R. A. Torrey, James M. Gray, C. I. Scofield, A. C. Dixon and A. J. Gordon. Numerous speakers involved in the Keswick movement were also frequent participants at the Northfield Conference.

59. Waldvogel-Blumhoefer (see note 2 above) 30

60. Dwight L. Moody, *Sowing and Reaping* (Chicago: 1896) 83

61. Quoted in Waldvogel-Blumhoefer (see note 2 above) 30. The author does not cite the source of her quote.

62. Dayton, *Theological Roots* (see note 4 above) 102. See also Stanley N. Gundry, *Love Them In: The Proclamation Theology of D. L. Moody* (Chicago: Moody Press, 1976) 154.

63. Gundry (see note 62 above) 154. Moody was also reticent on his eschatology, although he did have strong links with C. I. Scofield and the Dispensationalists.

64. For example, a report from 1877 in Moody's "Doctrinal Discourses" contains a sermon entitled "The Baptism of the Holy Spirit for Service."

65. Sarah A. Cooke, *The Handmaiden of the Lord; or, Wayside Sketches* (Chicago: S. B. Shaw, 1900) 42-43

66. James Gilchrist Lawson, *Deeper Experiences of Famous Christians* (Anderson, IN: Warner Press, 1911) 348

67. Lawson (see note 66 above) 348

68. Moody, *Secret Power* (New York: Fleming H. Revell, 1881) 51

69. Moody, *Secret Power* (see note 68 above) 49

70. Moody, *Secret Power* (see note 68 above) 51

71. Moody, *Secret Power* (see note 68 above) 62

72. Moody, *Secret Power* (see note 68 above) 62

73. Moody, *Secret Power* (see note 68 above) 62

74. Moody, *Secret Power* (see note 68 above) 62

75. Moody, *Secret Power* (see note 68 above) 50

76. Moody, as quoted in Waldvogel-Blumhoefer (see note 2 above) 40. The author does not cite the source of her quotation.

77. Waldvogel-Blumhoefer (see note 2 above) 61

Chapter 8

The Baptism of the Holy Spirit in the Teaching of A. B. Simpson's Contemporaries, Part 2: R. A. Torrey, A. J. Gordon, W. E. Boardman, Keswick Teachers

In this chapter, we continue our survey of "Revivalistic Reformed" teachers contemporary with Albert B. Simpson, focusing especially on their teaching concerning the baptism of the Holy Spirit. As we noted earlier, our inquiry is limited to the well-known leaders who, theologically and experientially, were closest to Simpson.

Reuben Archer Torrey (1856-1928)

The doctrine of the baptism of the Holy Spirit dominated the teaching ministry of R. A. Torrey. D. L. Moody encouraged the more scholarly Torrey to formulate a systematic view of the work of the Spirit, particularly as it related to the crisis of being empowered for ministry.[1] At most of the campaigns Moody conducted, he invited Torrey to preach his sermon entitled "The Baptism with the Holy Ghost."[2] Certainly Torrey's formulations were a major contribution to the intensification of the "empowering" motif in Deeper Life teaching at the turn of the century.[3]

Torrey acknowledged that the term *baptism of the Holy Spirit* had become popular in his day. He sought to show that the Scriptures

167

revealed flexibility in terminology when describing this experience. He cited a number of Scriptures—Luke 24:49, Acts 1:4-5; 2:4, 38; 4:8; 10:44-46; 11:15-17; and 19:2-6—to back his conclusion that the phrases "baptized with the Spirit," "endued with power from on high," "the promise of the Father," "the Holy Spirit fell upon them," "received the Holy Ghost" were interchangeable.[4]

Torrey asserted that this "baptism" was a "definite experience" and that believers would know whether or not they had received it. Referring to Luke 24:49, Torrey declared that the disciples would not have known when to stop "stay[ing] in the city" if the experience had not been definite. Furthermore, Paul's question (Acts 19:2) to the Ephesus believers assumes that they should know whether or not they had received the Holy Spirit.[5]

Torrey was also explicit in stating that the baptism of the Spirit was a work of the Spirit separate and distinct from His work in regeneration.[6] Torrey appealed to Jesus' statement in Acts 1:5 and the circumstances of Acts 8:12-16 as evidence that believers already regenerated had not received the baptism for service.[7] He went on to assert that the normative pattern was to receive the baptism immediately at conversion as is evident in Acts 2:43 and Acts 10:43.[8] Torrey observed, however, that in his day "the condition of the Church is not normal." He considered many believers to be in a deficient spiritual state, like "the Samaritan and Ephesian believers."[9] Remarking on First Corinthians 12:13—"We were all given the one Spirit to drink"—Torrey asserts that the Holy Spirit is the birthright of every believer. In his view, however, First Corinthians 12:13 does not imply that every believer is automatically empowered by the Spirit.[10] This aspect of the Spirit's ministry is not effective until the believer has by faith appropriated that empowering.

Always Connected with Testimony and Service

Torrey notes that the baptism of the Holy Spirit is always connected with testimony and service.[11] He is emphatic in his assertion that "the baptism of the Holy Spirit is not for the purpose of cleansing from sin, but for the purpose of empowering for service."[12] Specifically he refutes the idea of an instantaneous eradication of the sin nature. At the same time he does not deny the work of the Spirit in helping cleanse from sin.[13] Also, he notes that the believers referred to in Acts 2:44-46 and 4:31-35 evidenced a definite "moral uplift in their lives."

The other effect of the baptism of the Spirit, in Torrey's view, is a new consciousness or awareness of the Spirit. Up until "the baptism," believers are only dimly aware of the Spirit's presence. Torrey writes:

> It is one thing to have the Holy Spirit dwelling within us, perhaps dwelling within us way back in some hidden sanctuary of our being, back of definite consciousness, and something far different, something vastly more, to have the Holy Spirit taking complete possession of the one whom He inhabits.[14]

Torrey is careful to point out, however, that the Spirit has always been fully resident in the believer.

The necessity of the baptism of the Spirit is based primarily on the command and example of Christ. Torrey makes much of Jesus' instructions to the disciples that they were not to undertake the work of God until they had been prepared by God for the work (Luke 24:49; Acts 1:4, 5, 8).[15] Like others in his time, Torrey also pointed to the ministry of the Spirit in Jesus' own life, empowering Him for ministry. As Torrey's reasoning goes, if the Son of God needed the baptism of the Spirit in His life, how much more do we who serve God today.[16]

Torrey finds support for the continued possibility that believers may be baptized by the Spirit in Acts 2:39—"The promise is for you and your children and for all who are far off—for all whom the Lord our God will call." Torrey believed the "gift my Father promised" (Acts 1:4, 5) "poured out" (Acts 2:33) on the day of Pentecost was applicable to all believers.[17] Moreover, this promise is to be received consciously in every generation of believers. Torrey writes of this:

Whom is this gift for? "To you," says Peter to the Jews whom he was immediately addressing [Acts 2:39]. Then looking over their heads to the next generation, "And to your children." Then looking down all the coming ages of the Church's history to Gentile as well as Jew: "And to all that are afar off, even as many as the Lord our God shall call unto him." The baptism with the Holy Ghost is for every age in the Church's history. If it is not ours in experiential possession, it is because we have not taken what God has provided for us in our exalted Saviour.[18]

Believers Responsible for Ineffective Service

It appears here that Torrey sees this promise to be not so much the initial reception of the Spirit, but the "enduement with power from on high."[19] Torrey is adamant in his insistence that believers possess their full inheritance in Christ because of the effect the Holy Spirit will have on their ministry. He asserts that people will be held responsible by God for ineffectual ministry. He laments the fact that much of the preaching of his day was "in the energy of the flesh and not in the power of the Holy Spirit."[20] He declares:

> It is awfully solemn business preaching the gospel either from the pulpit or in quieter ways. It means death or life to those who hear; and whether it means death or life depends very largely on whether we preach it without or with the baptism with the Holy Spirit. We must be baptized with the Holy Spirit.[21]

From the tone of this plea it is easy to perceive how essential Torrey thought this empowering was.

Torrey devotes much space to how the baptism of the Spirit may be obtained. His principal text for this procedure is Acts 2:38: "Peter replied, 'Repent and be baptized, every one of you, in the name of Jesus Christ for the forgiveness of your sins. And you will receive the gift of the Holy Spirit.' " Torrey sees seven elements stated or implied in Peter's words.

1. "Repent" implies the necessity of conversion as the foundational step.

2. Torrey sees in that same word the importance of a "change of mind regarding sin," turning "from sin loving and indulging" to "sin hating and sin renouncing."[22] Torrey believed that the Lordship question was often the reason many had not received the baptism—they were unwilling to dedicate themselves completely to God.

3. A believer should be baptized in water. This was illustrated in Christ's life and accordingly is the normative event prior to the baptism of the Spirit.[23]

4. The next step, implied in Acts 2:38 but more explicitly in 5:32, is "obedience" or "total surrender to the will of God."[24] ". . . the Holy Spirit, whom God has given to those who obey him."

5 This obedience step must be followed by an intense, real desire to be baptized by the Spirit. Citing John 7:37-39—"Jesus . . . said, . . . 'If anyone is thirsty, let him come to me and drink' "—Torrey stresses the need to go before God with the right motive, denying any self-sufficiency. He emphasizes that God Himself is dishonored by an ineffectual ministry.[25]

A "Definite Asking for and a Definite Receiving"

6. There must be a "definite asking for and a definite receiving of the blessing."[26] Here Torrey asserts that the promises of God must be appropriated by His people. He asserts that as salvation, which is offered to all (see, for instance, John 3:16), demands a specific and intentional response, so also with the baptism of the Spirit. Torrey acknowledged that God gives the Spirit at conversion and that He henceforth indwells the believer (Romans 8:9). Yet that does not imply that the experiential realization of the power of the Spirit has come upon the believer. Torrey declares:

> As we have already seen, it is quite possible to have something, yes, much, of the Spirit's presence and work in the heart and yet come short of that special fullness and

work known in the Bible as the baptism or filling with the Holy Spirit.[27]

Torrey cites Luke 11:13—"If you . . . know how to give good gifts to your children, how much more will your Father in heaven give the Holy Spirit to those who ask him!"—and Acts 4:31—"After they had prayed, . . . they were all filled with the Holy Spirit and spoke the word of God boldly"—as key texts to support his view.

7. Unlike his contemporaries, Torrey did not advocate "tarrying" or "waiting" for the baptism of the Spirit. Citing Scriptures such as Acts 8:15-17, 9:17, 20; 10:44-46 and 19:6, he asserted that after Pentecost there was no interval between the time of asking and God's pouring out His Spirit.[28] The final element, therefore, was believing. Believing is based on confidence in God's assurance that He will give what He promises.[29] If a believer fulfills the requirements, he or she can be certain that God has answered. Torrey does not deny that there might be experiential enjoyment of this baptism, either concurrent with asking or at a later date.[30] However, in Torrey's view, fruit in ministry is the principal witness that a believer has indeed been baptized by the Spirit.

Torrey mentions the importance of an ongoing process of being filled with the Spirit. He prefers to use the term "filling" to describe this particular ministry of the Spirit. In this way Torrey clearly distinguishes the initial crisis—the "baptism" of the Spirit—from the ongoing process which ensues.[31]

In summation, Torrey displays a marked emphasis on power for service in his discussions of the baptism of the Spirit. Although believers receive the Spirit at conversion, the empowering—the baptism of the Spirit—must be specifically appropriated. Torrey also eliminates "tarrying for the Spirit" by denying that the baptism is necessarily experiential. This last is a marked departure from some of his contemporaries.

Adoniram Judson Gordon (1836-1895)

A. J. Gordon served for many years as the pastor of the famous

Clarendon Street Baptist Church in Boston. He was a frequent speaker at both Moody's Northfield conferences and Simpson's C&MA conventions.[32] Like Simpson, Gordon was involved in a wide range of endeavors, including the promotion of city evangelism, world missions, social agencies, healing and premillennialism.[33] He is an important figure to study because his activities closely paralleled those of Simpson. Author of many books, Gordon's most important work on the Holy Spirit is *The Ministry of the Spirit* (1894).

Unlike Moody and Torrey, Gordon's interest in the ministry of the Spirit does not flow from a utilitarian desire to receive more "power" for ministry. Gordon is primarily concerned that Christians understand the full implications of living in the age of the Spirit.[34] Although empowering for service is certainly a dimension of this new era of the Holy Spirit, it is a peripheral one. Gordon maintains that the principal task of the Spirit is to present "Christ in His entirety." By this Gordon means that the Spirit's work is to disclose the benefits of Christ's union with believers and then assist them in the realization of those benefits.[35] All discussions of the work of the Spirit, therefore, must relate to this realizing task.

Gordon emphasizes that the Holy Spirit was given to the Church on the day of Pentecost to help it embody Christ to the world.[36] Hence the "baptism of the Spirit" occurred only once at the inception of the Church, and the Spirit now dwells in the abode of the Church.[37] But Gordon quickly adds, "God's gift is one thing; our appropriation of that gift is quite another thing."[38] He asserts that in the divine economy there must always be active human response to God's promises. For this reason he writes:

> It seems clear from Scripture that it is still the duty and privilege of believers to receive the Holy Spirit by a conscious, definite act of appropriating faith, just as they received Jesus Christ.[39]

Hence, although the Spirit has been in "the abode" of the Church since Pentecost, a regenerated believer still may not necessarily have received the Holy Spirit.[40]

Gordon cites a number of texts in support of his position. Peter's words in Acts 2:38, in his opinion, indicate that repentance and the reception of the Spirit are two distinct elements: "Repent and be baptized . . . for the forgiveness of your sins. . . . And you will receive the gift of the Holy Spirit." Gordon insists, "Logically and chronologically the gift of the Spirit is subsequent to repentance."[41] Therefore he maintains that there is an additional work of the Spirit subsequent to "bringing men to believe and repent."[42]

This Subsequent Work Is Also Received by Faith

Referring to the question Paul asked the Galatians—"Did you receive the Spirit by observing the law, or by believing what you heard?"(3:2)—and his later statement—". . . that by faith we might receive the promise of the Spirit" (3:14)—Gordon states, "These texts seem to imply that just as there is 'faith toward our Lord Jesus Christ' for salvation, there is a faith toward the Holy Ghost for power and consecration."[43] Similarly he saw Paul's question to the believers he found at Ephesus—"Did you receive the Holy Spirit when you believed?"—as showing decisively "that one may be a disciple without having entered into possession of the Spirit as God's gift to believers."[44]

Finally, like others, he turns to Jesus Christ, the Archetype:

> Let us observe that Christ, who is our example in this as in all things, did not enter upon His ministry till He had received the Holy Ghost. Not only so, but we see that all His service from His baptism to His ascension was wrought in the Spirit.[45]

Gordon points out that, although Christ "was begotten by the Spirit," He needed the distinct event when the Spirit came upon him.[46] Moreover, he claimed that Jesus, when praying at the Jordan River (Luke 3:21-22), was very aware of Isaiah's words, "The Spirit of the LORD will rest on him" (11:2), thereby providing a basis for the believer's asking for the Spirit.[47]

Gordon prefers to call the reception of the gift of the Spirit "the enduement with the Spirit." He outlines three dimensions of this enduement: *First,* there is "the sealing of the Spirit," which occurs only once and consists of the impartation of the Spirit.[48] The Spirit grants assurance of divine ownership and of a summons to live a holy life.[49] *Second,* there is "the anointing of the Spirit," at which time God imparts power for ministry to the believer.[50] *Third,* there is "the filling with the Spirit," which occurs repeatedly in believers' lives since "our capacity is ever increasing and our need constantly recurring."[51]

From a reading of Gordon's *The Ministry of the Spirit,* it appears that he sees the (1) "sealing" and the (2) "anointing" as occurring at the time the believer exercises faith to appropriate the Spirit, while (3) the "filling" is, as was stated, an ongoing process.

No Set Formula

Although Gordon believed that it was the believer's privilege and duty to receive the enduement with the Spirit, he was reluctant "to prescribe any stereotyped exercises through which one must pass in order to possess [this benefit]."[52] A believer should on the one hand avoid preoccupation with theological quibbling, and on the other guard against seeking "striking spiritual experiences."[53] He does suggest that it is a helpful exercise to examine the crisis experiences of famous Christians.[54] Beyond this, the most important step is to exercise faith to appropriate the provision. Gordon defines faith as "an affirmation and an act, which bids eternal truth be present fact."[55]

Gordon describes the effect of the "enduement" in these words:

> We conceive that the great end for which the enduement of the Spirit is bestowed is our qualification for the highest and most effective service in the church of Christ. Other effects will certainly attain the blessing, a fixed assurance of acceptance in Christ, and a holy separateness from the

world; but these results will be conducive to the greatest and supreme end, our consecrated usefulness.[56]

Gordon defines "consecrated usefulness" as the task of proclaiming and displaying Christ to the world. Hence, while stressing that the enduement imparts effectual power for service, Gordon can never separate this power from the call to manifest Christ through transformed character. Accordingly, he sees sanctification as the process by which the Spirit makes "true in us what is already true for us in our glorified Lord."[57]

And how does the Holy Spirit produce the image of our glorified Lord in us? Through "the double process of mortification and vivification, the deadening and subduing of the old and the quickening and developing of the new."[58] At the same time, "the believer is required to be consciously and intelligently active in his own growth, . . . surrendering . . . to the divine action by living in the Spirit and praying in the Spirit and walking in the Spirit."[59]

Gordon condenses his view in the phrase, "Sinful in self, sinless in Christ." Believers are powerless on their own, but they have infinite resources available in Christ through the working of the Spirit.[60]

In summary, then, we can say that Gordon's pneumatology is Christocentric. Although he avoids the term "baptism of the Spirit," he does teach the need for a definite appropriation of the Spirit. The effect of the enduement of the Spirit is "consecrated usefulness," a concept which includes enabling both to proclaim Christ in service and to display Christ through a transformed life.

W. E. Boardman (1810-1886) and the "Higher Life" Movement

Three people are inextricably associated with the so-called "Higher Life Movement": W. E. Boardman, Robert Pearsall Smith and Hannah Whitall Smith.[61] All three were Americans, but they had their greatest influence on the fledgling Keswick movement in England.[62] The teaching of W. E. Boardman is of particular interest to us because his book, *The Higher Christian Life* (1859), had a profound influence on A. B. Simpson.[63] Moreover, although it was chronologically earlier than most of the other books we have thus far surveyed, a knowledge of Boardman's views helps us to understand the Christocentric focus of the Keswick movement.

It is impossible to understand accurately the concern of Boardman's book without being cognizant of the milieu in which he wrote it.[64] As we saw in chapter 1, the Oberlin and Methodist movements were having a great impact at the time with their teachings on Christian perfection. Boardman reacted to what he saw in these movements as an overemphasis on human agency. He therefore wrote *The Higher Christian Life* as a corrective. While maintaining people's need for a crisis experience, Boardman believed the object of that experience to be "the perception and reception of the Lord Jesus as [their] righteousness in sanctification."[65]

Boardman believed that God had provided for believers' sanctification as well as justification in the atonement. But the benefits of these provisions only took effect through distinct acts of faith.[66] There is a faith for justification and a faith for sanctification. Boardman argues that although both blessings are available at conversion, often believers only avail themselves of the latter provision later in life. The reason for this is that people more quickly apprehend the provision for the penalty of sin than they do the dynamics for overcoming the power of sin.[67] Moreover, as with the believers in Ephesus (Acts 19:2), many have

> . . . a *metenoya* [sic—a transliteration of the Greek word for repentance] conversion—a change of heart—and not yet a heart filled with faith of a present Saviour wrought in them by an indwelling Holy Ghost.[68]
>
> For this reason, most Christians go through a time of frustration and failure in the initial period after conversion.[69]

So Boardman calls for a "second conversion." The principal Scriptures he uses to back his viewpoint are Romans 7 and 8.[70] A part of the "second conversion" is the recognition that all our previous attempts to be holy through self effort are unavailing. Believers must acknowledge

> ... what Christ has already done for us, in tasting death for our sins, and what He is now to us in His living presence, power, care and love, watching over us day by day, and guiding us in all the struggles and issues of the present here upon the earth, and what He is now for us, as our Advocate, Mediator, and Friend in heaven above.[71]

Complete Dedication to God

This provision of Christ must be received by "faith," which Boardman defines as "that which gives all and takes all"; that is, complete dedication to God and acceptance of Christ's present work.[72]

As a result of this dedication, the surrendered believer will receive a conscious witness of Christ's indwelling.[73] Moreover, he or she has attained "sanctification." Boardman does not seem to use this term to signify that the righteousness of Christ is imputed to the believer, nor does he mean that the actual righteousness of Christ is imparted to the believer.[74] "Sanctification" seems to be the experiential "recognition" of Christ's provision for holy living and the confidence that this holiness will be realized in the believer's life. It is "a distinct plane of experience with its definite beginning."[75] Although there is a definite time when the believer enters "sanctification," the effect of sanctification is only progressively realized. Boardman contrasts this with the first conversion:

> In the one, the atonement has been made, and the moment it is accepted, the pardon is complete; in the other, although the righteousness of Christ is perfect in which the soul is to be clothed, yet the work of the unfolding heart to itself in its wants, and the unfolding of Christ to the heart from glory to glory, in His sympathizing love, and purifying

presence and power, as the soul shall be prepared to go onward and upward from faith to faith, is a work of time and progress.[76]

Boardman teaches a progressive deliverance "from conscious sinning plus progressive cleansing of heart and life."[77] As long as the believer "abides," he or she maintains this effectual ability to be transformed.[78]

Boardman refers to this "second conversion" as "the baptism of the Holy Spirit."[79] However, he says very little about the ministry of the Spirit in *The Higher Christian Life*.[80] In a later work, *In the Power of the Spirit* (1875), Boardman is more explicit in his explanation of the work of the Spirit. There he declares the "second conversion" to be the indwelling of the Spirit.[81] Concerning this baptism he writes:

> *The* baptism. *The* baptism, I say; not a baptism, but the gift of the Holy Ghost as an abiding, guiding, teaching, girding, strengthening [Presence].[82]

Although Boardman says more about the Spirit in this later book, the focus remains on the Spirit's ministry of revealing the indwelling Christ for sanctification.

In summary, then, Boardman uses the term *baptism of the Spirit* to denote the indwelling of Christ whereby believers receive sanctification. He makes minimal mention of the exact nature of the Spirit's work in this baptism. Boardman bases his concepts primarily on the struggle depicted in Romans 7 and the freedom found in Romans 8.

The Keswick Teachers

The final group of people we want to look at under the broad heading of "Revivalistic Reformed" consists largely of non-Americans who nevertheless had a significant voice in late 19th century America.[83] Men like F. B. Meyer, Andrew Murray and

Charles Inwood spoke at conferences held by both A. B. Simpson and D. L. Moody.[84]

The Keswick movement was the result of a rising concern in England for the people's spiritual life. This led to the famous "Union Meeting for the Promotion of Scriptural Holiness" at Oxford in 1874 and the "Convention for the Promotion of Scriptural Holiness" in Brighton the following year.[85] From 1875 onward, annual conventions were held at Keswick for the express purpose of enriching the spiritual life. Those attending the conferences came from a diversity of denominational affiliations. As the years passed, the Keswick convention also became a center for the promotion of foreign missions.

Keswick teaching was not as precisely defined as that of the Methodist-Holiness camp, for example. Moreover, there was a wide diversity of nuances and manners of expression among Keswick sympathizers. However, there was general agreement as to the central assertions of the movement. A survey of these assertions provides us a further comparison with the views of A. B. Simpson.

In contrast to D. L. Moody and particularly R. A. Torrey, Keswick teachers devoted much more attention to the Spirit's work in sanctification. Great emphasis was placed on the need for a decisive dedication and commitment to God's provision for holiness. This provision was Christ. Handley C. G. Moule, theologian of the movement, sums up this point well when he asserts:

> [Holiness] does not depend on wearisome struggles but on God's power to take the consecrated soul and to keep him. . . . Christ our righteousness, upon Calvary, received by faith, is also Christ our holiness, in the heart that submits to Him and relies on Him. . . . The Keswick teaching, then, presents the power of an indwelling Christ for deliverance from sin, freedom and the conquest of temptation from the tyranny of self. Christ is Victor![86]

Note how congruent this teaching is with that of W. E. Boardman. The explication of Keswick teaching is seen in the typical order of the Keswick conference week:

- Day One—the doctrine of sin and the necessity of forsaking intentional sinning
- Day Two—God's provision for sin through identification with Christ
- Day Three—consecration, what is involved in dedicating oneself to God
- Day Four—the fullness of the Spirit
- Day Five—Christian service[87]

A more detailed outline of the Keswick teaching is included in Appendix 5.[88]

Features of the Keswick Teaching

We should highlight several features of the Keswick teaching. *First,* Keswick placed great emphasis on the necessity of "death to self." Prior to receiving sanctification by faith and the "infilling of the Spirit," believers were urged to renounce sin. This decisive transaction extended beyond the recognition of being freed from slavery to the sin nature (Romans 6). It also included the actual cessation and renouncing of sinful practices.[89] Unless that was done, the conditions for receiving sanctification and "the infilling of the Spirit" had not been met. Hence, reception of these blessings, in the Keswick view, was predicated on this act of "death to self." While other groups emphasized the importance of dedicating themselves to God, they lacked the Keswick focus on the prior removal of specific sins which might hinder the reception of the promised blessings.

Second, Keswick teaching emphasized a distinct time when a believer received the "infilling of the Holy Spirit." This infilling could only follow the thorough cleansing and dedication we noted previously. The majority of the Keswick teachers avoided the use of the term "baptism of the Holy Spirit."[90] They acknowledged only "one 'baptism' of the Spirit once for all"; they taught that every believer was indwelt by the Spirit. However, they argued for a definite moment in which a person dedicated himself or herself to God and asked to be filled with the Spirit.[91] Pierson comments:

> Every disciple is at least entitled to claim his full share in that blessing [the historical outpouring of the Spirit on the day of Pentecost] and enter into pentecostal life and power, or rather to have it enter into him.[92]

Accordingly, a believer must exercise "faith" and thereby claim this promise.[93]

The *third* and final notable feature of the Keswick teaching is its Christocentric focus. Although "power over sin" and power for "holy serving" were among the privileges of the "infilling of the Spirit," "the revelation of Jesus Christ in the soul as an Indwelling Presence is the climax of it all."[94] Of this reality Pierson writes:

> The supreme end of the Holy Spirit's indwelling and inworking is to manifest the personal Christ as consciously in our possession and in possession of us. This is the mystery: *Christ in you.* The Spirit first takes the things of Christ and shows them to the believer; second, He testifies to Christ, and, third, He glorifies Christ. Note the three parts of this work as laid down in John xiv–xvi: Manifesting, witnessing, glorifying. He shows Christ in all His offices and relations; He makes Him real as an actual possession; and He clothes Him in glorious charms, so that we gaze on Him, enamored of His beauty and love. It is very different to have Christ revealed *without,* as a historic personage, and *within* as experientially and really Master and Lord. This latter, the Holy Spirit does, as the former is effected by the Word.[95]

For those immersed in Keswick teaching, this focus on Christ tends to eclipse any expansion on the other resultant effects of the Spirit's infilling.

F. B. Meyer (1847-1929), Keswick Spokesperson

F. B. Meyer was a key leader in the Keswick movement and also a speaker at some of Simpson's deeper life conferences. His writing is illustrative of the classic Keswick understanding outlined above. Thus a brief survey of his books is helpful to see how he expresses the views of the movement.

Meyer asserts that while many believers "historically and chronologically live on this side of Pentecost, experientially they are on the other side of Pentecost."[96] Meyer queries a believer this way:

> You have known the Holy Spirit regenerating and quickening and blessing you. But have you known Him infilling you with His mighty presence and power?[97]

Among the tests Meyer proposes to know whether a believer has been filled with the Spirit are these:

- Do you have victory over sin?
- Do you have "power to bear witness"
- Is "the Lord Jesus . . . a living reality" to you?[98]

Notice how this "test" parallels the Christocentric focus we saw earlier.

Those who do not experience these realities need to fulfill several conditions. They should realize that the Spirit indeed indwells them and that they merely have to appropriate His resources. They must be cleansed and dedicated to God and His service. In this regard, Meyer points out that any unyieldedness will prevent the effective experiencing of God's resources for holy living. Finally they must exercise faith:

> All God's dealings with men are on the same principle, by faith. By faith you are regenerated, by faith you are justified, by faith you are sanctified, by faith you receive the Holy

Ghost, by faith you receive Christ as the power of God into your life. It is all by faith.[99]

Meyer hence placed great emphasis on appropriating God's spiritual benefits through faith.

Summary

We have now outlined in this chapter and the last the three major streams of teaching on the baptism of the Holy Spirit contemporary with Simpson. We have also looked at the rationale, nature, procedure and results of the baptism. For a convenient although partial listing of the content of each of these views, see the following table. Note, however, that this table is a very brief recapitulation of what we have looked at in far greater detail in Chapters 7 and 8. For a more precise depiction, please consult the corresponding sections of the text.

	Methodist-Holiness	"Third Blessing" View	Asa Mahan
Baptism of the Holy Spirit	Distinct in time and content from conversion; also called "second blessing" or "second definite work of grace"	Distinct in time from conversion and the "second blessing" of entire sanctification	Moment of the Spirit's indwelling the believer
Results	Wesleyan understanding of sanctification along with power for service	Power for service	Holy living, but particularly power for service
Sanctification	Sanctification at a definite fixed time; Wesleyan understanding	Precedes empowering; understood along Wesleyan lines	
Indwelling of Spirit	Automatic at conversion	Automatic at conversion	Not automatic, but must be asked for; Spirit comes "upon a believer"

	Charles Finney	Dwight L. Moody	R. A. Torrey
Baptism of the Holy Spirit	The initial reception of the Spirit	Anointing of God for greater effectiveness in ministry	Distinct from regeneration
Results	Primarily power for service	Primarily power for service	Primarily power for service
Sanctification	The Spirit imparts Christ's provision for holy living	Not linked to the "baptism of the Holy Spirit"	Not linked to the "baptism of the Holy Spirit"
Indwelling of Spirit	A privilege to be asked for; not automatic	Automatically received at conversion	Automatically received at conversion

	A. J. Gordon	W. E. Boardman	Keswick
Baptism of the Holy Spirit	He didn't explicitly use this term; he asserted need for conscious appropriation of Holy Spirit	Point of the "indwelling of the Spirit"	Act of appropriation of God's blessings through faith
Results	Spirit fully discloses the benefits of union with Christ; "consecrated usefulness"	Primarily a new ability to lead a holy life	Holiness and power for service
Sanctification	Result of union with Christ	Result of union with Christ	New power to follow God
Indwelling of Spirit	Spirit "with" believer at conversion and comes with power at point of "enduement"	The Spirit "with" believer and then comes to fully indwell at baptism	Not linked to the baptism of the Spirit

Endnotes

1. Donald W. Dayton, *The Theological Roots of Pentecostalism* (Grand Rapids, MI: Zondervan, 1968) 102

2. Dayton, *Theological Roots* (see note 1 above) 103

3. Dayton, *Theological Roots* (see note 1 above) 102. In his book, *A Theology of the Holy Spirit: The Pentecostal Experience and the New Testament Witness* (Grand Rapids, MI: Wm B. Eerdmans, 1970) 45, Frederick Dale Bruner indicates that the Pentecostal movement viewed Torrey as the major source for their teaching on empowering for service.

4. R. A. Torrey, *The Baptism with the Holy Spirit* (New York: Revell, 1897) 13-14

5. Torrey, *Baptism* (see note 4 above) 14-15

6. Torrey, *Baptism* (see note 4 above) 17

7. Torrey, *Baptism* (see note 4 above) 17

8. Torrey, *The Person and Work of the Holy Spirit: As Revealed in the Scriptures and in Personal Experience* (London: James Nisbett, 1910) 177

9. Torrey, *Person and Work* (see note 8 above) 177

10. Torrey, *Person and Work* (see note 8 above) 177-178. Torrey states that this part of the baptism is not yet a matter of "real, actual, personal experience."

11. Torrey, *Baptism* (see note 4 above) 18. Torrey refers to Acts 1:5, 8; 2:4; and 4:31, 33.

12. Torrey, *Baptism* (see note 4 above) 18

13. Torrey, *Baptism* (see note 4 above) 19. Torrey writes, "It is our privilege to so walk daily and hourly in the power of the Spirit that the carnal nature is kept in the place of death."

14. Torrey, *Person and Work* (see note 8 above) 178

15. Torrey, *Baptism* (see note 4 above) 28

16. Torrey, *Baptism* (see note 4 above) 29-30. Torrey cites Acts 10:38 and the passages in Luke's Gospel (3:21, 22; 4:1, 14, 15, 18, 21) that attest to the work of the Spirit in Christ's life.

17. Torrey, *Baptism* (see note 4 above) 33

18. Torrey, *Baptism* (see note 4 above) 33-34

19. Torrey, *Baptism* (see note 4 above) 35

20. Torrey, *Baptism* (see note 4 above) 35-36. Torrey contrasts ministry performed "in persuasive words of wisdom" and that which is done "in demonstration of the Spirit and of power" (1 Cor. 2:4).

21. Torrey, *Baptism* (see note 4 above) 36

22. Torrey, *Baptism* (see note 4 above) 40

23. Torrey, *Baptism* (see note 4 above) 42
    Torrey, *Person and Work* (see note 8 above) 220

24. Torrey, *Baptism* (see note 4 above) 44
    Torrey, *Person and Work* 221

25. Torrey, *Baptism* (see note 4 above) 49. Torrey refers to the incident of Simon the Sorcerer in Acts 8:18-24 as an example of someone who had a wrong motive in seeking the baptism of the Holy Spirit.

26. Torrey, *Baptism* (see note 4 above) 51

27. Torrey, *Baptism* (see note 4 above) 52

28. Torrey, *Baptism* (see note 4 above) 62-64

29. Torrey, *Baptism* (see note 4 above) 55

30. Torrey, *Baptism* (see note 4 above) 58-59

31. Torrey, *Baptism* (see note 4 above) 69-70

32. Simpson included an article written by Gordon in one of his periodicals. See A. J. Gordon, "The Holy Spirit," *The Word, the Work and the World* (Apr 1885) 241-243.

33. C. Allyn Russell, "A. J. Gordon: 19th Century Fundamentalist," *American Baptist Quarterly* (Mar 1985) 62-63

34. Gordon, *The Ministry of the Spirit* (Philadelphia: American Baptist Publication Society, 1896) 24. Gordon maintained a threefold view of Salvation history. For more details on the prevalence of this view during the late 1800s, see chapter 1.

35. Gordon, *Ministry of Spirit* (see note 34 above) 24

36. Gordon, *Ministry of Spirit* (see note 34 above) 64

37. Gordon, *Ministry of Spirit* (see note 34 above) 69

38. Gordon, *Ministry of Spirit* (see note 34 above) 75

39. Gordon, *Ministry of Spirit* (see note 34 above) 76

40. Gordon saw a parallel between the logic employed by the Universalists and those who maintained that all automatically received the Spirit. Gordon pointed out that the Universalists of his day believed that on account of the incarnation of Christ all people were redeemed, regardless of their response to Christ. In Gordon's view, this was similar to the line of argument that suggested that since all the disciples received the Spirit on the day of Pentecost, everyone receives the Spirit today [Gordon, *Ministry of Spirit* (see note 34 above) 75-76].

41. Gordon, *Ministry of Spirit* (see note 34 above) 77

42. Gordon, *Ministry of Spirit* (see note 34 above) 77

43. Gordon, *Ministry of Spirit* (see note 34 above) 79

44. Gordon, *Ministry of Spirit* (see note 34 above) 79

45. Gordon, *Ministry of Spirit* (see note 34 above) 82

46. Gordon, *Ministry of Spirit* (see note 34 above) 83

47. Gordon, *Ministry of Spirit* (see note 34 above) 83

48. Gordon, *Ministry of Spirit* (see note 34 above) 88. Gordon writes, "In a word, the sealing is the Spirit Himself, now received by faith and resting upon the believer, with all the results of assurance, in joy, and in empowering for service, which must follow His unhindered sway in the soul."

49. Gordon, *Ministry of Spirit* (see note 34 above) 86-88. Concerning Divine ownership, Gordon cites John 6:27, Ephesians 1:13 and 2 Corinthians 1:21-22. About holy living, he discusses Ephesians 4:30.

50. Gordon, *Ministry of Spirit* (see note 34 above) 94-96

51. Gordon, *Ministry of Spirit* (see note 34 above) 91. In respect to the need for constant refilling, Gordon quotes from Godet: "Man is a vessel destined to receive God, a vessel which must be enlarged in proportion as it is filled and filled in proportion as it is enlarged" (source of citation not given by Gordon). Gordon refers to Ephesians 5:18—"Be filled with the Spirit"—and the refilling experienced by the apostles (Acts 4:31). Of Ephesians 5:18, Gordon comments, "The surrendered will, the yielded body, the emptied heart, are the great requisites to His incoming."

52. Gordon, *Ministry of Spirit* (see note 34 above) 99

53. Gordon, *Ministry of Spirit* (see note 34 above) 100

54. Gordon, *Ministry of Spirit* (see note 34 above) 100. Gordon mentions Finney, Wesley, Whitefield and Brainard Taylor as examples. It must be noted that his presentation of the experiences of these men is not always accurate, particularly with respect to Charles Finney.

55. Gordon, *Ministry of Spirit* (see note 34 above) 100. Gordon mentions the following prayer: "O Holy Spirit, I yield to Thee now in humble surrender. I receive Thee as my Teacher, my Comforter, my Sanctifier, and my Guide" (pages 81-82).

56. Gordon, *Ministry of Spirit* (see note 34 above) 82

57. Gordon, *Ministry of Spirit* (see note 34 above) 106

58. Gordon, *Ministry of Spirit* (see note 34 above) 113

59. Gordon, *Ministry of Spirit* (see note 34 above) 120

60. Gordon, *Ministry of Spirit* (see note 34 above) 122

61. Benjamin B. Warfield, *Perfectionism,* vol. 2 (Philadelphia: Presbyterian and Reformed Publishing Co., 1971) 464-465. See also Steven Barabas, *So Great Salvation: The History and Message of the Keswick Convention* (London: Marshall, Morgan and Scott, 1952) 16. The term itself comes from the title of Boardman's famous book, *The Higher Christian Life* (see note 65 below).

62. Robert Pearsall Smith withdrew from ministry shortly before the first meeting at Keswick in 1875. Prior to that he had been a leader in the events which culminated in the establishment of the Keswick convention, including serving as chairman of the Brighton conference.

    W. E. Boardman was involved in the inception of Keswick too. He continued to spread his higher life teachings in England and on the continent until his death in 1886. Boardman was also involved in the healing movement in England, participating in the Bethshan healing home. For a survey of the impact of these men on Keswick, see Barabas (see note 61 above) 15-28.

63. For more details, see Barabas (see note 61 above) 27. All of his chapter 1 and his endnote 111 are germane.

64. W. H. G. Thomas offers a rejoinder to Warfield's critique of the "Higher Life" movement [see Thomas, "The Victorious Life," *Bibliotheca Sacra* (Jul 1919) 267-288, and (Oct 1919) 455-467].

65. W. E. Boardman, *The Higher Christian Life* (Boston: Henry Hoyt, 1859) 38

66. W. E. Boardman (see note 65 above) 116-117

67. W. E. Boardman (see note 65 above) 140

68. W. E. Boardman (see note 65 above) 278

69. W. E. Boardman (see note 65 above) 140-142. Boardman uses the analogy of the conquest of Canaan. Having been delivered through the Red Sea and the Jordan, the Israelites soon found that they could not defeat the Philistines in their own strength. Boardman sees this as illustrative of our need to "depend on God's power *alone*" beyond both conversion and the initial sanctification experience in the Christian life.

70. W. E. Boardman (see note 65 above) 143

71. W. E. Boardman (see note 65 above) 252-253

72. W. E. Boardman (see note 65 above) 126

73. W. E. Boardman (see note 65 above) 206

74. See Warfield's analysis (see note 61 above) 483

75. W. E. Boardman (see note 65 above) 167, 187

76. W. E. Boardman (see note 65 above) 116-117. Elsewhere Boardman writes, "The soul is now placed in the hands of Christ, as the clay in the hands of the potter; and by faith, Christ is received by the soul as the Potter to mold it as His own sovereign will, into a vessel for the Master's own use and for the King's own table" (page 59).

77. W. E. Boardman (see note 65 above) 116

78. Boardman devotes a chapter to "abiding." See W. E. Boardman (see note 65 above) 321-323.

79. W. E. Boardman (see note 65 above) 198, 237

80. Most books of Christian theology written in the Civil War era were characterized by this Christocentric focus. See chapter 1 for the nature of teaching on holiness prior to the Civil War.

81. W. E. Boardman, *In the Power of the Spirit: Or, Christian Experience in the Light of the Bible* (1875) 89-90, as quoted in Warfield (see note 61 above) 490

82. W. E. Boardman, *In Power of Spirit* (see note 81 above) 102

83. Robert Mapes Anderson, *Vision of the Disinherited: The Making of American Pentecostalism* (New York: Oxford University Press, 1979) 41

84. A. E. Thompson, *The Life of A. B. Simpson* (New York: Christian Alliance Publishing Co., 1920) 110

85. For a good survey of this movement, see Melvin E. Dieter, "From Vineland and Manheim to Brighton and Berlin: The Holiness Revival in Nineteenth-Century Europe," *Wesleyan Theological Journal* (Spring 1974) 15-25.

86. Handley C. G. Moule, *Christ Is Victor* (London: Hodder and Stoughton, 1896) 64

87. Barabas (see note 61 above) gives a summary of this outline in his book. He asserts that this presentation had not changed significantly since the inception of Keswick in 1875.

88. Appendix 5 is essentially the same outline given by A. T. Pierson in *Forward Movements of the Last Half Century* (New York: Funk and Wagnalls, 1900) 32-38. Pierson, an American, became a strong advocate in the United States of Keswick teaching. His book presents the significant developments in Christianity during the late 1800s. It also sets forth an excellent overview of the Keswick message. Pierson and Barabas (see note 61 above) saw the movement essentially eye-to-eye.

89. See Appendix 5, "The Second Step," for an example of this emphasis.

90. Andrew Murray, *The Spirit of Christ: Thoughts on the Indwelling of the Holy Spirit in the Believer and the Church* (New York: A. D. F. Randolph and Co., 1888) 313, notes that Asa Mahan used this term, "baptism of the Holy Spirit," during his popular lectures at the Oxford and Brighton meetings. However, Murray points out that most of the Keswick teachers did not adopt Mahan's more radical teaching or his terminology. In his *Theological Roots* 105, Dayton says the most characteristic terms to denote the crisis of being infilled with the Spirit were "the fullness of the Spirit" and "the Spirit-filled life."

91. Pierson (see note 88 above) 36

92. Pierson (see note 88 above) 36

93. Compare "The Fourth Step," Appendix 5, and Pierson (see note 88 above) 36-37.

94. Pierson (see note 88 above) 37

95. Pierson (see note 88 above) 37-38

96. F. B. Meyer, *Back to Bethel* (Chicago: Moody Press, 1901) 90

97. Meyer, *Back to Bethel* (see note 96 above) 95

98. Meyer, *Back to Bethel* (see note 96 above) 97-101

99. Meyer, *A Castaway and Other Addresses* 92ff, as quoted in Bruner (see note 3 above) 340-341. Bruner provides no details as to the publisher or date of publication of this book.

Chapter 9

A. B. Simpson Compared with His Contemporaries, Part 1: Similarities between Simpson and His Contemporaries

As we noted back in the Introduction of this book, Simpson seemed to hold many of the same convictions regarding the baptism of the Holy Spirit that his contemporaries held.[1] But in several respects his views also seemed to differ from the views of his contemporaries. Our study is now at a point where the validity of that thesis may be demonstrated. Using material from the previous chapters, we shall undertake a comparative analysis of Simpson and his contemporaries. In this chapter our goal is to highlight the similarities in the views of Simpson and his contemporaries.

What Simpson Shared in Common with *All* His Contemporaries

As we might well surmise—and indeed have already discovered—there was not unanimity among those in his era, whom we can consider closest to Simpson "theologically and experientially," regarding their view of the baptism of the Holy Spirit. In attempting our search for shared viewpoints, therefore, it is necessary that we divide our inquiry under two headings: (1) What Simpson shared in common with *all* his contemporaries and (2) What Simpson shared in common with *some* of his contemporaries. We turn, first, to the first of these comparisons: the common ground between Simpson and all the ministry associates we have surveyed in the past chapters.

They All Believed the Benefits of Salvation Are Separate and Need to Be Realized Distinctly

Simpson and his contemporaries maintained that salvation encompassed many blessings. Although they thought of all these blessings as guaranteed by the finished work of Christ, they did not consider all of them to be received automatically at conversion. A believer had to apprehend each blessing and specifically ask for it in order for it to be realized. God is a respecter of a believer's volitional capacities, they held. Hence He will not impart a provision of salvation unless the believer knowingly and consciously asks for and receives it.[2]

Simpson and his contemporaries separated the blessings of justification and regeneration from God's blessings for sanctification and empowering for service. It appears from their writings that they think believers have no experience of these latter provisions prior to consciously asking for and receiving them.[3]

Such a view contrasts sharply with Simpson's Presbyterian Reformed background. The Reformed position asserts that all the benefits of salvation belong to a believer at conversion by virtue of his or her relationship to God. The degree to which these benefits are an experiential reality has no bearing on this fact. Consequently, for example, in the Reformed view the process of sanctification will occur from regeneration onwards. Simpson and the majority of his contemporaries, on the other hand, would declare that sanctification begins only after a believer has specifically received from God the resources to make this process possible.

A. B. Simpson, R. A. Torrey and A. J. Gordon are more explicit than some others in their assertion that the reception of the various blessings of salvation need not necessarily imply a lengthy time interval beyond regeneration.[4] The normative conversion pattern presented in the Scriptures, in their opinion, indicates that a believer should appropriate all of the provisions of salvation at the time of coming to Christ. They go on to suggest that the current state of the church is such that very few converts experience this normative pattern. Ignorance and deficient instruction—or disobedience on the part of the believer—are the primary causes of this impoverished state of the church. Consequently, the majority of believers need a second spiritual crisis in which the full provisions of salvation are consciously realized.

They Cited Similar Evidence to Support Their "Distinct Blessings of Salvation" Views

Our analysis of Simpson and his contemporaries indicates that they used similar arguments to support their view that sanctification and empowering for service are specific and distinct from justification and regeneration. The writers we looked at were especially fond of the book of Acts.[5] They contended that Acts demonstrates that

- people may be converted and yet not necessarily be experiencing all the provisions of salvation (for instance, the Ephesus believers mentioned in Acts 19:1-6)
- the coming of the Spirit upon believers is distinct from conversion, as Peter implies when he puts the "gift of the Holy Spirit" after repentance and baptism (Acts 2:38)[6]
- the nature of the reception of God's provisions is such that believers are distinctly conscious of having received them
- the "baptism of the Spirit" is for every generation of believers—"you and your children and for all who are far off" (Acts 2:39)
- complete consecration is necessary prior to receiving, subsequent to conversion, these promised provisions—"God has given [the Holy Spirit] to those who obey him" (Acts 5:32)

Romans 7 and 8 was also a popular text, especially with W. E. Boardman and the Keswick writers. They held these two chapters—Romans 7 denoting the wretched, losing struggle to walk God's way in human strength, and Romans 8, the glorious victory when through Jesus Christ the "Spirit of life" frees them from "the law of sin and death"—show the progression needed for entering the full Christian life.

A. J. Gordon's comment on Galatians 3:2, 14 is illustrative of the common view among the writers we have surveyed regarding the distinct reception of the provisions of salvation. He writes:

> These texts seem to imply that just as there is "faith toward our Lord Jesus Christ" for salvation, there is faith toward the Holy Ghost for power and consecration.[7]

Although Simpson shared similar views on this text and those mentioned above, we saw in chapter 4 that his principal texts were Jeremiah 31 and Ezekiel 36.

The significance of Christ's baptism in the Jordan River is given similar treatment in the writings of Simpson and his contemporaries. They interpreted this event to show that Christ specifically dedicated Himself to the Father. Consequently, the Holy Spirit came upon Jesus, empowering Him for life and ministry. Moreover, like the experiences recorded in Acts, Christ was held to have consciously recognized the transformation which occurred in his life. They also suggested that Christ's experience was paradigmatic for 19th century believers as well. It supported the necessity of consecration to God and a conscious reception of the divine provisions.

Finally, some of the writers examined in chapters 7 and 8, along with Simpson, cited as further evidence the testimonies of believers throughout church history who were filled with and purified and empowered by the Holy Spirit subsequent to their conversion.[8]

They All Agreed on a Similar "Entry Formula" for Realizing These Divine Blessings

Our study has indicated that Simpson and his contemporaries were in general agreement as to the manner in which the "blessings" of salvation were to be appropriated. Though their terminology and their views of the actual sequence varied somewhat, they nonetheless held to a similar entry formula.

The first step consisted of an awareness of need on the part of the believer and, along with the awareness of need, a comprehension of the divine provisions for that need. Next came the seeker's act of total dedication or "consecration" to God and His purposes. This step in essence dealt with the issue of "lordship." It was an affirmation on the seeker's part that he or she had completely yielded control to God. The third step was to request the specific blessing or provision the believer desired and needed. The content of this request would vary, depending on the person's understanding of the baptism of the Holy Spirit. For example, those who were influenced by R. A. Torrey would pray for the Holy Spirit to empower them for service. Those who followed Asa Mahan, on the other hand, were anxious for the promised Holy Spirit to indwell them.

All Agreed There Would Be a Conscious Awareness of Change

Simpson and his contemporaries shared the view that a believer should and would know that he or she had received the promised provision of God. The exact nature of this awareness, however, varied from teacher to teacher. R. A. Torrey and D. L. Moody asserted that the primary witness to this change was a more productive ministry. Others, particularly in the holiness group, tended to focus on the believer's newfound ability to lead a holy life. In addition to these external evidences, people like Asa Mahan, A. T. Pierson and A. B. Simpson suggested that there would also be some subjective witness, such as a new sense of the "indwelling Christ."[9]

All Agreed To Similarities in Their Personal Experiences

It is important to note that besides similarities in their theological positions, Simpson and his contemporaries had similar religious experiences. In chapter 2, we saw that Simpson underwent significant spiritual crises in 1874 and 1881. Each of these crises was marked by a period of intense awareness of need followed by a life-transforming encounter with God. Simpson's contemporaries whom we surveyed in chapter 3 testified to similar experiences. Certainly the motivating factors preceding these encounters with God varied, and so did their interpretations of what transpired as a result. For example, D. L. Moody perceived a lack of effectiveness in his ministry and subsequently experienced new "empowering." F. B. Meyer, on the other hand, was keenly aware of his failure to live a holy life. His new encounter with God gained him new insight into the dynamics of the spiritual life.[10] It is interesting to note, therefore, the correlation between the particular need of the writer and the subsequent emphasis present in his work. Moreover, the intensity of these personal experiences no doubt contributed to the emphasis laid in their writings on a definite, conscious spiritual crisis.[11] Little wonder, then, that their theological formulations shared many of the same features. After all, their spiritual experiences closely paralleled one another's.

What Simpson Shared in Common with *Some* of His Contemporaries

In addition to the Revivalistic-Reformed leaders mentioned in the previous section whose views Simpson generally shared, there were other contemporaries with whom Simpson could find some points of commonality. As we noted in chapter 7, Simpson was never directly associated with the Holiness-Methodist or the "Third-Blessing" groups. It is not surprising, therefore, to discover that his views tended to differ in some respects from theirs.[12] But even within the Revivalistic-Reformed group, where Simpson found his greatest affinity, he had views closer to some than to others. We want here to highlight these similarities, reserving for chapter 10 the areas of difference between Simpson and his contemporaries regarding the baptism of the Holy Spirit.

Simpson Agreed with Some of His Contemporaries on the Meaning of the Term, "The Baptism of the Holy Spirit"

This study has demonstrated that the term "baptism of the Holy

Spirit" had attained widespread usage by the turn of the century. However, its meaning and content were matters of widely varying interpretations. Asa Mahan and W. E. Boardman used the term to denote the specific reception of the Holy Spirit subsequent to regeneration. On this, Simpson wholeheartedly agreed. A. J. Gordon avoided the term, preferring "the enduement with the Spirit." However, his understanding of what took place when a person was endued corresponded with Simpson's understanding of what took place when a person was "baptized" with the Spirit. Moreover, Simpson, Mahan and Gordon would assert that the provisions for sanctification and power for service accompanied the reception of the Spirit.[13]

In contrast to this position, R. A. Torrey used the term "baptism of the Spirit" solely to denote the experience of being "empowered" with the Spirit. D. L. Moody maintained a similar view, although he chose to avoid the term, employing in its place "the Spirit came upon . . ." Keswick teachers preferred to speak of the "initial filling of the Spirit" or the "fullness of the Spirit." For them, this spiritual crisis denoted the moment in which the resources for holy living and empowered service were rendered experiential in a believer's life. They would deny that believers received the gift of the Spirit at this time.

Simpson Agreed with Some of His Contemporaries that the Holy Spirit Does Not Automatically Indwell at Conversion

Simpson, along with Mahan, Boardman and Gordon, did not believe that the Spirit indwells a believer without being specifically asked to do so.[14] Consequently they asserted that people could be Christians and not have the Spirit "in" them. They certainly did not deny that the Spirit was somehow present "with" the believer from conversion onwards. However, only when consciously requested to do so does the Spirit come "into" the believer. They saw special significance in Jesus' words to His disciples that the Spirit "lives with you and will be in you" (John 14:17). Simpson stated that a Christian who had the Spirit "with" him was essentially in the same state as an Old Testament believer. He had not yet moved into the new covenant realities promised in Jeremiah 31 and Ezekiel 36.

As we noted in chapter 4, Simpson used the illustration of a house in which the builder had not yet taken up residence to depict the contrast between the Holy Spirit's work in regeneration and his later indwelling. The newly constructed house is the regenerated believer. At the baptism of the Spirit, the Builder enters to reside.[15]

Simpson Agreed with Some of His Contemporaries that Holiness and Power for Service Must Be Related to the Baptism of the Holy Spirit

Simpson believed that the issues of holiness *and* power for service must be associated with the baptism of the Spirit. The Methodist-Holiness and Keswick teachers, along with Asa Mahan and A. J. Gordon, also believed that these issues were linked to this spiritual crisis. However, they varied on the precise interpretation of these provisions and the stress each should receive. As we noted in chapter 7, the Methodist-Holiness group understood the sanctifying aspect of the baptism along Wesleyan lines. However, their principal emphasis by the end of the 19th century was on the "empowering" provision. Asa Mahan also placed stress upon the empowering aspect of the baptism. The Keswick teachers, on the other hand, understood sanctification from a non-Wesleyan perspective. Furthermore, they tended to place more emphasis on the sanctification aspect than on the "empowering" aspect.

A. J. Gordon's position closely paralleled Simpson's. Simpson preferred to place the focus of his formulations on the Spirit's ministry in realizing the benefits of union with Christ. Holiness and empowering for service were the principal benefits. Hence, to receive the Holy Spirit was to receive all the potentiality that union with Christ could bring.

Simpson and Some of His Contemporaries Understood Sanctification Similarly

In chapter 2 we saw that Simpson's views on sanctification were initially shaped through reading W. E. Boardman's book, *The Higher Christian Life*. Along with Boardman, Simpson's views on this topic were similar to those of Mahan, Finney, Gordon and the Keswick teachers. They all believed that there was a "point" at which the provisions for sanctification were appropriated, ofttimes at a time well after conversion.

Moreover, each of these leaders explored in their writings how Christ provides for the believer's sanctification. In their view, Christ *is* the believer's sanctification; to receive Him is to receive sanctification. Objectively, this appears to imply that the complete resources for sanctification are provided through Christ and that these resources need to be progressively realized and applied. Subjectively, sanctification involves the conscious apprehension of the sufficiency of Christ and the rejection of mere self-effort to achieve godliness. Hence, sanctification is not so much the attainment of some state as it is the *obtainment* of divine resources for progressive transformation. Simpson, however, is much clearer than his contemporaries on the steps involved in the progressive growth dimension of sanctification.

Simpson Agreed with Some of His Contemporaries that the Holy Spirit is the Agent of Christ's Finished Work

As we saw above,[16] Simpson, along with Asa Mahan and A. J. Gordon, was very specific in tracing the connection between the work of the Holy Spirit and that of Christ. They pointed out that the provisions for holiness and empowering were the results of Christ's completed work. The Holy Spirit was the agent of the Trinity who applied these provisions of the ascended Christ. Others of their contemporaries were not always as explicitly clear in pointing out this relationship. W. E. Boardman, for example, devotes most of his book, *The Higher Christian Life,* to exploring the work of Christ. Yet he rarely mentions the ministry of the Spirit. The opposite is true in the writings of D. L. Moody and R. A. Torrey. They explore the work of the Holy Spirit in great detail, but they make little effort to relate it to Christ's completed ministry within the believer.

Simpson Agreed with Some of His Contemporaries about the "Indwelling of Christ" in the Believer

The concept of the "indwelling Christ" is frequently found in Simpson's writing.[17] W. E. Boardman and the Keswick movement, particularly H. C. G. Moule and A. T. Pierson, share this interest as well. In their thinking, the concept of the indwelling Christ seems to encompass two key elements. *First,* these writers stress the Holy Spirit's ministry of making Christ "real" to the believer. This emphasis goes beyond the Holy Spirit's work of merely testifying to the facts of Christ's life as recorded in the Scriptures. Rather it concerns the subjective sense of the actual presence of Christ manifesting Himself to the believer through the Spirit. Simpson took literally the Scriptures which spoke of Christ being "in" the believer.[18] It was his conviction that this conscious awareness of Jesus attended the baptism with the Holy Spirit. *Second,* the concept of the indwelling Christ is at the core of Simpson's view of sanctification.[19] Christ is deemed to be the One who reproduces His very character in the lives of those He indwells. The writings of Boardman[20] and the Keswick teachers[21] evidence a similar view.

What Lies Ahead

In this chapter we have explored the points of agreement between Simpson and his contemporaries who held, as he did, to a crisis encounter with God subsequent to conversion. With some of these fellow leaders, he agreed almost completely. With others, he and they had certain points of commonality.

In chapter 10 we shall find out where Simpson and his contemporaries differed in their views regarding the baptism of the Holy Spirit. Chapter 11 will explore Simpson's relation to the so-called "evidence doctrine" formulated by the incipient Pentecostals early in the 20th century—an era of painful schism for American evangelicals.

In chapter 12 we will address again Simpson's view of the baptism of the Holy Spirit and attempt to assess his formulation from our vantage point nearly a century later. A brief conclusion will complete our survey.

Endnotes

1. As noted in the introduction to chapter 7, the term "contemporaries" refers to those church leaders of Simpson's general era who were closest to him "theologically and experientially."

2. See, for example, A. B. Simpson's discussion on the will in chapter 5 under the heading "The Place of the Will in the Spiritual Life."

3. Moody and Torrey separated "power for service" from a believer's initial conversion. As we noted in chapters 7 and 8, however, they maintained that progressive sanctification did occur from conversion onward.

4. Simpson says: "There is every reason to believe that on the day of Pentecost and in the apostolic church, [conversion and the filling of the Spirit] were contemporaneous or close together in the actual experience of the believers. The difference is in the nature of things rather than in the order of time. The early Christians were expected to pass quickly into the baptism of the Holy Ghost and the fullness of their life in Christ; and when Paul came to Ephesus and found believers, his first question was, 'Have ye received the Holy Ghost since ye believed?' [Acts 19:2]. And when he found they had not, he immediately led them on to this deeper and fuller blessing" [Simpson, "The Crisis of the Deeper Life," *Living Truths* (Sep 1906)]. For R. A. Torrey, see Torrey, *The Person and Work of the Holy Spirit: As Revealed in the Scriptures and in Personal Experience* (London: James Nisbett, 1910) 177. For A. J. Gordon, see Gordon, *The Ministry of the Spirit* (New York: Fleming H. Revell, 1894) 75-76.

5. The Methodist-Holiness and "Third Blessing" writers along with Mahan, Moody, Torrey and Gordon.

6. See, for example, A. J. Gordon's discussion of this verse in chapter 8 at endnotes 40-41.

7. Gordon, *Ministry of Spirit* (see note 4 above) 79. As we noted in chapter 8, Gordon saw a parallel between the logic employed by the Universalists and those who maintained that all automatically received the Spirit in His fullness. Gordon pointed out that the Universalists of his day believed that

on account of the incarnation of Christ all people were redeemed, regardless of their response to Christ. In Gordon's view, this was similar to the line of argument that suggested that all the disciples received the Spirit on the day of Pentecost, and therefore everyone automatically receives the Spirit today. No so, argues Gordon (*Ministry of Spirit* 75-78).

8. Specifically Asa Mahan and Charles Finney.

9. See the section on Asa Mahan in chapter 7. For A. T. Pierson, a Keswick leader, see chapter 8. The section "The Indwelling Christ" in chapter 4 outlines Simpson's views on this subject.

10. Steven Barabas, *So Great Salvation: The History and Message of the Keswick Convention* (London: Marshall, Morgan and Scott, 1952) 182-190. Barabas chronicles the religious experiences of such Keswick people as F. B. Meyer, Handley C. G. Moule, J. Elder Cumming and Andrew Murray. Barabas observed that there were two distinct epochs in each of their experiences: a prior time in which they were undoubtedly sincere and earnest Christians, but sensed a lack in their lives, followed by another epoch of new awareness of God's provisions. This new epoch was entered through a crisis or crises of recognizing God's provisions and then accepting them as part of their lives. James Gilchrist Lawson's book, *Deeper Experiences of Famous Christians* (Anderson, IN: Warner Press, 1911), is indicative of the tremendous interest at the turn of the century in the phenomenon of religious experience, particularly "deeper" spiritual experience. The content of Lawson's book is devoted to exploring the crisis experiences of various figures throughout the history of the Church.

11. This raises the classic question of whether the experience of each of these writers determined their theology. That personal religious experience *does* influence every interpreter of the Scriptures is undeniable. The question is to what extent should a person allow experience to influence his or her interpretation. It appears that most of the writers in this survey sincerely acknowledged the danger. Moreover, Simpson in particular asserted that experience cannot be the basis of any doctrine. Still, he adds: "While no experience in itself is a sufficient foundation for a Christian doctrine, yet backed by such an array of Scripture as we have endeavored to present, we see . . . in these lives . . . eloquent appeals to us today . . . [to] 'present your bodies as a living sacrifice' [Romans 12:1], [to] 'tarry . . . till ye be endued with power from on high' [Luke 24:49]." [See Simpson, "The Baptism of the Holy Spirit: A Crisis or an Evolution?" *Living Truths* (Dec 1905) 715.] See also in chapter 5 the section entitled "Scriptural Support Simpson Found for His View." It seems fair, then, to state that Simpson, while recognizing the danger of basing doctrine on experience, believed that the Scriptures

amply authenticated his experience.

12. Simpson's immediate Alliance colleagues, however, included men with Methodist roots and education. Among them were George P. Pardington, Stephen Merritt and R. Kelso Carter (see the comments introducing "The Revivalistic Reformed View" in chapter 7).

13. In chapter 7 we saw that Asa Mahan tended to put more emphasis on the "empowering" dimension of the baptism. He does, however, refer to the implications of this experience for holy living.

14. This point is implicit earlier in this chapter (see the section "Simpson Agreed with Some of His Contemporaries on the Meaning of the Term, 'The Baptism of the Holy Spirit.' "

15. See chapter 4, under the section "Sanctification Explained." See also Simpson, *The Fourfold Gospel* (New York: Christian Alliance Publishing Co., 1887) 28, and "What Is the Difference between Sanctification and Regeneration?" *The Christian Alliance* (Mar 1888).

16. See "Simpson Agreed with Some of His Contemporaries that Holiness and Power for Service Must Be Related to the Baptism of the Holy Spirit" in this chapter.

17. Note, for example, the statement in the working document presented at the 1906 Conference for Prayer and Counsel Respecting Uniformity in the Testimony and Teaching of the Alliance, Section II.2.c: ". . . the indwelling of Christ in the heart of the consecrated believer *as a distinct experience*."

18. Simpson's main text was Colossians 1:27. See the discussion in chapter 4 under the heading "The Indwelling Christ."

19. Simpson declared that Christ's presence in the believer was the "mystery of the new life" and the "great mystical truth," something "Paul delighted in unfolding to the saints of the apostolic church" [Simpson, *Christ in the Bible*, vol. XIX (Galatians, Ephesians) (New York: Christian Alliance Publishing Co., 1904) 120]. Simpson made these comments while exploring such key texts as Colossians 1:27, Galatians 2:20 and 4:19.

20. See section on W. E. Boardman in chapter 8, especially with reference to the quotation given at endnote 76.

21. A. T. Pierson writes: "The supreme end of the Holy Spirit's indwelling and inworking is to manifest the personal Christ as consciously in our possession and in possession of us. This is the mystery: *Christ in you.* The Spirit first takes the things of Christ and shows them to the believer; second, he testifies to Christ; and, third, he glorifies Christ. Note the three parts of this work as

laid down in John xiv-xvi: Manifesting, witnessing, glorifying. He shows Christ in all His offices and relations; He makes Him real as an actual possession; and He clothes Him in glorious charms, so that we gaze on Him, enamored of His beauty and love. It is very different to have Christ revealed *without,* as a historic personage, and *within* as experientially and really Master and Lord. This latter, the Holy Spirit does, as the former is effected by the Word" [Pierson, *Forward Movements of the Last Half-Century* (New York: Funk and Wagnalls, 1900) 37-38]. This quotation appears in chapter 8 but bears repeating.

Chapter 10

A. B. Simpson Compared with His Contemporaries, Part 2: Differences between Simpson and His Contemporaries

I n chapter 9 we examined the similarities between Simpson and his contemporaries, especially regarding their views on the baptism of the Holy Spirit. That comparison indicated the presence of significant differences as well. Simpson's formulations contained elements and emphases that were quite distinct from others'. We want now to examine those elements in Simpson's writings that set him apart from his contemporaries.

Simpson Saw Water Baptism Related to the Baptism of the Spirit

Simpson's contemporaries devoted little attention in their writing to the significance of water baptism or to any possible relationship between it and the baptism of the Holy Spirit. R. A. Torrey, for example, simply mentions water baptism as one of the prior "steps" necessary to the baptism of the Spirit. Simpson, however, went beyond such a cursory glance to explore the biblical significance attached to water baptism.

Simpson deliberated long on this issue. He grappled with his own paedobaptistic heritage. He questioned as well the view that water baptism signaled little more than a person's willingness to join the visible church. As he worked through this issue of water baptism, Simpson came to the conclusion that God intended it to be closely associated with the concept of union with Christ Jesus and the new covenant promises of Jeremiah 31 and Ezekiel 36. In this respect, water baptism illustrated two things.[1] *First,* baptism was expressive of a believer's voluntary and irrevocable commitment to follow God. By submitting to baptism, the believer in effect announced his or her separation from the world and separation unto God. *Second,* baptism depicted the believer's union with Christ. Through this act a Christian should see himself as dying with Christ to his or her old life and being raised with Christ to his or her new resurrected life. Simpson thus believed that water baptism was intended to underscore for the believer the implications of the new covenant realities associated with his or her union with Christ.

In Simpson's view, the meaning of water baptism needed to be understood in relation to the baptism of the Holy Spirit. Both water baptism and Spirit baptism were aspects of union with Christ. Water baptism illustrated the antecedent responses necessary on the part of believers. The indwelling of the Spirit, through "the Baptism of the Holy Spirit," was the divine means for realizing the promises of the new covenant.

Accordingly, the importance of water baptism lay in its symbolism. Foremost was its depiction of the needed response on the part of the believer prior to his or her being baptized by the Spirit. Water baptism, as noted above, symbolized the decisive acts of separation and dedication which needed to occur at some point in the believer's new life.

Having attached such significance to water baptism, did Simpson insist on it before a believer sought to be baptized with the Holy Spirit? No. Simpson does not seem to imply that a believer must submit to water baptism prior to being baptized with the Spirit. For those who had already been baptized with the Spirit, water baptism served as a reminder of what union with Christ entailed.

In relating water baptism to the baptism with the Holy Spirit, Simpson stood relatively alone among his contemporaries.

Simpson's Pneumatology Was Christocentric

In chapter 1—and subsequently—we have noted that by the turn of the century, the doctrine of the person and work of the Spirit was prominent. As we saw in chapter 7, many of the writers of this time focused almost exclusively on the Holy Spirit. This was so of Asa Mahan, particularly his book, *The Baptism of the Holy Spirit.*[2] D. L. Moody and R. A. Torrey and many of the writers within the Holiness-Methodist and "Third Blessing" groups, likewise tended to focus almost exclusively on the Holy Spirit and His ministry of "empowering" believers.

Simpson avoided this imbalance evident in so many of his contemporaries.[3] His writings reflect a continued effort to link the work of the Spirit with the person of Christ. He believed this link was at the heart of New Testament teaching concerning the work of the Spirit.

This concern on Simpson's part is evident in several ways. *First,* while affirming the need to reexplore the doctrine of the Spirit, Simpson rejected positions which appeared to focus solely on the Spirit. In Simpson's opinion, such presentations violated the Scriptures which indicated that the Holy Spirit's principal ministry was the exaltation of Christ. Simpson asserted that the Spirit's ministry of empowering believers must be linked to Christ's continued work in the world. This work of the Spirit is ultimately for the glorification of Christ and the furtherance of His Church. *Second,* Simpson pointed out that it was the Spirit, as the agent of Christ's presence, who revealed Christ to the believer.[4] That great truth must not be neglected in any consideration of the work of the Spirit. Concerns like those indicate Simpson's resolve to present a pneumatology Christocentric in its focus.

Simpson, More Fully than Others, Explored the Work of the Spirit as the Agent of Union with Christ

Only a few of Simpson's contemporaries attempted to investigate the Spirit's work in assisting believers to realize the benefits of union with Christ. Mahan, in *The Baptism of the Holy Spirit,* declared the Spirit to be the agent of godliness. He did not, however, elaborate on the theme. Rather, Mahan merely cited this ministry to emphasize the believer's need to be baptized with the Spirit.

A. J. Gordon also alluded to this topic in his writing. We saw in chapter 8 that Gordon considered the Spirit's major ministry to be that of helping believers realize the benefits of their union with Christ. In particular, Gordon devoted space to explore how the Spirit reproduces the character of Christ in a believer. Beyond the scant reference in Mahan and these in Gordon, there was relatively little mention among Simpson's contemporaries of this important aspect of the Spirit's ministry.

The work of the Holy Spirit as the Agent of union with Christ is a dominant theme in Simpson's writing.[5] Simpson believed that this concept was at the heart of New Testament teaching; hence, he attached great significance to it in his writing.

In his books and articles Simpson explored the nature of union with Christ. He saw this union as including both judicial and experiential dimensions. Judicially, it provided for the forgiveness of sin; experientially, it made possible the moral transformation of believers. A. B. Simpson anchored these convictions in his understanding of the new covenant realities promised in Jeremiah 31 and Ezekiel 36. Not only would God provide the means for the forgiveness of sin, but He would also impart a new enabling to overcome the power of sin. This enabling was brought about through Christ's earthly life, His atoning death and His subsequent ascension and heavenly ministry of intercession.

Simpson believed that Jesus Christ lived His earthly life relying upon the power of the Spirit to carry out the will of the Father. His earthly life thus became a pattern for believers to emulate. Moreover, as a result of Christ's ascension, the Father God has sent the Holy Spirit to indwell believers. It is the indwelling Spirit who makes it possible for a believer to partake of the transforming grace procured by Christ.

The following quotations reiterate Simpson's assertions on this matter which were cited previously in chapter 4:[6]

> [The Holy Spirit] is the Executive of the divine Trinity, the supreme Guide and Overseer of the Church, and the sovereign Dispenser of all the gifts of the ascended Christ. Every grace which the Saviour has purchased and the Father is ready to bestow in His name must come through the hands of the Holy Ghost. As the Father committed all things to the Son, so the Son has committed all things to the Spirit, and it is through Him that we must receive the blessings which Christ died to purchase and lives to bestow.[7]

> [The Holy Spirit] is the Spirit of Christ. He resided in [Christ's] bosom during the three and a half years of His earthly ministry, and now He comes to us softened, coloured, and humanized by the heart of Jesus. . . . [He] brings to us the Master Himself in all that was really essential to His character and ministry. In a sense therefore the presence of the Spirit is the presence of Christ. As Jesus never did anything without the Holy Spirit, so the Holy Spirit never does anything without Jesus. It is His supreme delight to make Christ real to us and take of the things that are His and show them unto us.[8]

It is impossible for us to analyze, dissect or trace by any biological and psychological process the method of this divine mystery. This is all we can distinctly formulate— somewhere down in the depths of our subconscious being God through the Spirit takes up His abode. His actual personal presence is hidden from our consciousness, just as the hidden spring of that artesian well is far out of sight in the bowels of the earth. All we are conscious of is the manifestation of His presence from time to time in various influences, operations, emotions, and effects in our spirit and life. The Holy Spirit is just as truly in us when He makes no sign as when the fountains of joy are overflowing, or the waters of peace are softly refreshing our weary and troubled hearts.[9]

By living in dependence upon the Holy Spirit, the believer is enabled to begin to experience the promises of the new covenant.

Having outlined the significance of union with Christ, Simpson also explored the manner in which the Spirit transferred the provisions available by means of that union. Foremost, the Spirit transforms the believer into the image of Christ. He does this by transferring the qualities and graces of Christ's nature so that they become a part of the believer's character.[10] He also enables a believer to experience freedom from sin's power as the believer partakes of the freedom made possible through Christ's death. Furthermore, the Spirit sustains the believer by imparting to him or her the spiritual life of Christ.[11]

Simpson Believed that New Covenant Promises Are Rooted in Jeremiah 31 and Ezekiel 36

Jeremiah 31 and Ezekiel 36 were central texts in Simpson's writings. In chapter 4 we saw how Simpson's understanding of these texts shaped his view of such topics as "union with Christ," the work of the Holy Spirit, and the "steps" involved in the baptism of the Holy Spirit. The concept of the promised "new covenant" was also pervasive in his writing. In contrast, as we saw in chapter 3, the majority of Simpson's contemporaries were using the book of Acts, especially Acts 2:1-42, as their central text. This was particularly evident in the writings of the Methodist-Holiness and "Third Blessing" groups. We noted the same emphasis on the book of Acts among many in the Revivalistic-Reformed group, especially Asa Mahan and R. A. Torrey.[12]

It appears that one reason Simpson gave less prominence to Acts 2 was that he saw Pentecost as related to these new covenant promises in Ezekiel and Jeremiah. Pentecost was simply the historic event in which these new covenant promises were first realized.

Simpson Exercised Balance and Perspective Concerning the Benefits of the Baptism of the Holy Spirit

Simpson's formulation of the baptism of the Spirit was such that he attempted to present a balance between the issues of holiness and power. As we noted in chapter 1, Simpson lived in an era which was preoccupied with one or the other of these issues. From Simpson's perspective, however, the Scriptures affirmed the importance of both, not exalting one above the other. As a result, Simpson endeavored to maintain this balance in his writing. Moreover, he sought to show that there was a link between conformity to Christ and service for Christ.[13]

Simpson's manner of presenting the baptism of the Spirit also indicates that he wished to divert emphasis from the "blessings" to the "Blesser."[14] He was always careful to show that *God* was the source of "holy living" and "empowering." *Jesus Christ* had provided these benefits through the atonement; *God the Spirit* made them effective in the believer's life.

Because of this emphasis on the Godhead, Simpson is very non-utilitarian in the tone of his writings. Believers do not "use" God. They submit themselves to God and through the Spirit are enabled to undertake the tasks He leads them to do. Simpson is careful to point out that in all our activity as Spirit-filled believers, it is Christ who is continuing His work through the Spirit. By contrast, some proponents of the Spirit-filled life—R. A. Torrey in particular—focus much attention on seeking "the blessing," to the point of implying that the believer employs the Holy Spirit to enhance his or her own ministry.[15]

Furthermore, Simpson's formulations are very relational in nature. The blessings of union with Christ are contingent on the believer's continued relationship with the "Blesser." Consequently, Simpson is always careful to point out that unconfessed sin breaks the flow of God's blessing.

Simpson Explored More Deeply the Significance of Christ's Earthly Life

We have noted that the significance of Jesus' baptism in the Jordan River was a popular theme for exploration in Simpson's day.[16] However, we noted in chapter 3 that Simpson went far beyond this single event and attempted to understand the significance of Christ's entire earthly life.[17] He saw Christ as the perfect example of obedience to the Father. Simpson also explored the work of the Holy Spirit in Christ's life and ministry. He viewed Jesus as One who lived in full dependence on the Holy Spirit. Hence, Christ was and is the perfect Man in relationship with God through the enabling work of the Spirit. Moreover, Simpson also discussed how Christ, this perfect Man, ascended to heaven and is now manifested to us as the prototype into whose image the Holy Spirit wants to transform us.[18]

Simpson's Theology Was Always Trinitarian

There is a clear trinitarian theology present in Simpson's formulations. He studied carefully the life of Christ and grappled with how the three Persons of the Trinity relate to one another during Christ's earthly ministry. His resulting formulation portrays Christ as seeking and carrying out the will of the Father through the guidance and enabling of the Holy Spirit.[19] Our chapter 4 further indicated that Simpson attempted to search the role of the Trinity in the application of redemption.[20] Christ's atonement has secured forgiveness for sin as well as provision for breaking the power of sin. It is the Holy Spirit who reveals Christ. The Holy Spirit is the agent of transformation, conforming the believer into the image of Christ. This process in turn enables the believer to follow the example of Christ in being rightly related to the Father, loving Him and carrying out His will in the world.

Simpson Outlined a Relationship between the Baptism of the Spirit and Growth in God's Grace

Several of the writers we looked at in chapter 3 tended to focus unduly on the experience of Spirit baptism itself, giving little attention to what follows it.[21] Certainly Simpson's contemporaries acknowledged that growth occurs after the filling of the Spirit. In Simpson's teaching, however, he was always careful to show how the reception of the Spirit was related to growth in grace. For example, the 1906 document[22] that we have frequently referred to included a statement calling for

> . . . growth in grace and the deeper filling of the Holy Spirit as distinct from and the result of the definite experience of sanctification.

For all His attention to the initial baptism of the Spirit, Simpson maintained that this crisis merely completes a believer's entry into the Christian life. Once the believer has the presence of the Holy Spirit in all His fullness, he or she is called to progressive spiritual growth.

In chapter 6 we noted how Simpson presented the various aspects of growth in grace. He outlined the divine side of this process: the Spirit's task of revealing sin and the old sinful nature;[23] the putting to death of sin by the Spirit;[24] the Spirit's role of imparting God's grace for transformation; the Spirit's ministry of illuminating the Scriptures; the reality of God's "speaking" to the individual through the inner voice of the Spirit.[25]

Simpson also outlined the responsibilities of believers in the growth process: a continual attitude of separation from the world and dedication to God;[26] continued dependence on God's resources; the cultivation of the spiritual disciplines of prayer and meditation; learning to "walk in the Spirit."[27] Simpson also explored the ongoing process of remaining filled with the Spirit[28] as well as some of the problems which may occur in the believer's growth process.[29]

Topics like these indicate Simpson's desire to integrate the crisis experience of the Spirit's baptism with the progressive elements of the Christian's life and work.

Before we end this comparison of Simpson with his contemporaries, we need to address one possible caveat. Since our research of Simpson's writings has been more extensive than those of his contemporaries, are we justified in making the eight points stated in this chapter? Had we looked in greater depth at these contemporaries of Simpson, might we not have found similar emphases in their teaching and writing?

This objection is well taken. It is certainly true that we have attempted to examine only the major works on the "baptism of the Spirit" by these other writers contemporary with Simpson. But these writings were their major works. It is logical to presume that these writers would have included the emphases noted in this chapter had they deemed them important. Moreover, in many cases the books we examined were the *only* ones on this topic by the respective writers.[30] Accordingly, we must presume that these works are fairly representative of their views and present an adequate basis for our comparison. Furthermore, the differences noted in this chapter are evident even if only Simpson's *principal* books on this topic were used as a basis of comparison with his contemporaries (for example, *Wholly Sanctified, Walking in the Spirit* and *The Holy Spirit*, volumes 1 and 2). Surely this indicates Simpson's effort to present a well-rounded consideration on this subject—an effort that his ministry contemporaries did not attempt.

Conclusion

In this chapter and the preceding one we have examined both the points of similarity and the points of difference in the views of Simpson and his contemporaries regarding the baptism with the Holy Spirit. Simpson's understanding of the baptism and theirs coincided at many points. On the other hand, the eight distinctive aspects of the baptism present in Simpson's writings and noted in this chapter set him apart from all the others.

We began this study by proposing the thesis that Simpson's views on the baptism of the Holy Spirit were "distinct, although not unique." Our comparisons in this chapter and the preceding one, following our thorough examination of Simpson's writings and those of his contemporaries, substantiate that beginning proposition.

Endnotes

1. See chapter 5, "Water Baptism and the Baptism of the Holy Spirit," for Simpson's exploration of this topic.

2. Asa Mahan, *The Baptism of the Holy Ghost* (New York: Palmer and Hughes, 1870)

3. A. J. Gordon was the only exception to this. His writings also reflect a concern to preserve a Christocentric pneumatology.

4. See particularly chapter 4, "The Holy Spirit: Agent of Union with Christ."

5. See chapter 4, "The Holy Spirit: Agent of Union with Christ." It deals explicitly with this topic.

6. All of these quotations were cited in chapter 4, "The Holy Spirit: Agent of Union with Christ."

7. A. J. Gordon, *The Ministry of the Spirit* (New York: Fleming H. Revell, 1894) 438-439

8. Gordon, *Ministry of Spirit* (see note 7 above) 439. Simpson makes a similar statement when he writes: "The Holy Spirit is the Spirit that once dwelt in Christ, and He brings to us a spiritual Christ with a new touch and a higher form of manifestation than when He walked the earth of old and touched the bodies of men with His living hands" [A. B. Simpson, *Christ in the Bible,* vol. XIX (Galatians, Ephesians) (New York: Christian Alliance Publishing Co., 1904) 124].

9. Simpson, *When the Comforter Came* (New York: Christian Alliance Publishing Co., 1911), Day 7 (there are no page numbers in this book; each reading is intended for a day of the month). Simpson uses other figures as well to express "this extraordinary relationship" [see *Christ in Bible,* vol. XIX (Galatians, Ephesians) (see note 8 above) 121].

10. See chapter 4, "Sanctification and the Work of Christ" in context of the

discussion on Simpson's book *The Cross of Christ* (New York: Christian Alliance Publishing Co., 1910).

11. See chapter 4, endnote 62 and chapter 5, endnote 14. Simpson states: "We are sanctified by the indwelling life and power of the Holy Spirit in us filling our spirit, soul, and body with the life of Jesus Christ."

12. In chapter 7 we saw that Asa Mahan referred to Ezekiel 36 and Jeremiah 31 in reference to the promise of the Holy Spirit. However, his writing contains no detailed exploration of these two Old Testament Scriptures.

13. See A. B. Simpson's discussion on this relationship in chapter 6, "Personal Holiness and Spiritual Victory" and "Power for Service."

14. Simpson wrote a song, *Himself*, in which he relates his own spiritual journey pertaining to this Christocentric realization. This is the first stanza:

> Once it was the blessing,
>   Now it is the Lord;
> Once it was the feeling,
>   Now it is His Word;
> Once His gift I wanted,
>   Now the Giver own;
> Once I sought for healing,
>   Now Himself alone.

15. See chapter 8, "Reuben Archer Torrey (1856-1928)" and following two subheads.

16. See chapter 9, "Similar Evidence Supporting the Salvation Experience."

17. See chapter 3, "Christ Is Our Model."

18. See chapter 4, "Sanctification and the Work of Christ."

19. See chapter 3, "Christ Is Our Model" and "The Holy Spirit's Relationship to Christ."

20. See chapter 4, "The Indwelling Christ" and "The Holy Spirit: Agent of Union with Christ."

21. This is particularly evident in material of the Methodist-Holiness and "Third Blessing" writers. W. E. Boardman, Asa Mahan and Charles Finney also did not elaborate on this relationship. R. A. Torrey and D. L. Moody did not connect sanctification with the baptism of the Spirit; hence, they do not discuss this topic.

22. See Appendix 5. The reference here is to II.2.e.

23. See chapter 4, "Sanctification Explained."

24. See chapter 4, endnotes 87 and 88 and chapter 6, endnotes 10 and 11.

25. See chapter 6, "Walking in the Spirit."

26. See chapter 4, "Sanctification Explained."

27. See chapter 6, "Walking in the Spirit."

28. See chapter 6, "The Filling of the Spirit."

29. See chapter 6, "Subsequent 'Crisis' Experiences."

30. The majority of the writers surveyed in this study wrote only one or two books on the ministry of the Holy Spirit. This was the case with W. E. Boardman, A. J. Gordon, Asa Mahan and D. L. Moody. The Keswick teachers F. B. Meyer and A. T. Pierson likewise only wrote two books each on the ministry of the Holy Spirit.

Chapter 11

A. B. Simpson
and the "Evidence Doctrine"
of the Baptism of the Holy Spirit

No study of A. B. Simpson's views concerning the baptism of the Holy Spirit would be complete without an awareness of how he responded to the Pentecostal movement. In the previous chapters our concern was to compare Simpson and his views on the baptism of the Holy Spirit with his contemporaries who were doctrinally and experientially closest to him. In this chapter we want to see how Simpson related to those of a somewhat different theological perspective—those who insisted that speaking in tongues was a necessary evidence of the baptism of the Holy Spirit. To begin, we will examine the history and teaching of the Pentecostal movement. Then we want to briefly look at the response by some evangelicals to Pentecostalism. Finally, we shall see how Simpson responded, particularly to the issue of the so-called "evidence doctrine."

The Rise of Pentecostalism in America

Most scholars trace the beginning of the modern Pentecostal movement to an event which occurred at Bethel Bible College, Topeka, Kansas, on January 1, 1901. From their study of the book of Acts, a group of students there came to the conclusion that speaking in "tongues" was the initial outward evidence that a person had been baptized with the Holy Spirit. In prayer meetings at the school, numerous ones gave evidence to having received the "baptism." Charles Parham, the school's principal, took this new persuasion with him on his "revival meetings" throughout Missouri and Texas. And so this distinctive view of the baptism of the Spirit began to spread.

One of those who had been involved as a Bethel student was W. J. Seymour. He began to preach in various holiness churches in the South. In 1906, Seymour made a trip to Los Angeles, where he preached on the baptism of the Holy Spirit at a former Methodist church on Azusa Street. There the famous Azusa Street Mission revival began. Large numbers of people, including Methodists and Nazarenes, found themselves speaking in tongues. So remarkable was the phenomenon that soon the Azusa Street Mission was known throughout the United States and Europe. Many traveled to Los Angeles to observe what was happening there.[1]

From those beginnings numerous "Pentecostal" churches sprang up.

Until about 1908, the majority of Pentecostals came out of Holiness backgrounds, where sanctification was taught as a second definite work of God's grace. Now, in the experience of these Pentecostals, sanctification had been followed by a *third* work of God's grace—the baptism of the Holy Spirit—evidenced by the speaking in tongues.[2] But there were also many Pentecostals from Reformed or Baptist backgrounds, and they questioned such a "three-stage" view.

Three Stages or Two?

In 1908, William Durham, a Chicago holiness preacher who had received the "baptism" at the Azusa Street Mission, began to preach what he called the "finished work of Calvary." He reduced the Pentecostals' three stages to two. Under Baptist influence, he regarded conversion and sanctification as simultaneous. He says:

> I began to write against the doctrine that it takes two works of grace to save and cleanse a man. I denied and still

deny that God does not deal with the nature of sin at conversion. I deny that a man who is converted or born again is outwardly washed and cleansed but that his heart is left unclean with enmity against God in it. . . . This would not be salvation. Salvation is an inward work. It means a change of heart. It means a change of nature. It means that old things pass away and all things become new. It means that all condemnation and guilt is [sic] removed. It means that all the old man, or the old nature, which was sinful and depraved and which was the very thing in us that was condemned, is crucified with Christ.[3]

This question of a two- or three-stage pattern became very divisive within the Pentecostal movement. Denominations formed along the lines of this issue. The following table attempts to outline this difference of opinion:[4]

Parham/Seymour Three-Stage Pentecostals	*Conversion*, also called *regeneration*	*Sanctification*, distinct in time and content from conversion, also called "second blessing." The rationale behind this understanding of sanctification: the Holy Spirit can only enter purified hearts.	*Baptism of the Spirit* evidenced by speaking in tongues.
Durham Two-stage Pentecostals	*Conversion*, also called *regeneration*	*Baptism of the Spirit*, with speaking in tongues. Here sanctification is understood as a process continuing throughout life—known as the *Baptist understanding of sanctification*.	

While differing over the term *sanctification* and the number of stages of Christian initiation, all Pentecostals affirmed that the baptism of the Holy Spirit was evidenced by the gift of tongues. If one did not have tongues, he or she had not been baptized by the Spirit.

Pentecostalism spread rapidly throughout the United States from 1907 onwards. It influenced not only Holiness-Methodist denominations but Baptist and Reformed churches as well. Many, after receiving the gift of tongues, left these established churches, either voluntarily or were forced out over the issue of their new "baptism."

The reactions of these established churches to the exodus was negative. Church leaders voiced varying degrees of condemnation of the excesses and divisiveness of this new movement. Some went so far as to suggest that the church was being led astray by demons.[5] Cessationists (such as, for example, those of the Reformed tradition), who believed the spiritual gifts ceased with the apostolic era, continued to deny the legitimacy of any contemporary gift of tongues. Other groups, that until then had acknowledged the present-day validity of all the gifts, began to back off from their stance as the Pentecostal movement spread.

In this situation Simpson found himself embroiled. From 1907 onwards, he was forced to address the rising tongues movement. Like other evangelical denominations, The Christian and Missionary Alliance saw many departures from its ranks. Whole church congregations were swallowed up by the Pentecostals. It is fascinating to observe how Simpson reacted to the rising tide of the Pentecostal movement and the issue of the gift of tongues.

It is to Simpson's response that we now turn.

Simpson Acknowledged that Many Who Claimed to Have Received the Gift of Tongues Indeed Had

Large numbers of people within the C&MA were positively touched by God during the Pentecostal surge. Not only were they spiritually energized, but they also spoke in tongues. Simpson noted in his writing that these people had received an authentic gift of tongues. Addressing the church's General Council of 1907 in Nyack, New York, he declared:

> The sober and well considered reports of many of our workers left no doubt that God is now visiting His people in many places, with a special manifestation of power quite unusual even in the most profound revivals of our time, and that while there has been much fanaticism, there are undoubtedly well authenticated instances of the "gift of tongues" in connection with our work and meetings.[6]

Later that same year, Simpson writes:

> The work in Toronto [Canada] has passed through the new movement in connection with the gift of tongues without serious strain. There have been a few testimonies of God's special blessings in this direction, which have been frankly accepted as genuine, modest, and entirely scriptural, but the balance of truth has been carefully guarded.[7]

Robert A. Jaffray, the renowned C&MA missionary to China, Southeast Asia and Indonesia, received the gift of tongues. Simpson published a paper which Jaffray wrote concerning his experience and what God had taught him as a result.[8]

The Annual Report of The Christian and Missionary Alliance for 1907-1908 also mentions that many Alliance constituents had received authentic gifts of tongues from God:

> We believe there can be no doubt that in many cases remarkable outpourings of the Holy Spirit have been accompanied with genuine instances of the gift of tongues and many extraordinary manifestations. This has occurred both in our own land and in some of our foreign missions. Many of these experiences appear not only to be genuine but accompanied by a spirit of deep humility, earnestness, and soberness, and free from extravagance and error. And it is

admitted that in many of the branches and states where this movement has been strongly developed and wisely directed, there has been a marked deepening of the spiritual life of our members and an encouraging increase in their missionary zeal and liberality. It would, therefore, be a serious matter for any candid Christian to pass a wholesale criticism or condemnation upon such movements or presume to "limit the Holy One of Israel" [Psalm 78:41].[9]

No Wholesale Condemnation

The document goes on to outline several grave concerns Simpson saw in the "movement of tongues." We shall examine these shortly. It is interesting to note, however, that unlike many other evangelical leaders, Simpson stated that he could not "pass a wholesale criticism or condemnation upon" the Pentecostal movement.

Some who had identified with the Pentecostals accused Simpson and the C&MA of opposing the gift of tongues. Simpson pointedly responded to this assertion in a 1910 editorial in *The Christian and Missionary Alliance*:

The statement is made by unfriendly parties sometimes that the Alliance and its leaders are opposed to the manifestations of the gift of tongues in this age. This is wholly false. Our attitude has been often stated and is consistent and explicit. We fully recognize all the gifts of the Spirit, including "divers kinds of tongues" [1 Corinthians 12:10] as belonging to the Church in every age. And many of our most wise and honored workers both in the homeland and in the mission field have had this experience. But we are opposed to the teaching that this special gift is for all or is the evidence of the Baptism of the Holy Spirit. Nor can we receive or use to edification in our work and assemblies those who press these extreme and unscriptural views. We give and we claim charity and liberty, that those who have not this experience shall recognize in the Lord those who have it and use it to edification. And that those who have it, shall equally recognize those who have not this special form of divine anointing, but have the Holy Ghost in such other gifts as He is pleased to bestow upon one and another "severally as He will" [12:11]. On this Scriptural ground of truth, liberty and love, surely we can all meet and no other is practicable without error, division or fanaticism.[10]

Clearly Simpson did not deny the legitimacy of tongues as a gift bestowed by the Holy Spirit, but he opposed any teaching that made it the necessary evidence of the baptism of the Spirit. Moreover, many who authentically received the gift of tongues remained within the C&MA, preferring not to depart to the Pentecostal groups.

Simpson's Writing Reveals an Enlightened View of the Gift of Tongues

Simpson's view of the gift of tongues is rich and demonstrates his biblical understanding of tongues and their use. Simpson was by no means a cessationist; he believed all the spiritual gifts continued past the apostolic era. Referring to the gift of tongues addressed in First Corinthians 12:10, Simpson observes:

[Tongues] appears to have been a divine ecstasy, which lifted the soul above the ordinary modes and expressions of reason and utterance. As a profound German scholar expresses it, "Man contains three elements in his higher constitution; namely, the *pneuma*, the *nous* and the *logos*." That is, the spirit, the mind and the language. The spirit is the highest element and in the gift of tongues appeared to overlap the mind altogether and find its expression in speech, quite unintelligible to the person himself and yet truly expressing the higher thought and feeling of the exalted spiritual state of the subject. It may be a human tongue, or it may be a heavenly tongue. For the apostle distinctly speaks of both the tongues of men and angels. It was not always employed in the apostolic church as the vehicle of preaching to people of other languages, but was a channel of direct worship and adoration. "He that prophesieth speaketh unto men, but he that speaketh in an unknown tongue speaketh not unto men but unto God" [1 Corinthians 14:2-3].[11]

It is evident from this quotation that "tongues" in Simpson's view could either be human languages previously unknown to the speaker or a special heavenly language with which to adore and praise God.

To repeat, Simpson certainly was not opposed to the spiritual gift of tongues. But he strongly denied some of the teachings and practices which emerged from the Pentecostal movement. He states:

We are raising no question about the reality of the gift of tongues as one of the manifestations of the Holy Spirit in the Christian age. Our warning is against the danger of exaggerating it, of seeking it for its own sake rather than seeking the Spirit Himself, and of exercising it in an extravagant and unscriptural way to the dishonor of Christ, the disorder of His work and the division of His people. We appeal for the spirit of sanity as well as the spirit of power.[12]

Within that quotation lie the four fundamental issues that Simpson viewed as unscriptural in the Pentecostal movement:

- He denied that the gift of tongues was the necessary evidence of the baptism of the Holy Spirit.
- He disapproved of the gift-seeking inclination that marked those in the Pentecostal movement.
- He deemed the exercise of the gift of tongues in many Pentecostal meetings to be unscriptural.
- He deplored the divisive, elitist tendencies of many within

the Pentecostal movement.

We want now to look in greater depth at each of these points.

Simpson Denied that the Gift of Tongues Was the Necessary Evidence of the Baptism of the Holy Spirit

Simpson categorically rejected any teaching or inference that tongues were for all Spirit-filled believers or that they constituted the initial evidence of the baptism of the Holy Spirit. In the Annual Report of 1907-1908 Simpson declares:

> One of the greatest errors [of Pentecostals] is a disposition to make special manifestations an evidence of the baptism of the Holy Spirit, giving to them the name of Pentecost as though none had received the spirit of Pentecost but those who had the power to speak in tongues, thus leading many sincere Christians to cast away their confidence, and plunging them in perplexity and darkness, or causing them to seek after special manifestations of other than God Himself.[13]
>
> To say that the gift of tongues is the only proper evidence of having been baptized with the Holy Ghost is rash and wholly unscriptural, and places a mere manifestation of the Holy Ghost above His higher ministry of grace.[14]

In the former quotation, Simpson was reacting to the adverse effect Pentecostal teaching had upon many Alliance people and Alliance congregations. Such "evidence" teaching had resulted in much concern and confusion for many.

To those who had been thrown into confusion by Pentecostal teaching, Simpson wrote reassuringly that the baptism of the Holy Spirit had nothing to do with any bestowal of a particular gift:

> First of all let us carefully remember that the gifts of the Spirit are quite distinct from the grace of the Spirit, and that our possession of these gifts does not affect our personal

salvation and sanctification and our standing with God as subjects of His grace. [The gifts are] quite apart from the Holy Spirit's ministry in leading us to Christ for salvation and in bringing us into union with Him through consecration and the baptism of the Holy Spirit. The most pernicious error abroad today in connection with these gifts is to make them a necessary test of our having received the Holy Ghost, and come into the fulness of Christ.[15]

No one gift marked the person who had received the baptism of the Holy Spirit. Simpson asserted, rather, that the baptism of the Spirit was given

> . . . to every disciple who fully surrenders himself to God and may be received immediately by simple faith just as fully and completely as we receive Jesus Christ for forgiveness and justification in conversion.[16]

The baptism of the Spirit, therefore, was to be received immediately through an act of faith. The evidence of the Spirit's presence would be an increase in holiness and a new-found power for serving God—results we have already noted in chapter six.

Regarding gifts, Simpson taught that every disciple of Christ ought to have some gift for service.[17] Gifts are conferred by the sovereign will of the Spirit and are bestowed for the profit of the church. Simpson argued that it was ludicrous to suppose that all in the church would have the same gift of tongues; it ran completely counter to the body imagery used by Paul in First Corinthians 12. Moreover, it violated the transparent statements of Scripture (for example, First Corinthians 12:29-30) that not all have the same gift.[18]

Simpson Disapproved of the Excessive Gift-Seeking that Marked the Pentecostal Movement

Some within the Pentecostal movement advocated that a believer strive with God or "tarry" until He bestowed the gift of tongues.

They urged people to "abandon" themselves to the ministrations of the Spirit. Such "tarrying meetings" were often marked by wild excesses and emotionalism.

Simpson was not opposed to seeking God in a very concerted way. Moreover, an individual believer could certainly ask God for more effectiveness in ministry or for God to gift him or her for God's own glory. Indeed, in chapter 6 we saw that Simpson believed Christians might have many crises in their lives when God poured out His Spirit in powerful ways. However, the strivings after God that Simpson spoke of were not for a gift but for God Himself and a desire to see His mighty power released. A person should seek the Giver of the gifts, not the gifts themselves.

Simpson expressed concern that those who sought tongues by "abandoning" themselves to outside forces could possibly open themselves up to demonic counterfeits:

> There is always danger to earnest souls who are seeking at any cost the best gifts of the Holy Spirit that they may be as open to the influence of wicked spirits as to the Holy Ghost. Satan is the great mimic, and loves to imitate God and counterfeit the highest and holiest spiritual manifestations, and his choicest victims are honest, earnest, unsuspecting souls. Let us, therefore, not think that we are doubting God or questioning His leading if we "try the spirits" [1 John 4:1] and "prove all things" [1 Thessalonians 5:21]. There is a kind of "abandonment" urged by certain spiritual leaders that would throw our whole being open to any powerful influence and hypnotic control which the enemy might wish to exercise. It is a law in the spiritual world as well as in the natural that whenever there is a vacuum there is always some powerful current ready to sweep in and possess it. If, therefore, we leave our mind and will vacant and abandoned without any hand upon the helm, it is almost certain that the adversary will take advantage. There are good men and women that have literally been hypnotized by Satan or some of his agents, and with

the best intentions in the world have become deceived and deceivers.[19]

Simpson argued that true touches of the Holy Spirit could be authenticated by several tests, an issue which we will examine soon. Simpson also criticized the decorum of the "tarrying" meetings:

> There have been many instances where the [search for the] gift of tongues led the subjects and the audiences into the wildest excesses and were accompanied with voices and actions more closely resembling wild animals than rational beings, impressing the unprejudiced observers that it was the work of the devil.[20]

Simpson also reminded people that tongues, though a valid gift, was not given a high rank in the roster of gifts for the ministry of the church.[21] Legitimate seeking was to be limited to the "greater gifts" [1 Corinthians 12:31]—those which built up the whole church.

Simpson Deemed the Exercise of the Gift of Tongues in Many Pentecostal Meetings to Be Unscriptural

God has given absolute principles for discerning the authenticity of the gift of tongues, Simpson said. The proper use of this gift is also carefully regulated in the Scriptures. Simpson argued that these biblical principles must be strictly adhered to.

If a person believed he or she had received the gift of tongues, Simpson asserted that the person should not be reticent about testing to ascertain whether the gift was actually from God. As we noted above, Simpson believed not every spiritual experience was from the Holy Spirit. Concerning this discernment, he writes:

> God has nowhere told us that we are to surrender our personal responsibility and self-control even to the Holy Spirit. When [the Spirit] comes into a human heart He does

no violence to the nature which He Himself has given. It [sic] works in beautiful harmony with all our faculties; possessing, suggesting, inspiring, enabling, and elevating all our being, and yet not dethroning the reason or the will. One of the most important chapters of the New Testament, and one of special value at this time, is the fourteenth chapter of First Corinthians, and one of the most significant statements in that chapter is the thirty-second and thirty-third verses: "the spirits of the prophets are subject to the prophets, for God is not the author of confusion, but of peace, as in all the churches of the saints."[22]

Simpson insisted that the one who had authentically received the gift of tongues could exercise control as to when the gift was used—"not dethroning our will." At the same time, this quotation showed that the resulting "fruit" in a believer's life proved whether the gift was from God. The fruits of "peace and edification," along with the sense of God's "possessing, suggesting, inspiring, enabling and elevating all our being" authenticated a true bestowal from God.

Other Valid Tests

Simpson declared that the other tests of God's true working were "decency, order, self-control, soberness, edification and, above all, love." "Censoriousness, self-consciousness, and self-importance" indicated carnality, while "the supreme test of the Holy Spirit's operations is Christ-like holiness and love."[23]

Simpson asserted that love is placed within chapters 12-14 of First Corinthians to indicate that it is preeminently above the gifts and is to govern their use. Simpson repeatedly emphasized that love must be the motivation for the exercise of the gifts.

Concerning decorum, propriety and order in the use of the gifts, Simpson comments this way on Paul's instructions in First Corinthians 12 and 14:

"Let all things be done decently and in order" [Paul] admonishes [14:40]. "If any man speak in an unknown tongue, let it be by two or at the most by three, and that by course, and then let one translate, but if there be no translator, let him keep silence in the church and let him speak to himself unto God" [14:27-28]. "If anything be revealed to another that sitteth by, let the first speaker hold his peace, for ye may all prophesy one by one, that all may learn and all may be comforted. For God is not the author of confusion but of peace as in all the churches of the saints" [14:30-31, 33]. [Here Paul] unfolds a principle of the profoundest importance, "The spirits of prophets are subject to the prophets" [14:32]. The Holy Spirit does not carry us away in wild, irrational extravagance, but holds His communications subject to our sanctified judgement, and the order and edification of the whole assembly. It is the spirit of evil that rushes us and drives us to the excesses that bring dishonor and contempt upon the work and worship of God. How much cause we have to thank God for these wise and holy cautions and counsels! Let us be willing to heed and follow them.[24]

Simpson asserted, moreover, that interpretation was always necessary in the public use of tongues:

In a like manner the gift of tongues is followed by another gift, a sort of companion ministry called interpretation or translation. Because it is most important, as the apostle in the fourteenth chapter of [First Corinthians] states, the gift of tongues should not become a mere show or spectacle, but be for profit and edification; therefore [Paul] says, "Let him pray that he may translate, or else let him keep silent and speak to himself and to God" [14:28].

It must be seen that the supreme aim of the Lord in all the gifts of the Spirit is not so much to display His power only or attract attention to the instrument of the gift, as to really help, comfort and edify His people.[25]

In this way Simpson insisted that the spiritual gifts were to edify and were not for extravagant show. Ultimately the exercise of the gifts was for the growth of those in the church and the glorification of God.

Simpson Deplored the Divisive, Elitist Tendencies of Many within the Pentecostal Movement

In his 1907 annual report to the C&MA, Simpson noted that many caught up in the "tongues" movement became schismatic and withdrew from the Alliance:

> Another evil is the spirit of separation and controversy and the turning away of many of our people from the work to which God called them, to follow some novel teaching or some new leader, perhaps little known or tried. In several cases our Alliance work has been almost broken up by these diversions and distractions, and many have forgotten their pledges for the work of evangelization and become involved in separation and often bitterness and strife.[26]

Simpson denied that such an action by Christians could be the work of God. God was committed to unity:

> Surely the Spirit of Pentecost is the Spirit of peace and love and holy unity, and when we fully receive His baptism we shall be like them of old, of one accord and one soul.[27]

Conclusion

The issue of the evidence doctrine became a divisive one in the Alliance. As we have seen through Simpson's own allusions above, many left to join the Pentecostal movement. In spite of this, Simpson continued to emphasize that Christians should be open to all manifestations of the Spirit, at the same time using vigilance to be sure the exercise of spiritual gifts was according to the principles given by God Himself.

Simpson himself provides our conclusion:

> In conclusion let us not fear or ignore any of the gifts and manifestations of the Holy Ghost, no matter how extraordinary; but be prepared to expect God to reveal Himself to His people, especially in these last days, in many signal and glorious ways.
>
> At the same time let us not fear to exercise the spirit of discernment and to take ample time and measures to be sure that any alleged work bears the signs of God's approval and control. Let us especially watch lest even good movements become mixed with evil through the lack of discernment or carefulness. Let us not be afraid to exercise proper supervision and control in the Spirit over religious assemblies.[28]

Endnotes

1. Frank Bartleman, *How Pentecost Came to Los Angeles: As it Was in the Beginning* (Los Angeles: Privately printed, 1928) 58

2. Walter Hollenweger, *The Pentecostals* (London: SCM Press, 1972) 24

3. W. H. Durham, *Pentecostal Testimony* (Jun 1911)

4. This table was adapted from one found in Hollenweger (see note 2 above) 25

5. Hollenweger (see note 2 above) 25

6. A. B. Simpson editorial, *The Christian and Missionary Alliance Weekly* (8 Jun 1907)

7. Simpson editorial, *The Christian and Missionary Alliance Weekly* (6 Jul 1907)

8. Robert A. Jaffray, " 'Speaking in Tongues' —Some Words of Kindly Counsel," *The Alliance Weekly* (13 Mar 1909). This is an excellent article in which Jaffray outlines the great benefits the gift of tongues brought to him. At the same time, Jaffray strongly emphasizes that tongues were not the evidence of the baptism of the Holy Spirit. Jaffray asserted that God in His grace gave

this gift to some but, as the Scriptures indicate, it was not universal. The entire article is provided in Appendix 11.

9. *The Christian and Missionary Alliance Annual Report* (1907-1908) 9

10. Simpson editorial, *The Christian and Missionary Alliance Weekly* (30 Apr 1910) 78

11. Simpson, "Gifts and Graces," *The Christian and Missionary Alliance Weekly* (29 Jun 1907). The entire article is provided in Appendix 9.

12. "Spiritual Sanity," *Living Truths* (Apr 1907)

13. *Annual Report* (see note 9 above) 9

14. Simpson, "Gifts and Graces" (see note 11 above) 303

15. Simpson, "Gifts and Graces" (see note 11 above) 302

16. Simpson, "What is Meant by the Latter Rain?" *Living Truths* (Oct 1907) 38

17. Simpson, "Gifts and Graces" (see note 11 above) 302. Referring to First Corinthians 12:7, Simpson remarked: "There is no place for idlers and drones, and there is no excuse for a fruitless Christian. God has power and work for all who will yield themselves to Him for His service and glory."

18. Simpson, "Gifts and Graces" (see note 11 above) 302

19. Simpson editorial, *The Christian and Missionary Alliance Weekly* (16 Mar 1907) 121. Elsewhere, Simpson wrote: "God does not ask us to give up our sanity and to become passive subjects to hypnotic influence, either from Himself or any other being. He has given to us our own rational nature and He acts in harmony with it. If we give ourselves up to spells and influences, irrespective of our judgement or reason, we are just as likely to be taken possession of by evil spirits as by good. This is the very way in which the trance medium in clairvoyance and spiritualism becomes possessed with the spirit of Satan. . . .

    "It is right to wait upon God for the fulness of His blessing, it is right to wait with an open heart and a listening ear, but God will never blame us for vigilance in proving the spirits and 'discerning things that differ.' If He has anything to say to us He will give us ample time to be sure that He is saying it. The Spirit of Christ is the 'spirit . . . of power, and of love, and of a sound mind' [2 Tim. 1:7]." [From "Latter Rain?" (see note 16 above) 38.]

20. Simpson editorial, *The Christian and Missionary Alliance Weekly* (2 Feb 1907) 49

21. Simpson, "Gifts and Graces" (see note 11 above) 303

22. Simpson editorial (see note 19 above) 121

23. Simpson editorial (see note 7 above) 313

24. Simpson, "Gifts and Graces" (see note 11 above) 303

25. Simpson, "The Ministry of the Spirit," *Living Truths* (Aug 1907) 444

26. *Annual Report* (see note 9 above) 11

27. *Annual Report* (see note 9 above) 11

28. Simpson, "Gifts and Graces" (see note 11 above) 303

Chapter 12

An Assessment of A. B. Simpson's View of the Baptism of the Holy Spirit

The previous chapters of this study have served to substantiate the validity of our thesis: that the view of A. B. Simpson regarding the baptism with the Holy Spirit was distinct, but not unique. The task now remains to assess that view. To do so, we will use a twofold approach. First, we shall seek to understand *why* Simpson formulated his view as he did. Second, we shall try to highlight the strengths in Simpson's view of the baptism of the Holy Spirit. As a result of this twofold exploration, we should be able to make an intelligent assessment of Simpson's thought on the subject.

As we have seen, Simpson's view on the baptism of the Holy Spirit was both similar to and dissimilar from those of his contemporaries. The questions naturally arise, Why the similarities? Why the dissimilarities? We turn first to seek answers to those questions.

An Explanation for the Similarities of Viewpoint between Simpson and His Contemporaries

There are a number of reasons to account for the similarities in view between Simpson and his contemporaries. Foremost among these is the obvious fact that they all were influenced by a similar theological milieu. In chapter 1 we noted some of the theological presuppositions which gained widespread influence in 19th century America. Most notable among these were the ones forwarded by John Wesley, Phoebe Palmer and Charles Finney.

As we noted, Wesley was the first to divide the benefits of salvation into distinct blessings that could be received separately. Wesley also elevated the believer's role: the believer had to actively respond to God. In Wesley's view, God's work was contingent on a believer's response to the divine initiative. This was in contrast with the Reformed view that minimized human agency. Wesley also put forth the idea that there was a "crisis point" in which a believer entered into the full blessings of the Christian life.

Palmer intensified these ideas and added her own emphases on the necessity of "consecration." Whereas Wesley gave more room for a gradual outworking of the blessings of God, Palmer expected immediate results once a person "entered" the fuller Christian life. Charles Finney served to spread Wesleyan teaching into American Calvinist circles, presenting his own form of holiness teaching, which came to be termed "Oberlin Perfectionism."

By the late 1800s, therefore, the American theological milieu was greatly affected by these doctrines. And all of them find some degree of correspondence in the views of the writers we surveyed in our study.[1]

Not only were the writers whom we looked at influenced by similar doctrine, but they also had similar concerns. In chapter 1 we saw how and why "holiness" and "power" became central issues in the late 1800s. These leaders perceived the church in America to be in an anemic condition. Moreover, America was faced with tremendous cultural challenges—challenges that did not leave the church unaffected. It is little wonder, then, that all of the surveyed writers, in their theological formulations, attempted to deal with these issues. Moreover, all of them were very interested in how God's offered blessings could be realized, and all were inclined to affirm the need of a "crisis experience" for their appropriation. Thus these common concerns were a further reason for a similarity of viewpoint on the baptism of the Holy Spirit.

Each of the surveyed writers, moreover, had some degree of contact with his or her contemporaries. In chapter 1 we saw the numerous conferences in the United States where these Christian leaders regularly addressed the issues of "holiness of life" and "power for service." Those from divergent traditions within the Protestant church often spoke at these conferences. Simpson, for example, invited D. L. Moody, R. A. Torrey, A. J. Gordon and several of the Keswick teachers to address his Deeper Life conferences. These speakers certainly influenced those who were present and served to promote similarities of expression. Beyond that, the leaders we surveyed were aware of the writings of their contemporaries, making for a cross-fertilization of thought among them and promoting similarities of expression.

Another strong factor in the similarity was personal religious experience. As we saw in chapter 9, all of the writers we looked at testified to a specific time when they entered into a radical new relationship with God. Moreover, all of them regarded their prior life as somehow deficient. The effect of this common spiritual journey accentuated their concern that every Christian know a similar crisis moment.

There is a fifth reason to account for the similarities. All of the writers shared similar vocations. They were either ministers or evangelists or itinerant speakers—shepherds of God's flock. When they saw believers living below the potential that God had provided for them, they responded with pastoral concern. They urged a course of action that had worked for them. And when those same people were wonderfully transformed, their conviction concerning the validity of what they preached and taught was reinforced.

An Explanation for the Differences Between Simpson and His Contemporaries

That leaves us the remaining question: Why did Simpson differ in some respects from his contemporaries? A partial explanation is intimated in the differences we noted in chapter 10. Simpson's view of the baptism of the Holy Spirit demonstrated theological thoughtfulness which many of his contemporaries lacked.

We saw this distinguishing feature in Simpson's attempt to link his view of the baptism of the Holy Spirit with such issues as union with Christ, growth in grace, the work of the Spirit and water baptism.[2]

Simpson also explored other issues which his contemporaries did not. Simpson articulated a solid Trinitarian theology in all his Deeper Life teaching.[3] Simpson explored the interrelationship within the Trinity in the application of Christ's redemption.

Further, Simpson insightfully examined the link between Christ's earthly life and the Christian's.[4] The idea that Christ Jesus, in His relationship to the Father, is the pattern Man is a concept not mentioned by any of Simpson's contemporaries.

This theological thoughtfulness in Simpson's writing may be attributed to both his character and background. Simpson was concerned for truth. His Presbyterian upbringing and seminary education had provided him rigorous theological training. It had disciplined him to be theologically precise. When in the course of his life he was confronted with new views and new concepts—some of them significant departures from the Reformed teaching he had once embraced—Simpson first had to thoroughly test these new understandings against the Scriptures and work through all of their implications. Certainly this background factor accounts in large part for Simpson's more developed understanding of the baptism of the Holy Spirit.

In addition, the biography of A. B. Simpson indicates that his temperament was such that he did not make decisions quickly or without considerable reflection. His spiritual and theological journey of transformation began well before his crisis in 1874 and continued through 1881. This lengthy development meant that his views were seasoned by considerable reflection. The qualities of the man account for the quality of his exposition.

Other Factors

There were other factors. In the introduction we noticed that Simpson attempted to define himself with respect to his contemporaries. In chapters 3 through 6 and chapter 10 we saw that Simpson not infrequently pointed out imbalances in the work of his contemporaries. His responses to weaknesses he saw in the pronouncements of his contemporaries shaped his own expressed position. He believed his views were a corrective to some things his contemporaries were urging.

An example is in the working paper adopted by the 1906 Conference for Prayer and Counsel Respecting the Uniformity in the Testimony and Teaching of the Alliance. In the section dealing with the results of the baptism of the Holy Spirit, there is this statement:

> II.2.b. The baptism of the Holy Ghost <u>as a distinct experience</u>, not merely for power for service, but for personal holiness and victory over the world and sin [underlining in the original].

The tenor of the clause "not merely for power for service, but for personal holiness," as we saw, indicates Simpson's reaction to the rather utilitarian power focus which had risen in the teaching of his day. Elsewhere he noted:

> It is a common and most paralyzing view that the Holy Spirit is simply an enduement of power for service and has no direct connection with our personal character and holiness.[5]

We noted that Simpson, both in his theological formulations and in his teaching and preaching, was always careful to present a balance between these two blessings of the baptism.[6] Since the Scriptures did not exalt either one over the other, neither would Simpson. Hence he reacted to those views that evidenced this imbalance.

Regarding the issue of "power," Simpson was careful to state that Christian life and ministry always flowed from a person's character. "Being" preceded "doing." The following quotation illustrates Simpson's concern. Referring to the "power" mentioned in Acts 1:8, he writes that Christ's provision of the Holy Spirit was

> . . . power to be, rather than to say and do. Our service and testimony will be the outcome of our life and experience. . . .[7]

Furthermore, Simpson asserted that one could not "use" the power of the Spirit. Rather, in his discussions on the empowering work of the Spirit he was careful to point out that the Spirit is a divine Person who uses people but is not Himself used. Believers are not to grieve Him. They are to be responsive to His divine leading.

The Focus Must Be on Jesus Christ

Simpson also stressed that the focus of the work of the Spirit must always be linked to the person of Christ. This too was a corrective to the tendency at the turn of the century to be preoccupied with the third Person of the Trinity.[8] Simpson believed that his view accurately captured the New Testament's emphasis on the Holy Spirit's principal task of exalting Christ. Hence, in Simpson's opinion, one could never exclude this relationship from any discussion about the Holy Spirit.

Simpson also believed that dialogue concerning the Holy Spirit should always be linked to the work of Christ. The Spirit applied the benefits secured through Christ's atoning sacrifice. God's provision for holy living and empowering for ministry came through Christ and was realized in the believer's life by the Spirit. Once again his desire to reflect New Testament teaching dictated that this interrelationship could not be absent from his formulations. Simpson accordingly found himself differing with many of his contemporaries who did not draw this link. Many of them simply talked about the "blessings" of "the baptism." Simpson desired to emphasize an issue that the Scriptures emphasized.

In chapter 10 we saw that Simpson sought to relate water baptism to the baptism of the Holy Spirit. We noted in contrast that his contemporaries gave no consideration to water baptism in their formulations. But the New Testament attaches great significance to this event in a believer's life. Simpson saw that water baptism represented our union with Christ in His death and resurrection, a union realized through the power of the Holy Spirit. Beyond that, he was convinced that water baptism symbolized the believer's act of dedication to God prior to being baptized by the Holy Spirit. Hence, in Simpson's view water baptism needed to be related to Spirit baptism.

One Further Facet

There is one further facet to be considered in accounting for the differences present in Simpson's work from that of his contemporaries. One of the most notable features of Simpson's theology is the centrality he attaches to the "new covenant" texts of Jeremiah 31 and Ezekiel 36.[9] In chapter 4 we noted that Simpson believed these texts to be the key to understanding the significance of union with Christ. They also explained the nature of the baptism of the Holy Spirit. Speaking of the new covenant promises in Jeremiah 31:31-34, Simpson says:

> This is the work of the Holy Ghost. This is the meaning of sanctification. This is the great purpose of Christ's redemption and His indwelling in the heart of the believer through the Spirit. It is God who undertakes this covenant. . . . It is the power of the divine grace to keep from sin, and to lead us into righteousness and holiness.[10]

Simpson's use and explication of the term *new covenant* set him apart from his contemporaries. Discovering the reasons for the centrality of these texts will thus further assist us in understanding the differences between Simpson's work and that of his contemporaries.

The origin of Simpson's fascination with the "new covenant" texts is difficult to trace. Nowhere in his writing, either autobiographical or otherwise, does Simpson indicate where he first came upon this idea.[11] As we examine the influences upon his life, however, we discover some clues. In chapter 2 we saw that W. E. Boardman's book, *The Higher Christian Life,* was particularly significant in Simpson's life. The book led to his spiritual crisis in 1874 and helped shape his ideas concerning sanctification. But the book nowhere mentions the verses in Jeremiah 31 and Ezekiel 36, nor does it discuss the "new covenant" concept.

In contrast, another formative book in Simpson's life did explore these matters. Walter Marshall's *The Gospel Mystery of Sanctification* contains an extensive examination of the "new covenant" promised by God.[12] The nature and implications of union with Christ are also central themes in this book. Simpson respected Marshall's views on the results of union with Christ and he cited Marshall in some of his writing.[13]

Putting these clues together, it appears that Marshall's book imparted to Simpson this idea of God's promised provision for the believer in the "new covenant." It seems likely, therefore, that Marshall's book may have served to awaken Simpson's search to experience these "new covenant" provisions. However, it was not until after he had read Boardman in 1874 that Simpson believed he had attained them. As a result of reading *The Higher Christian Life,* he realized that he simply needed to ask and receive by faith these provisions which Christ had made available.

Whatever the origins of Simpson's interest in the "new covenant" may have been, we saw that these passages provided Simpson with a foundation for understanding the significance of God's work in Christ.[14] As he investigated the New Testament, he saw that the Spirit offered believers the possibility of participating in the benefits of Christ's finished work. In Simpson's view, Christ had not only provided for the forgiveness of sin but he had also provided for the ability to overcome the power of sin. These truths profoundly impacted Simpson's life, and he had a burning desire to communicate them to others. This tremendous concern of Simpson's, therefore, accounts for the prominence of Ezekiel 36 and Jeremiah 31 in his writings.

Qualities of Strength Found in Simpson's Deviations from His Contemporaries

Our investigation is now at the juncture where the strengths of Simpson's views can be highlighted.

First, Simpson must be commended for the attention he gives to the interrelationship of the baptism of the Holy Spirit with contextual considerations. As we noted above, he never let the baptism of the Holy Spirit stand in isolation. He joined it with water baptism, growth in grace and the Spirit's role in helping the believer realize all the provisions available through his or her union with Christ. In this respect, Simpson's view displays a quality of internal consistency and coherence not present in the writings of many of his contemporaries.

Second, Simpson explored and developed issues that most of his contemporaries either did not think about or neglected to explicitly state in their formulations. Each of the issues mentioned in chapter 10 indicates this attention to detail that was a hallmark of Simpson's work. Obviously Simpson wanted to go beyond a simple presentation of the "how to" of receiving the baptism of the Holy Spirit. He attempted to provide a fully developed rationale based on what he saw as the scriptural arguments for the specific reception of the Spirit. He traced the promises in the Old Testament for such a "baptism." He explored the significance of the Holy Spirit in Christ's life as well as the significance and meaning of Christ's sending the Holy Spirit after His ascension. He also detailed the Spirit's application of the benefits of Christ's work subsequent to the baptism.

Third, Simpson's exploration of growth in grace indicates his concern to make clear what occurs subsequent to the baptism of the Spirit. He grappled with the nature of Christian growth, the manner in which it occurred and some of the problems that believers might experience in the process.[15] His concern for this topic indicates that Simpson desired to move beyond a simplistic picture of the Christian life. This fact is of great importance. Those who quote Simpson are prone to focus on what he says about the initiatory step into the Deeper Life, overlooking his wealth of material on what follows that initiation.

Fourth, Simpson correctly presents the New Testament perspective on the person of the Holy Spirit. He calls for the recognition of the Spirit as a Person to be acknowledged and honored. Simpson rightly criticizes the utilitarian tone of some of his contemporaries.[16] Believers cannot "use" the Holy Spirit. As well, Simpson correctly keeps discussion on the Person and work of the Spirit centered on

Christ Jesus. He accurately captures the New Testament emphasis: the primary ministry of the Holy Spirit is to exalt Christ.

Fifth, Simpson keeps Christianity supernatural. His writing indicates an openness and desire for the vital experience of God and His power in daily living. The Christian should live a life qualitatively different from the non-Christian because God Himself indwells him or her. At the same time, Simpson's call for a supernatural experience avoided the then-current preoccupation with experience-seeking or some specific gift or manifestation. In an era when some evangelicals shunned anything supernatural and the Pentecostals were preoccupied with the supernatural, Simpson displayed a remarkable balance.

Finally, Simpson accurately and effectively embraced both holy living and empowered service. He continually affirmed that both were provisions of Christ's finished work; hence, neither one could be exalted above the other. His presentation on these matters provides the reader with a rich picture of the full provision in Christ that God intends for the believer.

> Once it was the blessing,
>   Now it is the Lord;
> Once it was the feeling,
>   Now it is His Word.
> Once His gift I wanted,
>   Now the Giver own;
> Once I sought for healing,
>   Now Himself alone.
>
> Once 'twas painful trying,
>   Now 'tis perfect trust;
> Once a half salvation,
>   Now the uttermost!
> Once 'twas ceaseless holding,
>   Now He holds me fast;
> Once 'twas constant drifting,
>   Now my anchor's cast.

Once 'twas busy planning,
  Now 'tis trustful prayer;
Once 'twas anxious caring,
  Now He has the care.
Once 'twas what I wanted,
  Now what Jesus says;
Once 'twas constant asking,
  Now 'tis ceaseless praise.

Once it was my working,
  His it hence shall be;
Once I tried to use Him,
  Now He uses me.
Once the power I wanted,
  Now the Mighty One;
Once for self I labored,
  Now for Him alone.

Once I hoped in Jesus,
  Now I know He's mine;
Once my lamps were dying,
  Now they brightly shine.
Once for death I waited,
  Now His coming hail;
And my hopes are anchored
  Safe within the vail.

(Refrain)
All in all forever,
  Jesus will I sing;
Everything in Jesus,
  And Jesus everything.

"Himself"
By A. B. Simpson

Endnotes

1. This is *not* to say that Simpson and his contemporaries understood these issues in precisely the way Wesley, Palmer and Finney understood them.

2. For Simpson's views on union with Christ, see chapter 10, "Simpson's Pneumatology Was Christocentric," "Simpson, More Fully than Others, Explored the Work of the Spirit as the Agent of Union with Christ," and "Simpson Believed that New Covenant Promises Are Rooted in Jeremiah 31 and Ezekiel 36." For growth in grace, see chapter 10, "Simpson Outlined a Relationship between the Baptism of the Spirit and Growth in God's Grace." For the work of the Holy Spirit, see chapter 10, "Simpson's Pneumatology Was Christocentric," and "Simpson, More Fully than Others, Explored the Work of the Spirit as the Agent of Union with Christ." For water baptism, see chapter 10, "Simpson Saw Water Baptism Related to the Baptism of the Spirit."

3. See chapter 10, "Simpson's Theology Was Always Trinitarian."

4. See chapter 10, "Simpson Explored More Deeply the Significance of Christ's Earthly Life."

5. A. B. Simpson editorial, *Living Truths* (Mar 1906) 130. This quotation appears also in chapter 6.

6. See chapter 6, "Personal Holiness and Spiritual Victory" and "Power for Service."

7. Simpson, *The Holy Spirit, Or Power from on High,* vol. II (New York: Christian Alliance Publishing Co., 1896) 79-80. This quotation appears also in chapter 6, "Power for Service."

8. See chapter 10, "Simpson's Pneumatology Was Christocentric."

9. See chapter 4, "Sanctification and the New Covenant of Jeremiah 31 and Ezekiel 36." Simpson believed that God's provisions for holiness and power were promised in the Old Testament. It was through Christ's work that these provisions were accomplished. The new covenant brought believers into union with Christ and by the ministry of the Spirit they were able to experience the provisions of this union. It was necessary, however, for the believer to be baptized with the Spirit before he or she could begin to experience these benefits.

10. Simpson, *Holy Spirit,* vol. II (see note 7 above) 227-228. This quotation was

cited in chapter 4, "Sanctification and the New Covenant of Jeremiah 31 and Ezekiel 36."

11. I have read most of Simpson's published material without finding a reference as to where the idea originated.

12. Walter Marshall, *The Gospel Mystery of Sanctification* (London: Publisher unknown, 1692) 13. Marshall at one point writes, "God restores His people to holiness by giving them 'a new heart, and a new spirit, and taking away the heart of stone out of their flesh, and giving them a heart of flesh' " (page 13). The reference is to Ezekiel 36:26.

13. Appendix 3 presents an extensive quote which Simpson cited from Marshall (see note 12 above). The passage provides an overview of Marshall's concept of union with Christ. In chapter 2 we saw that Marshall's book was initially influential in imparting the assurance of salvation to Simpson as a teenager.

14. See chapter 3, "Christ Is Our Model," and chapter 4, "Sanctification and the New Covenant of Jeremiah 31 and Ezekiel 36."

15. See chapter 6, "The Spiritual Journey of the Believer after the Baptism."

16. R. A. Torrey was the most notable of these. For an analysis of his teaching, See chapter 8, "Reuben Archer Torrey."

Conclusion

Distinct but Not Unique

In this study we have explored Simpson's view in relation to his contemporaries' on the baptism of the Holy Spirit. In this finale we want to highlight the results of our examination and draw an appropriate conclusion.

From the outset, we have worked on the premise that we can understand Simpson's views on the baptism of the Holy Spirit only as we are aware of the context within which he ministered and wrote. Indeed, this procedure is the very essence of historical theology.

Our investigation uncovered numerous factors in 19th century America that combined to produce an intense interest in the Holy Spirit. There were sociological and ecclesiastical factors. By the late 1800s, urbanization, immigration and industrialization had produced significant changes in American society—changes that posed intricate challenges for the church. But traditional forms of church life and ministry seemed inadequate to meet these challenges. Moreover, there was a growing perception by many that the spiritual vitality of most Protestant churches was at low ebb. There was a tremendous incongruity between Christian life as depicted in the Scriptures and Christian life as exemplified by most church members. Society was becoming secular, and the church seemed powerless to stem the tide. Only a return to New Testament vitality would enable the church to meet this assault.

Paralleling these factors, significant theological shifts were occurring in America's Protestant milieu. First, several of the presuppositions underlying Methodism became widely accepted. As a result, many within both the Methodist-Holiness and even the Reformed traditions sought the "full blessings" of salvation. To experience these blessings became a pervasive concern in the American evangelical milieu.

Second, from the 1860s onward, many viewed the book of Acts as the answer to the problems facing the church. Until then, they had viewed Acts as descriptive in nature—simply history. Now they saw it as prescriptive—holding within that history a formula for divine resources to enable the church to face its battles.

Third, Premillennial eschatology gained widespread acceptance in the late 1800s. Belief in the imminent return of Jesus Christ intensified the church's interest in worldwide evangelization.

These theological shifts prompted Christians to investigate afresh the Holy Spirit's ministry of equipping believers for service.

The culmination was an intense search for solutions to the problems facing the church. Two questions became vital concerns of those searching for solutions: How could a believer live a holy life? And, how can a believer experience the power of the Spirit promised at Pentecost (Acts 2:39)? These related questions prompted people to seek to understand how holy living and power for service could become present-day realities in their lives. And that quest led naturally to a reexploration of the person and work of the Holy Spirit, the agent of both sanctification and divine power.

Further, if this holiness of life and empowerment for service was bestowed at some point after a sinner had repented and been born again, what was that point of entry and how did the believer achieve it? The resulting formulation regarding the entry point was commonly called "the baptism of the Holy Spirit."

Their Commonalities

This study has demonstrated that Simpson and his contemporaries, having shared the common theological context outlined above, held many points in common in their understanding of the baptism of the Holy Spirit. Foremost was belief that the provisions which God supplies in salvation are not automatically received and realized at conversion. A person must recognize each provision specifically and specifically ask God to impart it to him or her. They believed that the Scriptures present an "entry formula" for obtaining these promised provisions: a recognition of need, an awareness from the Scriptures that God has made provision for the need, a total consecration to God and a request for the specific benefit promised. Simpson and his contemporaries also asserted that God would effect definite changes in the believer's life as a result of this quest.

Simpson found more agreement with some of his contemporaries than with others. The term *baptism of the Holy Spirit* or *baptism with the Holy Spirit* was a flexible metaphor during this era. Simpson took it to mean the moment when the Holy Spirit begins fully to indwell the believer as opposed to His merely being "with" him or her. In this regard, Simpson and some of his contemporaries did not believe that the Holy Spirit automatically "indwelt" a believer at regeneration. The Spirit had to be invited in specifically.

Moreover, they believed that since the Spirit is the agent of sanctification and empowering for service, both these issues must be related to the baptism of the Holy Spirit. Having received the baptism—and, hence, the Spirit in His fullness—a believer had the potentiality for progress in both sanctification and empowered service. These teachers also maintained a common understanding of the term *sanctification*. Sanctification was not a crystallized state but rather the appropriation of the divine resources to live a holy life. Christ, in their view, had provided for the believer's sanctification in the atonement.

Simpson and several of his contemporaries were also careful to highlight the relationship between the ministry of the Holy Spirit and the finished work of Christ on the cross. Furthermore, they emphasized the "indwelling Christ"—the mystical presence of Christ in the believer through the agency of the Holy Spirit.

Their Significant Differences

While Simpson's views in many ways were similar to those of his contemporaries, we saw as well some significant differences in viewpoint. No other writer of those we surveyed followed the theme of the "new covenant" that Simpson found in Jeremiah 31 and Ezekiel 36 and saw fulfilled at Pentecost. In these two Old Testament passages he saw the key to understanding the nature of God's provisions for holy living and powerful service.

Simpson reflects on the relationship between water baptism and the baptism with the Spirit. No other writer did this.

Simpson presents a fuller exploration of the nature and benefits of union with Christ in his writings than did most of his contemporaries. He formulated a detailed explanation as to the role of the Spirit as the Agent of that union with Christ.

Simpson also displays a balance and breadth concerning the benefits of the baptism of the Holy Spirit not present in the writings of the majority of his contemporaries.

Simpson probes the specific work of the individual Persons of the Trinity in relationship to the Christian life.

Simpson presents a clear relationship between the baptism of the Holy Spirit and the Spirit-filled believer's subsequent growth in grace.

The evidence is clear that Simpson's views on the baptism of the Holy Spirit share many common features with the views of his contemporaries. At the same time, his views were marked by significant differences. Though in general Simpson's views were not unique, his formulation concerning the baptism of the Holy Spirit was distinct. We may therefore summarize his view with the words *distinct, but not unique.*

Finally, we need to highlight the great value this survey can have for us as we close out this current century. Like the church of Simpson's day, the church today faces great challenges, both in North America and worldwide. Concern for spiritual renewal is also growing in many segments of the church. People do not simply wish to go through the motions of religious formality. They hunger for authenticity and a sense of "connectedness" with God. For us today, we may learn much from Albert B.Simpson.

A Rich Theology of Experience

Simpson presents us with a rich theology of experience. He

tackled the problem of moving from *knowledge* about God and His blessings to *experiencing* God and His blessings. Returning to Simpson's imagery cited at the conclusion of chapter 5, we are reminded that Christianity is a two-sided coin. There is the objective dimension: our position *in Christ*. And there is the subjective dimension: our experience of *Christ in us*. Simpson reminds us that Christianity affirms both.

Current portrayals of the Christian life tend to stress one aspect or the other. Simpson reminds us we must embrace both, neither fearing experience nor neglecting truth. At the same time he calls us to be continually open to the Spirit of Jesus Christ. Christianity is supernatural, it is life-related; and if we know Christ authentically, the results should overflow into the lives of many others.

To his generation—and to ours—Simpson insists that the truth he has endeavored to demonstrate

> . . . is intensely practical. So long as people think they have it all, there is little incentive to rouse themselves and claim their full inheritance, but when God's people see that like Israel of old, they are still toiling in the wilderness under His displeasure, that they are neglecting a great salvation, that they are out of fellowship with Christ and grieving the Holy Ghost, motive is supplied of overwhelming power and they are led to heart searching, humiliation and unceasing prayer, and a new impulse comes into their lives like a great tidal wave over the ocean of love, and an experience comes to their souls as much higher than conversion as conversion is better than the old life of flesh and sin.
>
> This is the deepest need of the church today. One such consecrated, Spirit-filled life means a score of souls for God. "Let us therefore fear lest the promise being left us of entering into his rest any of you should seem to come short of it" [Hebrews 4:1].

> O brother, give heed to the warning
> And obey His voice today;

The Spirit to thee is calling,
  Oh, do not grieve Him away.

Oh, come now in complete surrender,
  Turn back from thy doubt and sin;
Pass on from Kadesh to Canaan
  And a crown and kingdom win.[1]

Endnote

1. A. B. Simpson, "The Baptism of the Holy Spirit: A Crisis or an Evolution?" *Living Truths* (Sep 1905) 714-715

Bibliography

Books by Albert B. Simpson

Unless otherwise noted, all books by Simpson were published by A. B. Simpson's publishing house, The Christian Alliance Publishing Company (now Christian Publications).

All in All: Or, Christ in Colossians. 1901.
Christ in the Bible. Vol. 13 Matthew. 1904.
Christ in the Bible. Vol. 14 Mark. 1910.
Christ in the Bible. Vol. 14B Luke. 1905.
Christ in the Bible. Vol. 10 John, Acts. 1891.
Christ in the Bible. Vol. 16 Acts. 1902.
Christ in the Bible. Vol. 11 Romans. 1894.
Christ in the Bible. Vol. 17 1 Corinthians. 1904.
Christ in the Bible. Vol. 18 2 Corinthians. 1904.
Christ in the Bible. Vol. 19 Galatians, Ephesians. 1904.
Christ in the Bible. Vol. 20 Phil., Col., Thess. 1903.
Christ in the Bible. Vol. 21 Thess., Tim., Titus. 1920s.
Christ in the Bible. Vol. 22 Hebrews. 1920s.
Christ in the Bible. Vol. 22A James. 1920s.
Christ in the Bible. Vol. 23 Peter, John, Jude. 1920s.
The Christ of the Forty Days. 1890.
The Christ Life. London: Morgan & Scott. 1888.
The Cross of Christ. 1910.
Danger Lines in the Deeper Life. 1897.
Days of Heaven on Earth. 1897.
Echoes of the New Creation. 1903.
The Fourfold Gospel. 1887.
The Fullness of Jesus. 1886.

The Gospel of Healing. 1886.
The Holy Spirit: Or, Power from on High. 2 vols. 1895-1896.
In Heavenly Places. 1892.
A Larger Christian Life. 1890.
The Life of Prayer. 1890.
The Old Faith and the New Gospels. 1911.
Present Truth. 1897.
The Story of The Christian and Missionary Alliance. 1900.
Walking in the Spirit. 1889.
When the Comforter Came. 1911.
Wholly Sanctified. 1890.

A. B. Simpson periodical articles

All listed articles appeared in one of two periodicals:

1. Simpson's "official" church magazine, which bore several titles from its inception in 1882 until his death in 1919:

- *The Word, the Work and the World* (Jan 1882-Dec 1887)
- *The Christian Alliance* (Jan 1888-Jul 1889)
- *The Christian Alliance and Missionary Weekly* (Aug 1889-Dec 1893)
- *The Christian Alliance and Foreign Missionary Weekly* (Jan 1894-Dec 1896)
- *The Christian and Missionary Alliance Weekly* (Jan 1897-Nov 1898)
- *The Christian and Missionary Alliance* (Dec 1898-May 1899)
- *The Christian and Missionary Alliance Weekly* (Jun 1899-Sep 1911)
- *The Alliance Weekly (Oct 1911-)*

2. *Living Truths,* a monthly magazine edited and published by Simpson but not identified with either his New York City Gospel Tabernacle or with the North American organizations he later founded.

Unless marked *Living Truths,* the articles are from Simpson's official church magazine (see #1 above). The titles of all articles are in alphabetical order and, in the case of duplicate titles, in chronological order.

"The Abiding Life." 9 May 1908.

"The Abiding Life." 27 Mar 1915.

"All the Blessings of the Spirit." 29 Sep 1906.

"The Anointing." 18 Jan 1919.

"Baptism, and Baptism of the Holy Spirit." 17 May 1902.

"The Baptism with Fire." 16 Nov 1894.

"The Baptism with the Spirit." 30 Sep 1892.

"The Baptism of the Holy Spirit: A Crisis or an Evolution?" *Living Truths.* Dec 1905.

"Be Filled with the Spirit." 6 Nov 1895.

"The Blessings of the Spirit." 17 Oct 1914.

"Christ, Our Model, Motive and Motive Power." *Living Truths.* May 1903.

"The Christian Life a Christ Life." *Living Truths.* Jan 1906.

"The Conferences in Great Britain." Sep 1885.

"The Connection between the Holy Spirit and External Blessing." 20 Jul 1894.

"The Crisis of the Deeper Life." *Living Truths.* Sep 1906.

Editorial. Jun 1899.

Editorial. Jul 1899.

Editorial. Nov 1899.

Editorial. 9 Dec 1905.

Editorial. 30 Dec 1905.

Editorial. *Living Truths.* Mar 1906.

Editorial. 31 Mar 1906.

Editorial. 19 May 1906.

Editorial. 2 Jun 1906.

Editorial. *Living Truths.* Jul 1906.

Editorial. 21 Jul 1906.

Editorial. *Living Truths.* Nov 1906.

Editorial. *Living Truths.* Feb 1907.

Editorial. *Living Truths.* May 1907.
Editorial. 12 Jun 1909.
Editorial. 30 Apr 1910.
Editorial. 1 Mar 1913.
"Evolution or Revolution." *Living Truths.* Jun 1904.
"Failure and Sin after Sanctification." Mar 1888.
"Farther On." 1 Sep 1907.
"Farther On, concluded." 28 Sep 1907.
"Filled with the Spirit." 26 Nov 1904.
"Full Salvation." 15 Dec 1917.
"The Gift of Tongues." 12 Feb 1892.
"The Gift of Tongues." *Living Truths.* Dec 1906.
"Gifts and Graces." 29 Jun 1907.
"God's Part in Sanctification." 11 Mar 1905.
"God's Provision for His People's Sanctification." 26 Jun 1891.
"The Holy Ghost." 24 Apr 1909.
"The Holy Spirit." Apr 1885.
"The Holy Spirit." 22 May 1891.
"The Holy Spirit and the Gospel." 4 Mar 1905.
"The Holy Spirit and the Ministry." *Living Truths.* Sep 1904
"The Holy Spirit in the Life of the Lord Jesus Christ." 15 May
     1895.
"How Is Christ Made unto Us Sanctification?" Mar 1888. "How
     to Enter In." 27 Apr 1912.
"How to Receive Divine Healing." Aug 1885.
"The Ministry of the Spirit." *Living Truths.* Aug 1907.
"Misapprehensions Respecting Sanctification." Apr 1888.
"The Need of a Deeper Spiritual Life." 3 Jul 1909.
"The Old Orchard Convention—The Holy Spirit." Sep 1886.
"Paul, a Pattern of Full Salvation." 21 Aug 1909.
"A Personal Testimony." 2 Oct 1915.
"Phases and Phrases of the Deeper Life." *Living Truths.* Oct 1902.
"The Place of the Will in the Spiritual Life." 11 Mar 1892.
"The Power of Stillness." Oct 1909.
"Prevailing Prayer." 24 Apr 1915.
"Receive Ye the Holy Ghost." 17 Nov 1893.

"Reckon, Recognize, Realize." 3 Feb 1893.

"The Residue of the Spirit." 5 Oct 1912.

"Rest, Perfection and Faith." 28 Jun 1919.

"Revival Movements." Apr 1907.

"Rivers of Living Water." 3 Mar 1906.

"Sanctification." Jun 1885.

"Sanctification." 11 Sep 1891.

"Sanctification." 3 Aug 1894.

"Sanctification." *Living Truths.* Dec 1903.

"Sanctification." 19 Jan 1901.

"Sanctification and Growth." 17 Jul 1891. "Sanctification and Growth in Grace." Mar 1888.

"Sanctification by the Grace of Christ." 4 May 1894.

"Sanctification in Romans." 30 Jun 1893.

"Sanctification More than Cleansing." Feb 1888.

"Sanctification through Death and Resurrection." 27 Apr 1894.

"Sanctification through the Spirit." 11 May 1894.

"The Secret of Prayer." *Living Truths.* Mar 1904.

"Sinning against the Spirit." 25 Feb 1911.

"Some Aspects of the Holy Spirit." *Living Truths.* Jul 1905.

"Special Spiritual Gifts." *Living Truths.* Dec 1906.

"The Spirit-Filled Life." 16 Nov 1907.

"The Spirit-Filled Life." 13 Jul 1918.

"The Spirit of the Lord Is upon Me." Mar 1883.

"Spiritual Counterfeits." *Living Truths.* Dec 1906.

"Spiritual Sanity." *Living Truths.* Apr 1907.

"Spiritual versus Ecclesiastical Gifts." *Living Truths.* Jun 1905.

"A Story of Providence." *Living Truths.* Mar 1907.

"The Supernatural Gifts and Ministries of the Church." Jan 1898.

"Tarry." *Living Truths.* Sep 1907.

"Theories about Sanctification." 9 Sep 1892.

"Three Types of Religious Experience." 8 Oct 1910.

"The Training and Sending Forth of Workers." 30 Apr 1897.

"What Is Meant by the Latter Rain?" 19 Oct 1907.

"What Is the Difference between Sanctification and Regeneration?" Mar 1888.

"Why Our People Give So Much for Missions." *Living Truths.* Nov 1905.

"The Work of the Christian and Missionary Alliance." 13 May 1916.

Miscellaneous A. B. Simpson material

"Christian and Missionary Alliance." *New Schaff-Herzog Encyclopedia of Religious Knowledge.* Vol. 3. Gen. ed. S. M. Jackson. New York: Funk & Wagnalls, 1908-1912.

"The Genius of the Alliance." *Twenty Sermonettes.* Ed. William T. MacArthur. New York: Christian Alliance Publishing Co., n.d.

"Letters from Abroad." 1871.
"Simpson's Diary." 1879.
"My Own Story." N.d.
   In *Simpson's Scrapbook.* Compiled by C. Donald McKaig. Regina, SK: Canadian Bible College/Canadian Theological Seminary Archibald Library archives.

"Himself." Camp Hill, PA: Christian Publications, n.d.—originally an address delivered at Bethshan, London, in 1885 and first printed that year.

"Paper on the Uniformity in the Testimony and Teaching of the Alliance." The Conference for Prayer and Counsel, May, 1906.

Books by Other Authors

Anderson, Robert Mapes. *Vision of the Disinherited: The Making of American Pentecostalism.* New York: Oxford UP, 1979.

Arthur, William. *The Tongue of Fire: Or, The True Power of Chris-*

tianity. New York: Harper & Brothers, 1865.

Barabas, Steven. *So Great Salvation: The History and Message of the Keswick Convention*. London: Marshall, Morgan & Scott, 1952.

Bartleman, Frank. *How Pentecost Came to Los Angeles: As it Was in the Beginning*. Los Angeles: Privately printed, 1928.

Baxter, Richard. *The Saints' Everlasting Rest*. Abridged by Benjamin Fawcett. New York: American Tract Society, n.d.

Bloch-Hoell, Nils. *The Pentecostal Movement: Its Origin, Development and Distinctive Character*. Oslo: Universitetsorlaget, 1964.

Bloesch, Donald. *The Crisis of Piety: Essays toward a Theology of the Christian Life*. Grand Rapids, MI: Eerdmans, 1968.

Boardman, Mary M. *Life and Labors of W. E. Boardman*. London: Benrose & Sons, 1886.

Boardman, William E. *The Higher Christian Life*. Revised edition. Boston: Henry Hoyt, 1871.

Bruner, Frederick Dale. *A Theology of the Holy Spirit: The Pentecostal Experience and the New Testament Witness*. Grand Rapids, MI: Eerdmans, 1970.

Chrisman, C. H., and Turnbull, W. M., eds. *The Message of The Christian and Missionary Alliance*. New York: Christian Alliance Publishing Co., 1925.

Cooke, Sarah A. *The Handmaiden of the Lord: Or, Wayside Sketches*. Chicago: S. B. Shaw, 1900.

Dayton, Donald W. *Discovering an Evangelical Heritage*. New

York: Harper & Row, 1976.

—. *The Theological Roots of Pentecostalism.* Grand Rapids, MI: Zondervan, 1986.

—. Preface. *Late Nineteenth Century Revivalist Teachings on the Holy Spirit. New York and London: Garland Publishing, 1985. Reprint of Secret Power* by D. L. Moody, *Receive Ye the Holy Ghost* by J. Wilbur Chapman and *The Baptism with the Holy Spirit* by R. A. Torrey.

Dieter, Melvin Easterday. *The Holiness Revival of the 19th Century.* Metuchen, NJ: Scarecrow Press, 1980.

Findlay, James F., Jr. *Dwight L. Moody: American Evangelist 1837-1899.* Chicago: U of Chicago P, 1969.

Finney, Charles G. *An Autobiography.* Edited and Condensed by Helen Wessel. Minneapolis: Bethany Fellowship, 1977.

—. *Lectures on Revivals of Religion.* Revised and edited by William Henry Harding. London: Morgan & Scott, 1910.

—. *Power from on High: A Selection of Articles on the Higher Spiritual Life.* London: Victory Press, 1946.

—. *The Promise of the Spirit.*

Frank, Douglas W. *Less than Conquerors: How Evangelicals Entered the Twentieth Century.* Grand Rapids, MI: Eerdmans, 1986.

Gordon, A. J. *The Ministry of the Spirit.* New York: Fleming H. Revell, 1895.

—. *The Twofold Life: Or, Christ's Work for Us and Christ's Work in Us.* New York: Fleming H. Revell, 1896.

—. *The Holy Spirit in Missions.* London: Hodder and Stoughton, 1896.

Gordon, Ernest B. *Adoniram Judson Gordon: A Biography.* New York: Fleming H. Revell, 1896.

Gundry, Stanley N. *Love Them in: The Proclamation Theology of D. L. Moody.* Chicago: Moody Press, 1976.

—. and Kenneth S. Kantzer, eds. *Perspectives on Evangelical Theology.* Grand Rapids, MI: Baker, 1979.

Hartzfeld, David F., and Charles Nienkirchen, eds. *The Birth of a Vision: Essays on the Ministry and Thought of Albert B. Simpson.* Beaverlodge, AB: Buena Book Services, 1986.

Heron, Alasdair I. C. *The Holy Spirit.* Philadelphia: Westminster P, 1983.

Hills, A. M. *Holiness and Power for the Church and the Ministry.* Cincinnati: Revivalist Office, 1897.

Hollenweger, Walter. *The Pentecostals.* London: SCM P, 1972.

Hunter, Harold D. *Spirit-Baptism: A Pentecostal Alternative.* New York: UP of America, 1983.

Jones, Charles E. *Perfectionist Persuasion.* Metuchen, NJ: Scarecrow P, 1974.

—. *A Guide to the Study of the Holiness Movement.* Metuchen, NJ: Scarecrow P, 1974.

Knapp, Martin Wells. *Out of Egypt into Canaan: Or, Lessons in Spiritual Geography.* Boston: McDonald and Gill, 1889.

Lawson, James Gilchrist. *Deeper Experiences of Famous Christians.* Anderson, IN: Warner P, 1911.

Lovelace, Richard F. *Dynamics of Spiritual Life: An Evangelical Theology of Renewal.* Downers Grove, IL: Inter-Varsity P, 1979.

Mahan, Asa. *Baptism of the Holy Ghost.* New York: Palmer & Hughes, 1870.

—. *Out of Darkness into Light: Or, The Hidden Life Made Manifest.* London: Wesleyan Conference Centre, 1877.

Marsden, George M. *Fundamentalism and American Culture: The Shaping of Twentieth-Century Evangelicalism, 1870-1925.* New York: Oxford UP, 1980.

Marshall, Walter. *Gospel Mystery of Sanctification.* London: n.p., 1692. MacDill AFB, FL: Tyndale Bible Society, n.d.

McLoughlin, William G. *The American Evangelicals, 1800-1900.* New York: Harper & Row, 1968.

Meyer, F. B. *Back to Bethel.* Chicago: Moody P, 1901

Miller, Perry. *The Life of the Mind in America from the Revolution to the Civil War.* New York: Harcourt, Brace & World, Inc., 1965.

Moody, Dwight L. *Secret Power.* Reprint ed. Ventura, CA: Regal Books, 1987.

—. *Sowing and Reaping.* Chicago: n.p., 1896.

Morrison, H. C. *The Baptism of the Holy Ghost.* Louisville: Pentecostal Herald, 1900.

Moule, Handley C. G. *Christ Is Victor.* London: Hodder and Stoughton, 1896.

Murray, Andrew. *The Spirit of Christ: Thoughts on the Indwelling of the Holy Spirit in the Believer and the Church.* New York: A. D. F. Randolph and Co., 1888.

—. *The Full Blessing of Pentecost.* New York: Fleming H. Revell, 1908.

—. *The Master's Indwelling.* New York: Fleming H. Revell, 1908.

Niklaus, Robert L., John S. Sawin and Samuel J. Stoesz. *All for Jesus: God at Work in The Christian and Missionary Alliance over One Hundred Years.* Camp Hill, PA: Christian Publications, 1986.

Orr, J. Edwin. *The Fervent Prayer.* Chicago: Moody P, 1974.

—. *The Second Evangelical Awakening.* London: Marshall, Morgan & Scott, 1955.

Packer, James Innell. *Keep in Step with the Spirit.* Old Tappan, NJ: Fleming H. Revell, 1984.

Palmer, Phoebe. *Faith and its Effects: Or, Fragments from My Portfolio* New York: n.p., 1854.

—. *Four Years in the Old World.* New York: W. C. Palmer, Jr., 1870)

—. *The Promise of the Father.* Boston: H. V. Degen, 1859.

Pardington, George P. *Outline Studies in Christian Doctrine.* New York: Christian Alliance Publishing Co., 1916.

—. *The Still Small Voice.* New York: Christian Alliance Publishing Co., n.d.

—. *Twenty-five Wonderful Years.* Intro. by A. B. Simpson. New York: Christian Alliance Publishing Co., 1914.

Pierson, Arthur T. *Forward Movements of the Last Half Century.* New York: Funk & Wagnalls, 1900.

Reynolds, Lindsay. *Footprints: The Beginnings of The Christian and Missionary Alliance in Canada.* Toronto: C&MA in Canada, 1982.

Sandeen, Ernest R. *The Roots of Fundamentalism.* Chicago: U of Chicago P, 1970.

Sangster, W. E. *The Path to Perfection.* New York: Abington-Cokesbury, 1943.

Scharpff, Paulus. *The History of Evangelism: Three Hundred Years of Evangelism in Germany, Great Britain, and United States of America.* Trans. Helga Bender Henry. Grand Rapids, MI: Eerdmans, 1966.

Smith, Timothy L. *Called unto Holiness: The Story of the Nazarenes.* Kansas City, MO: Nazarene Publishing House, 1962.

—. *Revivalism and Social Reform: American Protestantism on the Eve of the Civil War.* New York: Harper & Row, 1965.

Stevenson, Herbert F. *Keswick's Authentic Voice.* Grand Rapids, MI: Zondervan, 1959.

Stoesz, Samauel J. *Understanding My Church.* Rev. ed. Camp Hill, PA: Christian Publications, 1984.

Sweet, Leonard I., ed. *The Evangelical Tradition in America.* Macon, GA: Mercer UP, 1894.

Sweet, W. W. *The American Churches: An Interpretation.* New York: Cokesbury P, 1947.

Synan, Vinson. *The Holiness-Pentecostal Movement in the United States.* Grand Rapids, MI: Eerdmans, 1971.

—, ed. *Aspects of Pentecostal-Charismatic Origins.* Plainfield, NJ: Logos International, 1975.

Thomas, W. H. Griffith. *The Holy Spirit of God.* London: Longmans, Green and Co., 1913.

Thompson, A. E. *The Life of A. B. Simpson.* New York: Christian Alliance Publishing Co., 1920.

Torrey, Reuben Archer. *The Baptism with the Holy Spirit.* New York: Fleming H. Revell, 1897.

—. *The Person and Work of the Holy Spirit: As Revealed in the Scriptures and in Personal Experience.* London: James Nisbet, 1910.

—. *How to Obtain Fullness of Power.* New York: Fleming H. Revell, 1897.

Tozer, Aiden Wilson. *Wingspread: Albert B. Simpson—A Study in Spiritual Altitude.* Harrisburg: Christian Publications, 1943.

Warfield, Benjamin B. *Perfectionism.* Philadelphia: Presbyterian & Reformed Publishing Co., 1971.

Wells, David F., and John D. Woodbridge, eds. *The Evangelicals: What They Believe, Who They Are, Where They Are Changing.* Grand Rapids, MI: Baker, 1975.

Weber, Timothy P. *Living in the Shadow of the Second Coming:*

American Premillennialism 1875-1982. Grand Rapids, MI: Zondervan, 1983.

Articles by Other Authors

Anonymous. "A Presbyterian Minister Baptized." *The Canadian Baptist.* 24 Nov 1881.

Anonymous. "According to the Papers." *Simpson's Scrapbook* Comp. C. Donald McKaig. Canadian Bible College/Canadian Theological Seminary Archibald Library archives, n.d.

Beere, Emma F. "Recollections of a Secretary," and "Simpson Anecdote." *Simpson's Scrapbook.* Comp. C. Donald McKaig. Canadian Bible College/Canadian Theological Seminary Archibald Library archives, n.d.

Brennen, Katherine Alberta. "Mrs. A. B. Simpson, the Wife: Or, Love Stands." N.c.: n.p., n.d.

Buckman, Margaret May. "My Father." *Simpson's Scrapbook.* Comp. C. Donald McKaig. Canadian Bible College/Canadian Theological Seminary Archibald Library archives, n.d.

Dayton, Donald W. "Asa Mahan and the Development of American Holiness Theology." *Wesleyan Theological Journal* 9 (Spring, 1974): 60-69.

—. "The Doctrine of the Baptism of the Holy Spirit: Its Emergence and Significance." *Wesleyan Theological Journal* 13 (Spring, 1978): 114-126.

Gordon, A. J. "The Holy Spirit." *The Word, the Work and the World* (Apr 1885).

Hamilton, James E. "Nineteenth Century Holiness Theology: A Study of the Thought of Asa Mahan." *Wesleyan Theological Journal* 13 (Spring, 1978): 51-64.

Jaffray, Robert A. " 'Speaking in Tongues'—Some Words of Kindly Counsel." *The Christian and Missionary Alliance Weekly* (13 Mar 1909).

Johnson, James E. "Charles G. Finney and Oberlin Perfectionism." *Journal of Presbyterian History* 46 (Mar 1968): 42-57 and 46 (Jun 1968): 128-138.

Lowrey, Asbury. "Is the Baptism of the Holy Ghost a Third Blessing?" *Divine Life (Sep 1879) 47.*

MacKenzie, Kenneth. "My Memories of Dr. Simpson." *The Alliance Weekly* (7 Aug 1937).

Menzies, William. "The Non-Wesleyan Origins of the Pentecostal Movement." *Aspects of Pentecostal-Charismatic Origins.* Ed. Vinson Synan. Plainfield, NJ: Logos International, 1975. 87-96.

Noel, Mark A. "The Great Awakenings." *Evangelical Dictionary of Theology.* Ed. Walter A. Elwell. Grand Rapids, MI: Baker, 1984.

Russell, C. Allyn. "A. J. Gordon: 19th Century Fundamentalist." *American Baptist Quarterly* 4 (Mar 1985): 61-89.

Shelley, Bruce. "Sources of Pietistic Fundamentalism." *Fides et Historia* 5 (Fall/Spring, 1972): 68-78.

Smalley, William F. "The Christian and Missionary Alliance." *Twentieth Century Encyclopedia of Religious Knowledge: An Extension of the New Schaff-Herzog Encyclopedia of Religious*

Knowledge. Vol. 2. Gen. ed. Lefferts A. Loetscher. Grand Rapids, MI: Baker, 1955.

Smith, Timothy L. "The Doctrine of the Sanctifying Christ: Charles G. Finney's Synthesis of Wesleyan and Covenant Theology." *Wesleyan Journal of Theology* 13 (Spring, 1978): 92-113.

Stevens, W. C. "The Latter Rain." *Living Truths* (Sep 1907).

Stoesz, Samuel J. "The Doctrine of Sanctification and The Christian and Missionary Alliance." A paper presented at the staff retreat of Canadian Bible College/Canadian Theological Seminary, August, 1980.

Wacker, Grant. "The Holy Spirit and the Spirit of the Age in American Protestantism: 1880-1910." *Journal of American History* 72 (Jun 1985): 45-62.

Dissertations and Master's Theses

Brown, Raymond. "Evangelical Ideas of Perfection: A Comparative Study of the Spirituality of Men and Movements in Nineteenth Century England." Diss. U of Cambridge, 1964.

Cartmel, Daryl. "The Missionary Policy and Program of A. B. Simpson." Thesis. Kennedy School of World Mission, Hartford Seminary Foundation, 1962.

Lee, Mark W. "The Biblical View of the Doctrine of the Holy Spirit in the Writings of A. B. Simpson." Thesis. Wheaton Col., 1952.

McGraw, Gerald E. "The Doctrine of Sanctification in the Published Writings of Albert Benjamin Simpson." Diss. New York U, 1986.

Schenk, Ray W., Jr. "A Study of the New Testament Basis for the Teaching of Dr. Albert B. Simpson on Divine Healing." Thesis. Wheaton Col., 1968.

Waldvogel-Blumhoefer, Edith L. "The Overcoming Life: A Study in the Reformed Evangelical Contribution to Pentecostalism." Diss. Harvard U, 1977.

Weideman, Donald C. "An Evaluation of A. B. Simpson's Idea of Sanctification from the Biblical Perspective." Thesis. Wheaton Col., 1966.

Wheelock, Donald R. "Spirit Baptism in American Pentecostal Thought." Diss. Emory U, 1983.

Wilson, Ernest Gerald. "The Christian and Missionary Alliance: Developments and Modifications of Its Original Objectives." Diss. New York U, 1984.

Appendix 1

A List of Books by A. B. Simpson

This bibliography follows the detailed catalog prepared by John S. Sawin (Nov 1984). At the time, Sawin was archivist for the International Headquarters of The Christian and Missionary Alliance. His work is used by permission.

Unless otherwise noted, all Simpson titles—some of them issued posthumously—were originally published in New York by The Christian Alliance Publishing Company (1888-1928) or its early predecessor, The Word, Work and World Publishing Company (1882-1887). Titles still in print may be secured from

Christian Publications
3825 Hartzdale Drive
Camp Hill, Pennsylvania 17011

Inquire of Christian Publications for information and prices. See Appendix 12 for a listing of those books by and about Simpson that are currently in print.

All in All: Or, Christ in Colossians. 1901.
The Apostolic Church: Or, First Corinthians. 1898.
Back to Patmos: Or, Prophetic Outlook on Present Conditions. 1914.
The Berachah Yearbook for 1886. 1885.
The Berachah Yearbook for 1887. 1886.
     (Promotional publications for Simpson's New York church.)
But God. 1899.
The Challenge of Missions. 1925.

The Christian Alliance Yearbook for 1888. 1887.

The Christian Alliance and the International Missionary Alliance Yearbook for 1893. 1892.

Christ in the Bible. Vol. 1 Genesis, Exodus. 1888.

Christ in the Bible. Vol. 2 Lev.-Deut. 1889.

Christ in the Bible. Vol. 3 Joshua. 1904.

Christ in the Bible. Vol. 4 Judges, Ruth. 1902.

(From *Danger Lines* and *Making Jesus King.*)

Christ in the Bible. Vol. 5 Sam., Kings, Chron. 1902.

(Part is from *Making Jesus King.*)

Christ in the Bible. Vol. 6 Kings and Prophets. 1903.

Christ in the Bible. Vol. 7 Isaiah. 1905.

Christ in the Bible. Vol. 8 Life of Christ. 1888.

Christ in the Bible. Vol. 9 Matt., Mark, Luke. 1889.

Christ in the Bible. Vol. 10 John, Acts. 1891.

Christ in the Bible. Vol. 11 Romans. 1894.

Christ in the Bible. Vol. 13 Matthew. 1904.

Christ in the Bible. Vol. 14 Mark. 1910.

Christ in the Bible. Vol. 14B Luke. 1905.

(Sermons; not a reprint of part of volume 9.)

Christ in the Bible. Vol. 15 John. 1904.

(A slightly edited reprint of the first part of volume 10.)

Christ in the Bible. Vol. 16 Acts. 1902.

(Sermons; *not* a reprint of part of volume 10.)

Christ in the Bible. Vol. 18 1 & 2 Corinthians. 1904.

(Part is from *The Apostolic Church.*)

Christ in the Bible. Vol. 19 Galatians, Ephesians. 1904.

(A reprint of *Free Grace* and *The Highest Christian Life.*)

Christ in the Bible. Vol. 20 Phil., Col., Thess. 1903.

A reprint of *The Sweetest Christian Life, All in All* and *The Epistles of the Advent.*)

Christ in the Bible. Vol. 21 Thess., Tim., Titus. 1920s.

(Material from volume 20 augmented by Simpson sermons.)

Christ in the Bible. Vol. 22 Hebrews. 1920s.

(A reprint of *Within the Veil.*)

Christ in the Bible. Vol. 22A James. 1920s.

    (A reprint of *Practical Christianity.*)

Christ in the Bible. Vol. 23 Peter, John, Jude. 1920s.

    (A reprint of *Words of Comfort* and *Messages of Love.*)

Christ in the Bible. Vol. 24 Revelation. 1905.

    (A reprint of *Heaven Opened.*)

Christ in the Tabernacle. 1888.

The Christ Life. London: Morgan & Scott. 1888.

    (Subsequent editions have added three more chapters.)

The Christ of the Forty Days. 1890.

A Cloud of Witnesses. 1887.

The Coming One. 1912.

The Cross of Christ. 1910.

Count Your Blessings. 1900.

    (A Bible prayer and promise for each day.)

Danger Lines in the Deeper Life. 1897.

Days of Heaven on Earth. 1897.

    (A daily devotional.)

The Discovery of Divine Healing. 1903.

    (Ten of the 13 chapters are from *Friday Meeting Talks, No. 3.*)

Divine Emblems in the Book of Genesis. 1888.

Divine Emblems in Exodus. 1888.

Earnests of the Coming Age. 1921.

Echoes of the New Creation: Or, Messages of the Cross, the Resurrection and the Coming Glory. 1903.

Elim: Its Wells and Palms. 1905

Epistles of the Advent: Or, Christ in Thessalonians. 1901.

Evangelistic Addresses. 1926.

The Fourfold Gospel. 1887.

    (Originally four chapters; two more were added later.)

Free Grace: Or, Christ in Galatians. 1901.

Friday Meeting Talks, No. 1. 1894.

Friday Meeting Talks, No. 2. 1899.

Friday Meeting Talks, No. 3. 1900.

    (Addresses Simpson gave at his Friday afternoon healing and consecration meetings.)

From the Uttermost to the Uttermost. 1914.

(The story of Josephus Pulis, an alcoholic turned saint.)

The Fullness of Jesus: Or, Christ Life in the New Testament. 1886.

The Gospel of Healing. 1886.

(Subsequent editions—during Simpson's life and after—have seen editorial changes. Probably Simpson's best-selling book.)

The Gospel of the Kingdom. 1887.

A Great Missionary Movement. 1892.

(Tracts regarding Alliance missionary work, and the Annual Report for 1891.)

Heart Messages for Sabbaths at Home. 1899.

(Four sermonettes for each month of the year, plus a 13th month covering the "Fourfold Gospel.")

The Heavenly Vision. 1896.

Heaven Opened: Or, Expositions of the Book of Revelation. 1899.

He Is Risen. 1887.

Henry Wilson: One of God's Best. 1908.

(Chapters 5-9 are by Simpson; the rest by Wilson's daughter, Madele.)

The Highest Christian Life: Or, Expositions of the Book to the Ephesians. 1898.

Holy Ghost Ministries. 1901.

(A reprint of seven chapters from *The King's Business*.)

The Holy Spirit: Or, Power from on High. 2 vols. 1895-1896.

In Heavenly Places. 1892.

Hymns of the Fourfold Gospel and the Fullness of Jesus. 1890.

(Words only; no music scores.)

In Heavenly Places. 1892.

Inquiries and Answers. 1886.

In the School of Christ: Or, Lessons from New Testament Characters. 1889.

In the School of Faith. 1907.

(Part is a reprint of *Seven Stars*.)

Is Life Worth Living? 1899.

Jesus in the Psalms. 1892.

The King's Business. 1886.

The Land of Promise: Or, Our Full Inheritance in Christ. 1888.
A Larger Christian Life. 1890.
Larger Outlooks on Missionary Lands. 1893.
    (Diary of Simpson's 1893 around-the-world trip.)
Life More Abundantly. 1912.
    (Devotional readings for 31 days.)
The Life of Prayer. 1890.
The Lord for the Body. 1925.
    (A reprint from *Discovery of Divine Healing* and *Inquiries and Answers.*)
The Love-Life of the Lord. 1890.
    (Sermons from the Song of Songs.)
Making Jesus King. 1897.
Memorial Names. 1890.
Messages of Love. 1900.
    (Expositions of First John.)
Michele Nardi, the Italian Evangelist. 1916.
Millennial Chimes. 1894.
    (A collection of 62 Simpson poems.)
Missionary Messages. 1925.
The Names of Jesus. 1891.
Natural Emblems of Spiritual Life. 1887.
The Old Faith and the New Gospels. 1911.
Paul: The Ideal Man and Model Missionary. 1896.
Practical Christianity 1901.
    (Expositions of James.)
Present Truth. 1897.
Providence and Missions. 1898.
Salvation Sermons. 1925.
The Self-Life and Christ Life. 1897.
Service for the King. 1900.
    (Seven sermons from *The King's Business.*)
Seven Stars in the Firmament of Faith. 1890.
    (Seven chapters from *In the School of Faith.* No copy of this book has been found.)

The Songs of the Spirit. 1920.

(One hundred sixteen of Simpson's poems published posthumously.)

Standing on Faith: Or, Talks on the Self-Life. London: Marshall, Morgan & Scott, 1932.

(Simpson sermons from six previously published books, selected by the publisher.)

The Story of The Christian and Missionary Alliance. 1900.

(A promotional publication.)

The Sweetest Christian Life. 1899.

(Expositions of Philippians.)

Walking in Love. 1892.

Walking in the Spirit. 1889.

We Would See Jesus. 1910.

(Devotional readings for 31 days.)

When the Comforter Came. 1911.

(Devotional readings for 31 days.)

Wholly Sanctified. 1890.

Within the Veil. 1900.

(Expositions of Hebrews.)

Words of Comfort for Tried Workers. 1901.

(Expositions of First Peter.)

Appendix 2

The Conference for Prayer and Counsel Respecting Uniformity in the Testimony and Teaching of the Alliance, May 25-28, 1906

[This transcript of the original document is in the archives of the Archibald Foundation Library, Canadian Bible College/Canadian Theological Seminary, Regina, Saskatchewan. Section II is also quoted in chapter 3. In chapter 3 we used this document as an interpretive guide to Simpson's writings. The italics are in the original transcript.]

Conference for Prayer and Counsel Respecting Uniformity in the Testimony and Teaching of the Alliance

The Committee appointed by the Board to prepare a plan for conference on the matters above stated, recommend that such conference be held immediately before the annual Council at Nyack [New York] in the beginning of June and that as many as possible of our Alliance workers throughout the country be invited and urged to attend.

The importance of unity upon a common basis of testimony and teaching is becoming more and more urgent, and the need of prayer for the great objects which we hold in common is emphasized at this time as never before. In connection with this conference the following plan is suggested:

1. That it shall be held for at least three days, and that at least one hour of each session shall be given to prayer and the rest of the time to conference respecting our Alliance testimony and teaching.

2. That the various subjects covered by this report be introduced by a short paper not exceeding fifteen minutes and followed by five- or ten-minute addresses by the members of the conference.

3. That a Committee be appointed by the conference for the purpose of carefully following the various discussions and drawing up a brief paper to be submitted to a subsequent meeting and adopted as the sense of the conference upon the matter in question.

4. That specific subjects be taken up at the various meetings of the Council for prayer and made the subject of earnest, united, believing intercession.

5. The following outline of subjects to be discussed is respectfully submitted as a basis for the deliberations of the proposed conference:

I. Open Questions

That the conference recognize certain matters of teaching and testimony as not within the direct province of the Alliance, but open questions about which our brethren agree to differ and hold in mutual charity their individual convictions according to their various denominational connections and previous teachings. These questions include:

1. Church government
2. The subjects and mode of baptism
3. The doctrines known as Calvinism and Arminianism
4. Various ceremonies and practices such as feet washing, etc.

II. Our Distinctive Testimony

1. Christ, our Savior, always assuming that we stand unequivocally upon the Deity of Christ, His vicarious sacrifice and the necessity of regeneration through the power of the Holy Spirit

2. Christ, our Sanctifier, assuming the following essential points:

   a. a definite second blessing, *distinct in nature,* though not necessarily far removed in time, from the experience of conversion

   b. the baptism of the Holy Ghost as *a distinct experience,* not merely for power for service, but for personal holiness and victory over the world and sin

   c. the indwelling of Christ in the heart of the consecrated believer *as a distinct experience*

   d. sanctification by faith *as a distinct gift* of God's grace to every open and surrendered soul

   e. growth in grace and the deeper filling of the Holy Spirit *as distinct from* and the result of the definite experience of sanctification

It is understood that all our Alliance officers and teachers are at liberty to present the truth of sanctification in such phases and phrases as [their] own convictions warrant, in general accordance with the above specifications, but with the understanding that such extreme views as are sometimes taught under the name of "eradication" or "suppression" shall not be presented in an aggressive or controversial spirit toward those who differ.

III. Divine Healing

It is understood the Alliance holds and teaches:

1. The will of God to heal bodies of those who trust and obey Him by His own direct power without means

2. The atonement of Christ for the body

3. The life of the risen Christ for our mortal frame received by faith

4. The ordinance of anointing and laying on of hands with proper recognition of the necessity of faith on the part of the individual anointed

5. Power over evil spirits through the name of Jesus

6. The disclaiming of all merit or individual power on the part of the worker, and the constant recognition of the name of Jesus as the source of all supernatural power

IV. The Lord's Coming

1. The Alliance holds and teaches the personal and premillennial coming of the Lord Jesus

2. [blotted out—unreadable]

3. Liberty is accorded to our teachers in connection with the various opinions held about Antichrist, the Tribulation, the Last Week of Daniel, Rapture, etc., but with the understanding that any spirit of antagonism and strife toward those who may hold different opinions is discountenanced

Committee: Henry Wilson, J. D. Williams, A. E. Funk, F. H. Senft, A. B. Simpson

An Extended Quotation
from Walter Marshall's
The Gospel Mystery of Sanctification

[The quotation that follows may be found in the most recent reprint of Marshall's work (Welwyn: Evangelical Press, 1981) 40-42. A. B. Simpson cites this quote in *The Cross of Christ* (New York: Christian Alliance Publishing Co., 1912) 90-93. He prefaces Marshall's comment by stating: "The resurrection of Jesus Christ is the efficient cause of our sanctification. I cannot better express this great truth than by quoting the following paragraphs from an old and little known volume that is worthy of permanent and wide circulation, Marshall's *Gospel Mystery of Sanctification*." Marshall's influence on Simpson is noted in chapter 4, "Sanctification and the New Covenant of Jeremiah 31 and Ezekiel 36."]

The end of Christ's incarnation, death and resurrection was to prepare and form a holy nature and frame for us in Himself. [This new nature was] to be communicated to us by union and fellowship with Him; [He did not intend] to enable us to produce in ourselves the first original of such a holy nature by our own endeavors.

1. By His incarnation there was a man created in a new holy frame after the holiness of the first Adam's frame had been marred and abolished for the first transgression; and this new frame was far more excellent than even the first Adam's was, because man was really joined to God by a close, inseparable union of the divine and human nature in one person—Christ; so that these natures had

communion each with the other in their actings, and Christ was able to act in His human nature by power proper to the divine nature, wherein He was one God with the Father.

Why was it that Christ set up the fallen nature of man in such a wonderful nature of holiness in bringing it to live and act by communion with God living and acting in it? One great end was, that He might communicate this excellent frame to His seed that should by His Spirit be born of Him and be in Him as the last Adam the quickening Spirit; that as we have borne the image of the earthly so we might bear the image of the heavenly (I Cor. 15:45, 49), in holiness here and in glory hereafter. Thus He was born Emmanuel, God with us; because the fullness of the Godhead with all holiness did first dwell in Him bodily, even in His human nature, that we might be filled with that fullness in Him (Matt. 1:23; Col. 2:9, 10). Thus He came down from heaven as living bread, that, as He liveth by the Father, so those that eat Him may live by Him (John 6:51, 57), by the same life of God in them which was first in Him.

2. By His death He freed Himself from the guilt of our sins imputed to Him, and from all that innocent weakness of human nature which He had borne for a time for our sakes. And, by freeing Himself, He prepared a freedom for us from our whole nature condition; which is both weak as He was, and also polluted with our guilt and sinful corruption. Thus the corrupt nature state which is called in Scripture the "old man," was crucified together with Christ, that the body of sin might be destroyed. And it is destroyed in us, not by any wounds which we ourselves can give it, but by our partaking of that freedom from it, and death unto it, that is already wrought out for us by the death of Christ; as is signified by our baptism, wherein we are buried in Christ, by the application of His death to us (Rom. 6:2, 3, 4, 10, 11).

"God sending His own Son in the likeness of sinful flesh, and for sin" (or, "by a sacrifice for sin," as in the margin) "condemned sin in the flesh; that the righteousness of the law might be fulfilled in us, who walk not after the flesh, but after the Spirit" (Rom. 8:3, 4).

Let these Scriptures be well observed, and they will sufficiently evidence that Christ died, not that we might be able to form a holy nature in ourselves, but that we might receive one ready prepared and formed in Christ for us, by union and fellowship with Him.

3. By His resurrection He took possession of spiritual life for us, as now fully procured for us, and made to be our right and property by merit of His death, and therefore we are said to be quickened together with Christ. His resurrection was our resurrection to the life of holiness, as Adam's fall was our fall into spiritual death. And we are not ourselves the makers and formers of our new holy nature, any more than of our original corruption, but both are formed ready for us to partake of them. And by union with Christ, we partake of that spiritual life that He took possession of for us at His resurrection, and thereby we are enabled to bring forth the fruits of it; as the Scripture showeth by the similitude of a marriage union, Romans 7:4: "We are married in Him that is raised from the dead, that we might bring forth fruit unto God."

Appendix 4

Simpson's Contrasts of Conversion and Sanctification

[The chart that follows is taken from Gerald E. McGraw, "The Doctrine of Sanctification in the Published Writings of Albert Benjamin Simpson" (diss., New York U, 1952) 461. In this chart McGraw presents his interpretation of how he saw Simpson's contrasts of these two doctrines. There is reference to this chart in chapter 4, "Sanctification and the New Covenant of Jeremiah 31 and Ezekiel 36."]

Justification/Regeneration	Sanctification
[God] counts us righteous	[God] makes us righteous
Pardon of sin	Power of sin [broken]
Imputed righteousness	[Imparted] righteousness
Peace *with* God	The peace *of* God
Birth of the soul	Baptism [with the Holy Spirit]
Birth of the new life	Separation between this new life and the old sinful self

Brings life	Brings victorious life
Regenerated by the Spirit	Received Him in His fullness
Raised from the dead [spiritually]	Married unto [Christ to] bring forth fruit unto God
Germ of the seed	Summer fullness
Holy Spirit creates [the sinner] anew	[The Spirit] enters our inmost being
New heart in [the believer] while the old nature still remains	Dominion over sin and self by the indwelling life of Jesus
New heart and new spirit	[Jesus'] Spirit within
Robe of righteousness [clean robe]	Beauty of holiness [marriage robe]
In [Christ]	[Christ] in [the believer]

Appendix 5

Steps to and in the Blessed Life

An Outline of
Biblical Teachings
After the
KESWICK PLAN

The Keswick plan is Definite, Complete, Progressive.

It has a definite Beginning, Course, and Culmination.

Six successive Steps are indicated, all of which are deemed important.

The Basis of all, is the Conviction that "*the average Christian Life is too often grievously destitute of real Spiritual Power, and is Essentially Carnal; and that it is the duty and privilege of every Child of God to enter at once into 'Newness of Life,' and walk henceforth in the power of Christ's Resurrection.*"—Phil. iii. 10.

The First Step.—Instant abandonment of Sin, and of every weight which prevents or hinders Holy Living.—Eph. iv. 22-24. Rom. vi. 11-13. Heb. xii. 1, 2.

The Second Step.—A deadly blow is aimed at SELF in its seven prominent forms— 2 Cor. v. 14, 15.

1. Self Trust.—Rom. x. 1, 2.
2. Self Help.—John xv. 4-6.
3. Self Will.—James iv. 13, 15.

4. Self Seeking.—Matt. xvi. 24, 25.
5. Self Pleasing.—Gal. vi. 14.
6. Self Defense.—1 Pet. ii. 19-23; iii. 16.
7. Self Glory.—Gal. vi. 14.

Crucified with Christ. I crucify the Pleasures of Ambition, Avarice, Covetousness, Appetite, Amusements.—Eph. v. 11.

We are dead to Ambition save as we desire "to be found in Him."

Dead to Avarice, save as we "covet earnestly the best gifts."

Dead to Appetite, save as we "hunger and thirst after righteousness."

Dead to the amusing and alluring Pleasures of the World—the Theater, the Dance, the Card Table, the Opera, the Wine Cup.

A new practical center around which the life may revolve, is found—

HIS LIFE.

I will seek in everything to please my Master, as the Lord and Sovereign of my Life.

I will seek in everything to please my neighbor, for his good, unto edification.

The Third Step.—The Absolute Surrender of the *Will* to God in *Obedience.*—Rom. x. 9. 1 Cor. xii. 3.

"No man can serve two masters."

The Fourth Step.—The Infilling of the Spirit, claimed by Faith apart from feeling.—Rom. iv. 21.

(a) The Infilling of the Spirit as Sealing.—Eph. i. 13, 14.
(b) The Infilling of the Spirit for Power.—Acts i. 8.
(c) The Infilling of the Spirit for Teaching and Holy Serving. Col. iii. 16. 1 John ii. 27.

The Fifth Step.—The Revelation of Jesus Christ as an Indwelling Presence.—Matt. xxviii. 20. John xiv. 17, 23. Gal i. 6. Heb. xi. 17.

The Sixth Step.—The *Privileges* and *Victories* of this Higher and Deeper Life.

    (a) The Rest of Faith.—Rom. v. 1, 2. Heb. iii. 7 to iv. 11.
    (b) Power over Sin.—1 Cor. xv. 56, 57. Rom vi. 4; viii. 2.
    (c) Passion for Souls.—Rom. ix. 1, 2.
    (d) Conscious Fellowship with God.—1 John 1-3.
    (e) Growing Possessions of the Promises.—2 Pet. i. 4.
    (f) Prevailing Prayer—John xv. 7. Jas. v. 16, 18. 1 John v. 14, 15.

"Having therefore these promises, dearly beloved, let us cleanse ourselves from all filthiness of the flesh and spirit, Perfecting Holiness in the fear of the Lord."—2 Cor. vii. 1.

"Wherefore come out from among them and be ye separate, saith the Lord, and touch not the unclean thing, and I will receive you, and will be a Father unto you; and ye shall be my sons and daughters, saith the Lord Almighty."—2 Cor. vi. 17, 18.

Appendix 6

The Baptism of the Holy Spirit, a Crisis or an Evolution
A. B. Simpson

Is the baptism of the Holy Spirit a distinct blessing or is it simply a deeper development of the experience of conversion? Is the indwelling of Christ in the believer's heart a definite promise to the consecrated believer, or is it received at regeneration and simply revealed and manifested as a later stage of progressive Christian experience? This is a question of much practical importance and divides the teachers of deeper spiritual truth into two important classes.

I. The Arguments for the Progressive Theory

Those who believe in what we shall call in this paper the progressive theory, hold that the Holy Spirit is given at conversion to every believer, and there is no subsequent receiving of the Spirit, although there are many successive stages in the revelation of Christ to the soul, and the realization of the Spirit's fullness.

1. A favorite passage and the strongest argument which they present is Romans viii. 9-10: "But ye are not in the flesh, but in the Spirit, if so be that the Spirit of God dwell in you. Now if any man have not the Spirit of Christ, he is none of His. And if Christ be in you, the body is dead because of sin; but the Spirit is life because of righteousness." At the first glance, this seems to be a very convincing argument, but it will bear much investigation.

In the first place, it is possible for a truly converted soul to be in the flesh and not in the Spirit. Writing to the Corinthians, the Apostle Paul distinctly says, "I, brethren, could not speak unto you as unto spiritual, but as unto carnal, even as unto babes in Christ. For ye are yet carnal, for whereas there is among you envying and strife and divisions, are ye not carnal and walk as men?" No one will deny that these were Christians. They were brethren. They were "babes in Christ," and yet they were carnal. They were in the flesh. They were not pleasing God. They were not subject to the law of God, but they were the children of God. Therefore the apostle in Romans viii. 9 is speaking not of all Christians, but of those Christians who are no longer in the flesh, but have received the Spirit of God and have become spiritual simply through the Holy Spirit.

In the next place the words, "If any man have not the Spirit of Christ, he is none of His," does not mean necessarily that such an one is not a Christian, but rather that he has not yet surrendered to Christ in such a sense that he belongs to Him. Christ may be ours and yet we not fully His. This is the great difference between the two classes of Christians that we find everywhere to-day. The one class has surrendered to Christ and belongs to Him. The other has not yet recognized the divine Ownership and given up the self-life. "Christ is mine," is one thing. "I am Christ's" is another. In the Song of Solomon the bride begins by saying, "My Beloved is mine," but ends by the deeper confession, "I am my Beloved's." It is when we reach this deeper experience, and can truly say, "I am the Lord's," that the glorious words, I. Corinthians iii. 22, 23: "All things are yours and ye are Christ's and Christ is God's." All things are not ours till we are all the Lord's. Therefore in Romans xii. 1 the apostle appeals to those who have already experienced the mercies of God and are brethren, "I beseech you, brethren, by the mercies of God, that ye present your bodies a living sacrifice, holy, acceptable unto God, which is your reasonable service." The passage therefore in Romans viii. 9, 10, does not necessarily prove that if we have not yet received the Holy Ghost, we are not Christians or saved persons, but rather that we are yet carnal and belong partly to ourselves. The same is true of the 10th and 11th verses: "If Christ be in you, the body is dead because of sin, but the Spirit is life because of righteousness. But if the Spirit of Him that raised up Jesus from the dead dwell in you, He that raised up Christ from the dead shall also quicken your mortal bodies by His Spirit that dwelleth in you." This really describes a very balanced Christian experience, an experience in which the Holy Spirit so dwells in us and Christ is so embodied in us that we are able to receive His quickening life in our bodies. Our physical life is practically the temple and the home of the Holy Ghost, and as such He cares for it, keeps it and heals it. To say this is the experience of every Christian would be taking a good deal for granted.

2. Another argument for the indwelling of Christ in all believers is II. Corinthians xiii. 5: "Know ye not your own selves how that Jesus Christ is in you, except ye be reprobates?" The hasty inference of a superficial reader would be that if we do not have the indwelling of Christ in our hearts we are doomed and damned. Now this is all due to an erroneous reading of the passage. On reference to Rotherham's version or the admirable notes of Conybeare and Howson on this passage, an intelligent reader will observe that the word "reprobate" is translated disapproved. The apostle has just been speaking of a test that he proposes to have whether the Corinthians are walking in the complete will of God or not, and this is to be made evident either by his being disapproved or they being disapproved when the test comes. Indeed, he says he will be glad to be disapproved that they may be approved in that test because this will be to him the best evidence that they are right with God. "We are glad," he adds, "when we are weak and ye are strong; we wish also your perfection." The same word is used in the apostle's fine figure in I. Corinthians ix. 27, to the rewards of the Father. The word is translated "castaway," in our old English version, but every Bible student knows that this is entirely wrong. Literally it is "disapproved." The reference is to the race and the apostle's fear lest having preached the Gospel to others, when the prizes are distributed at the end of the race, he should miss his crown and be disapproved by the judge. He has no idea of being lost at all, but

simply losing the great reward of the victor. Therefore here in the passage first quoted he simply means that if Christ is not in them, they are disapproved; they are not living up to the high standard of Christian life which they should. They are coming short of their privilege and duty. Surely, no one will deny this. But this is a very different matter from being an unsaved man or woman. On the contrary, there is the strongest implication that they are saved, but coming short of Christian privileges and duties.

3. The next argument of our friends, the evolutionists, is founded upon the promise of the Apostle Peter on the day of Pentecost, "Repent and be baptized every one of you in the name of Jesus Christ for the remission of sins, and ye shall receive the gift of the Holy Ghost. For the promise is unto you and to your children and to all that are afar off, even as many as the Lord our God shall call." Now, we do not for a moment question that the promise of the Holy Spirit is for every sinner, for all the promises are offered freely through His grace to any that will accept the Saviour, but that does not mean that they are all received at the same moment. When you enter a house, you enter the several rooms in order, and you must pass from chamber to chamber. It is so in the experiences of the deeper Christian life. You come into the vestibule and then you pass on to all the apartments until at last you reach the observatory at the top, but you don't get there the first step. Peter was simply announcing the fullness of our great salvation and telling them all that God had for them, and yet there was much still reserved for them even after their conversion. We are willing, however, to concede that the baptism of the Holy Ghost may be received at the very same time a soul is converted. We have known a sinner to be converted, sanctified and saved all within a single hour, and yet each experience was different in its nature and was received in proper order and by a definite faith for that particular blessing. What we contend for is that the baptism of the Holy Spirit is a distinct experience, and must be received by a definite faith, and this involves the crisis: a full surrender and an explicit preparation of the promise of God by faith.

4. Another proof text quoted by our friends is Acts v.32: "The Holy Spirit whom God hath given to all them that obey Him."

Therefore if we are obedient Christians we must have the Holy Spirit. But this is just what we are contending for: that multitudes of Christians are not obedient Christians. They have not surrendered to the will of God. They have not given up the world and sin. They have not presented their bodies a living sacrifice and therefore they do not enjoy the indwelling of the Holy Spirit, because they do not obey Him.

5. A very strong text used by our friends is I. Corinthians iii. 16: "Know ye not that we are the temple of God and that the Spirit of God dwelleth in you? If any man defile the temple of God, him shall God destroy, for the temple of God is holy, which temple ye are." This passage, it is said was addressed to carnal Christians, even to "babes in Christ," and therefore all such Christians must be the temples of God and have the Holy Spirit. In answer to this it is enough to say that there were evidently two classes of Christians in the church at Corinth, and that the apostle alternately addresses these two classes. Speaking to the one class he says, "In everything ye are enriched so that ye come not behind in any gift, waiting for the coming of our Lord Jesus Christ.

And yet, in the next breath he says, "There is evil among you. Ye do wrong and defraud, and that your brethren. Ye are carnal and walk as men." Paul expected them to apply the shoe where it would fit. Substantially he says this in I. Corinthians x. 15: "I speak as to wise men. Judge ye what I say." Some of them were the temples of God. Others were too unholy to be the temples of God. The passage, II. Corinthians vi. 16-18, where he says, "What agreement hath the temple of God with idols? For ye are the temple of the living God; as God hath said I will dwell in them and walk in them, and I will be their God and they shall be My people. . . . Wherefore come out from among them and be ye separate, saith the Lord, and touch not the unclean thing, and I will receive you. And I will be a Father unto you, and ye shall be My sons and daughters, saith the Lord Almighty." Here most plainly the condition of separation is insisted upon before God will come in and dwell in them and walk in them and receive them. Putting these two Scriptures together the argument of our brethren falls to pieces, and the necessity of a very thorough spiritual preparation for the indwelling of Christ is made plain.

6. In the twelfth chapter of I. Corinthians verse 7, it is said, "The manifestation of the Spirit is given to every man to profit withal," and verse 13, "For by one Spirit are we all baptized into one body, whether we be Jews or Gentiles." In these two passages the apostle is speaking of two distinct things. In verse 13 it is our union with Christ as His body that is referred to. Now, there is no doubt that every believer the moment he accepts Christ is united to the body of Christ. The word "by" should be "in" here. Are we all baptized into one body? That is a very different thing from the individual reception of the Holy Ghost. The apostle refers to this in the next clause, "We have all been made to drink into one Spirit." Some one has finely illustrated this by the figure of the bottle in the sea, and the sea in the bottle. It is possible for the bottle to be in the sea and the sea not be in the bottle. It is possible for us to be in the Spirit and in Christ by the faith that saves and yet not have the Spirit of Christ in us by the faith that sanctifies. The seventh verse, however, has special reference to the supernatural gifts of the Spirit in healing, teaching, speaking with tongues, etc. "These," he says, "are given to every man to profit withal." He means that every Christian may have the enduement of power without respect of persons in the measure in which he will profit thereby and use this great gift to the best account. But this very word "profit" implies certain conditions. The gift is for those that will make good use of it. It is, therefore, implied that before receiving it there shall be evidences of very deep sincerity and consecration, and every readiness to use it according to the will and for the glory of God. Even the apostles were required to tarry until they be endued with power from on high. This was not a gift that could be lightly assumed, but a profound experience calling for the most earnest and protracted preparation.

But time and space will not permit us to prosecute farther this side of the argument. Let us turn now to some proofs of the other view: namely, that the indwelling of Christ and the Baptism of the Holy Spirit constitute a definite experience and a second blessing and involve a very real crisis in our spiritual life.

1. The strongest proof we know is derived from the experience

of the Master Himself, our glorious Forerunner. He was born of the Spirit, as we read in Luke i. 35: "The Holy Ghost shall come upon thee, and the power of the Highest shall overshadow thee: therefore also that holy thing which shall be born of thee shall be called the Son of God." But he was not baptized with the Spirit until His thirtieth year. Then when He made a complete surrender of His life to the Father and assumed the cross and the work of redemption in His baptism at the hands of John, the heavens were opened and the Holy Ghost ascended upon Him and abode. From that time there was a new personality added to the Son of man, and all His words and works were spoken and performed in dependence upon the power of the Holy Ghost.

Now, our Lord was our Forerunner. "As He is so are we also in this world." Like Him we are born of the Spirit and like Him we too must be baptized with the Spirit. There comes a time when a new personality is added to ours and we go forth to life's conflicts and duties no longer alone, but in union with Him who has come to be our very life and all-sufficiency. It is the same as the bride who has hitherto walked alone through life, but there comes a day when another life is united to hers, and two go forth to life's toils and trials, and yet not two, but one, and henceforth he is her strength, he is her support, he is her guide, and she goes forth leaning upon her beloved. That is exactly what comes to pass when we receive the Holy Ghost and the Lord to dwell within.

2. The experience of the disciples before and after Pentecost is equally clear and convincing on this point. Up to that time, they were undoubtedly saved men and women, but after Pentecost there came to them an entirely new experience involving not only power for service, but power for holiness and righteousness in their own lives. The men were as changed as their ministry. "With great power gave the apostles witness to the resurrection of Jesus Christ and great grace was upon them all."

3. The promise of Christ to His disciples that the Comforter should come was accompanied with very clear conditions and definitions. Speaking of Him, He says, "He dwelleth with you and shall be in you:" (John xiv. 17). He identifies the coming of the

Comforter with His own indwelling. "At that day, ye shall know that I am in the Father and ye in Me and I in you." And yet His coming to abide is connected with a Spirit of devotion and obedience. "If a man love Me," He says; "he will keep My words and My Father will love him and We will come unto him and make our abode with him" (John xiv. 23). He had already said, John xiv. 21: "He that hath My commandments and keepeth them, he it is that loveth Me: and he that loveth Me shall be loved of My Father, and I will love him and will manifest Myself to him." Christ's indwelling is here connected with a spirit of love and obedience. Who will say that the men and women that are loving and living for the world and trying to have barely enough religion to save them from the flames of hell, are fit subjects for such an experience? Is it not a degration of such a glorious promise to make such an application of it?

4. The promise of Ezekiel respecting the coming of the Holy Ghost clearly distinguishes it from conversion. First we have the promise of conversion (Ezek. xxxvi. 25, 26): "Then will I sprinkle clean water upon you and ye shall be clean: from all your filthiness and from all your idols will I cleanse you. A new heart also will I give you and a new spirit will I put within you: and I will take the stony heart out of your flesh and I will give you an heart of flesh." All this very clearly refers to the forgiveness of sins, justification by faith and regeneration by the power of the Holy Spirit. This is the new heart received in conversion. But now there comes another promise transcendently greater and not to be confused with all this: "And I will put My Spirit within you and cause you to walk in My statutes, and ye shall keep My judgments and do them." This is the baptism of the Holy Ghost. This is not our Spirit, but His Spirit. We have received our new spirit, but now in this His Spirit comes to dwell, the divine and infinite Spirit of God. The effect of this is to cause us to walk in His statues and to keep His judgments and do them. It does not say to encourage us, to instruct us, but to "cause" us. Therefore if this is not its effect, the Holy Ghost somehow has failed. How is it therefore if all Christians have received the Holy Ghost to dwell in them that the Holy Ghost has

not caused them to be obedient? He does not say He will try to cause them, but He will cause them, and this is the great first cause, and above all, our second cause. Would we not naturally conclude that the people that are not walking in His statutes and keeping His judgments and doing them, have not received this causing power?

5. The types which we find in ancient Israel foreshadow this deeper life and second blessing. When Israel went out of Egypt, they typified our conversion, but when they entered the land of promise and crossed the Jordan, they set forth our coming in the "rest which remaineth for the people of God." There was surely a very great difference between these two experiences, and it was marked in the most significant manner and a great heap of stones set up so that there never could be any mistake about it in the minds of their children. Even in the earlier chapters of their wilderness life, we have a fine illustration of this deeper life. The Holy Spirit was set forth by the pillar of cloud and fire that went before them. This was their experience during the first year after leaving Egypt, but on the first day of the second year, something very different came to pass. The tabernacle was finished and dedicated and solemnly handed over to God, and then that mystic cloud came down and no longer led them from the sky or the mount, but took up its abode in the very bosom of the tabernacle as the Shekinah Presence of God, the Holy of Holies, and henceforth we read that God spoke to them, not from the mount, but from between the cherubim. This is exactly what comes to pass when we receive the Holy Ghost. God moves down into our heart and henceforth the throne of grace is not yonder in the skies, but within us, and

"Christ is never so distant from us
    As even to be near;
He dwells within our inmost being,
    And makes our heaven here."

The appeal of the Apostle Paul to the Galatians, Galatians iv.19: "My little children, of whom I travail in birth again until Christ be formed in you," makes it very plain that these were his little children who had been born through an earlier experience of soul travail on his part, and now he is travailing in birth for another blessing: that Christ may be formed in them. The logical force of the truth itself needs no emphasizing.

7. Space will only permit us to add one more argument, namely: that the experiences of the saints of God both in the Scriptures and in modern Christian life, involves this deeper blessing. Jacob came to his Peniel and through a divine transformation came forth no longer Jacob but Israel, a prince with God. Job dies to his self life, and came out with a new experience and blessing. Isaiah saw himself unclean and received the touch of fire that sanctified and sent him forth to his glorious service. Joshua, notwithstanding all the victories of the wilderness, had to meet the angel of the Lord and die to his own leadership before he could bring Israel into the land. Paul went through the struggle of the seventh chapter of Romans, and by a definite revelation of Christ came out of the eighth chapter of the Christ life filled with the Holy Ghost. It was after meeting with some Moravian saints who had found the "secret of the Lord," that John Wesley became changed and filled with the Holy Ghost, and set the world on fire. The same experience has been multiplied in scores and hundreds of saintly lives in these last days, and while no experience in itself, is a sufficient foundation for a Christian doctrine, yet backed by such an array of Scripture as we have endeavored to present, we see much more in it in these lives which are eloquent appeals to us today, saying, "I beseech you therefore by the mercies of God that ye present your bodies a living sacrifice, holy, acceptable unto God, which is your reasonable service." "Tarry ye till ye be endued with power from on high." "Abide in Me and I in you."

In conclusion, the truth that we have been endeavoring to demonstrate is intensely practical. So long as people think they have it all, there is little incentive to rouse themselves and claim their full inheritance, but when God's people see that like Israel of old, they are still toiling in the wilderness under His displeasure, that they are neglecting a great salvation, that they are out of fellowship with Christ and grieving the Holy Ghost, motive is supplied of overwhelming power and they are led to heart searching, humiliation and unceasing prayer, and a new impulse comes into their lives like a great tidal wave over the ocean of love, and an experience comes to the soul as much higher than conversion as conversion was better than the old life of flesh and sin.

This is the deepest need of the Church today. One such consecrated, Spirit-filled life means a score of souls for God. "Let us therefore fear lest the promise being left us of entering into His rest any of you should seem to come short of it."

"Oh, brother, give heed to the warning
    And obey His voice today;
The Spirit to thee is calling,
    Oh, do not grieve Him away.

"Oh, come in complete surrender,
    Turn back from thy doubt and sin;
Pass on from Kadesh to Canaan,
    And a crown and kingdom win."

Appendix 7

The Crisis of the Deeper Life

A. B. Simpson

This is the title of a new volume by Rev. George P. Pardington, Ph.D., Professor of Homiletics and Church History in the New York Missionary Institute, and published by the Alliance Press Company, New York. It is evidently intended for wide public circulation, for the price is so low, only twenty-five cents, that it is within the reach of those in the humblest circumstances. Within the compass of less than two hundred pages this little manual unfolds with rare simplicity, scripturalness and spiritual power, the very heart of the consecrated life.

The title is itself a message, most timely and suggestive, striking as it does at the most dangerous error of modern thought, the principle of evolution which has permeated, not only scientific and philosophical thought, but given form to very much of the current religious opinion regarding spiritual things. While Herbert Spencer labored to apply the doctrine of evolution to all the facts of nature and human life, the theologians have carried it to the higher realm of religion and tried to explain the Bible and the entire Christian life as well as the progress of Christianity in the world and the future destiny of the earth itself on the principle of natural development. The tendency of all this is to leave God out, to do away with the directly supernatural and to reduce Christianity practically to Rationalism.

According to these teachers, salvation itself is religious culture and the response of man's will and life to a natural germ of spiritual life which God has implanted in every human heart. "God is inside of every man," they tell us; "turn into the center of your being and there you will meet Him. Follow the higher nature, obey the voice that calls you to the best and you will grow better by the habit of obedience and gradually develop along the lines to which the heavenly voice is ever calling you." This is not regeneration but self-culture and makes man his own savior with, of course, a certain measure of help from the divine principle within him.

But even those who do concede a real new birth through the working of the Holy Spirit and a divine act of justification by faith through the atonement of the Lord Jesus Christ, fall back again upon the principle of evolution by explaining all the later experiences of Christian holiness as the gradual unfolding of the germ implanted in us at regeneration. As the acorn contains in itself all the parts of the noble oak, which is afterwards to rise from the germ when planted in the soil, as the egg contains in the little embryo the whole of the living bird that is afterwards to come forth from the shell through the process of incubation, so the new born Christian contains in his regenerated spirit everything that is yet to unfold, even unto the day when he shall stand before the throne "without spot or wrinkle or any such thing." All that is necessary, therefore, is to develop, to cultivate, to foster this new life and "grow in grace" until by a gradual process of spiritual development, we shall be conformed to the perfect likeness of Christ, our Pattern and our living Head.

Now all this leaves no place for a crisis after conversion. There may be marked uplifts, there may be a deeper and deeper realization of our privileges and rights in Christ, there may be more complete surrender and a more perfect recognition of our high calling, there may be a deeper filling with the Holy Spirit as we receive more light and yield more fully to it, but all this is but part of the process of spiritual development which was begun at conversion and which will go on until we reach perfection.

But in all this, our beloved brethren overlook the fact that nature is not the perfect symbol of the supernatural. The mighty transformation which grace brings to us is transcendently beyond any power in the natural world, or any image by which it may be unfolded. The very essence of the Christian life is that it is a Divine life, it is God in us and must be brought about by God Himself. All that has been said about regeneration and the growth of the new man is true, but there is another stupendous fact beyond this and that is, that besides the new heart and the new spirit that God gives us, He comes to dwell in it, to make it His temple and to add to all its new impulses and dispositions His own Divine nature and His own Almighty presence. The promise of Ezekiel is not only that He will give us a new heart and a new spirit but mightier than all He says, "I will put My Spirit within you and cause you to walk in My statutes and keep My commandments and do them." Into the new heart which Christ gives us He Himself comes to dwell and "the life which I now live in the flesh I live by the faith of the Son of God, who loved me and gave Himself for me." There are two distinct personalities in the sanctified life; the one is the new spirit of the believer, the other is the Holy Spirit of Jesus Christ, bringing the Master's presence and uniting us to Him in the fellowship of His life and power.

We are not without illustrations of this, even in nature itself. The power of steam which, until the advent of electricity, was the great force of our modern industrial life, is created by a distinct crisis in the boiler, in which this mighty force is generated. Up to a certain point the water is pure and clean, it is also warm, nay, hot. But there comes a point when a complete transformation takes place and that water ceases to be water and rises to a new element, that elastic vapor, steam, which moves the piston, drives the engine and carries our commerce over land and sea. That new power of steam is a fine emblem of that higher life into which we come when the regenerated spirit passes out of the human into the Divine, out of itself into God, and henceforth, the power of this divinely quickened life is not merely a renewed man, following the highest impulses of his new nature but a Divine personality, God Himself, wholly possessing him, absolutely controlling him and enabling him to realize the splendid ideal of the apostle Paul, when he says, "Whereunto I also labor, striving according to His working which worketh in me mightily." Again he says, "It is God who worketh in you both to will and to do of His good pleasure."

The Holy Scriptures have many beautiful parables and patterns of this supernatural life. Eve, the type of the bride of Christ, was not only taken from Adam and created a distinct personality herself, but Eve was married to Adam and his own life was added to hers in the most intimate of all earthly unions. So we are not only created anew in Christ Jesus but we are united to Christ Jesus in such a way that all the strength of His life flows into us and He simply relives His own life in the members of His body. Christ's own conception and birth were accomplished through the Holy Ghost and became a true type of our new birth. But later there came to Him a new and distinct experience, when the heavens were opened and the Holy Ghost descended upon Him and abode with Him, and all His work and all His words thenceforth were in the power, not of His own personal wisdom and strength, but of the Holy Ghost that dwelt within Him. How perfectly this corresponds to that deeper, higher, mightier crisis that comes to us when we, too, receive the Holy Ghost and pass from the human to the Divine, from our endeavoring to God's best.

There needs to be no long interval between these two experiences. There is every reason to believe that on the day of Pentecost and in the Apostolic church, they were contemporaneous or close together in the actual experience of believers. The difference is one in the nature of things rather than the order of time. The early Christians were expected to pass quickly into the baptism of the Holy Ghost and the fullness of their life in Christ; and when Paul came to Ephesus and found believers, his first question was, "Have ye received the Holy Ghost since ye believed?" And when he found they had not he immediately led them on to this deeper and fuller blessing. Dr. Torrey in a recent address in the city of Chicago remarked that the greatest need of the church today was an army of Spirit-filled men to go forth and ring in the ears of the professing Christians of America this old question, "Have ye received the Holy Ghost since ye believed?"

Dr. Pardington sums up the steps that lead to this blessed experience with great clearness and force. We cannot render our readers a better service than by quoting the headlines of some of these paragraphs:

I. A Step of Entire Surrender.

Another name for surrender is consecration. But as consecration is really a divine work, surrender is a better term. The Christian can yield his heart and life, but he cannot consecrate them; only God can do that. Thus, the Old Testament priests did not consecrate themselves: Moses, acting for Jehovah, consecrated them; the priests could only yield themselves to be consecrated. (Leviticus viii. 1-13; Romans vi. 13; xii. 1.)

Surrender is giving up—a yielding to God. The believer must lay his whole life on the altar, relinquish all right to its control, and count himself henceforth and forever the Lord's. Surrender is a painful act. It means separation; it means sacrifice; it means self-denial; it means death. Before we come to know Christ as our Saviour we learn something of the meaning of surrender. It costs the sinner a good deal to give up the world with its pleasures and attractions. It is hard for him to separate himself from old associates and detach himself from old associations. But when we come to know Christ as our Sanctifier we learn the deeper meaning of surrender. It is one thing to give up the world; it is quite another thing to give up oneself. Yet this is what the Master requires of His disciples:

"If any man will come after Me, let him deny himself, and take up his cross, and follow Me." (Matthew xvi. 24.)

Now, self-denial, which is the essence of surrender, does not mean giving up things; it means giving up self. Self is securely seated upon the throne of the heart, and stoutly refuses to abdicate in favor of Christ. But union with Christ means participation in His death. Now, in any form death is painful and terrible, at least in contemplation; and it is perfectly natural that the self-life within us should shrink from the ordeal of crucifixion with Christ. Yet there is no escape therefrom, if we are ever to know the liberty and delight of a life of deliverance from the dominion of sin and from the tyranny of the flesh. Therefore, like our blessed Lord we must become "obedient unto death, even the death of the cross." (Philippians ii. 8.) The self-life may shrink and quiver with pain; yet we must take our place with the Lord on the cross; and by a deliberate and determined act of the will hold ourselves there, while the Holy Spirit passes the iron of judgment and death through our souls.

Surrender to God must be voluntary, complete and final.

II. An Act of Appropriating Faith.

The gift of the Holy Ghost is received not only by a step of entire surrender but also by an act of appropriating faith. These two conditions must go together and in this order. Surrender is yielding to God; faith is taking from God. Again, surrender is negative and passive, while faith is positive and aggressive. Moreover, just as the step of surrender must be voluntary, complete, and final, so the act of faith must be definite, vital and appropriating.

In the act of faith through which we receive the Holy Spirit we must believe that God takes all that we give Him and that we take all that God gives us. On the Lord's side there will be no failure in taking; of this fact we may feel assured. He Who has prompted the step of surrender will not refuse the gift that we bring. When we lay our hearts and lives unreservedly upon the altar, Christ accepts our offering and seals it eternally His. Moreover, the altar sanctifies the gift.

Nor on our part will there be failure in taking, if we remember that Christ gives Himself far more freely and unreservedly to us than we give ourselves to Him. Let us not wait for a thrill of emotion before we count God true to His word. The Divine order is fact, faith, feeling. Whatever God says we must believe just because He says it; and then feeling will follow in its time as a matter of course. According to a converted heathen child, "Faith is believing a thing hard enough to act as if it was so." Therefore, when we have taken the step of surrender, let us count God faithful in meeting us and in giving us all our faith has dared to claim.

The importance of fully recognizing the spiritual crisis to which we have referred, is emphasized by the fact that God is moving on through all these spiritual unfoldings to a still grander crisis in the fulfillment of prophecy and the redemption of the world. The evolutionist expects this to come through the gradual working of the social and moral religious forces, which are at present molding human society. But this is not the teaching of God's Word. The coming kingdom is not to be a development, but a revolution. The New Jerusalem will never be built out of the stones which men's wisdom and culture are chiseling today in the quarries of time. That fair city is to "descend out of heaven from God, prepared as a Bride adorned for her husband." The Millennial Age will not be an evolution but a revolution. Therefore, all along the way redemption is wholly Divine and when the Consummation comes this shout shall echo through the heavens and the ages to come; "Salvation unto Him that sitteth upon the throne and unto the Lamb."

Appendix 8

Spiritual Sanctity

A.B. Simpson

One of our public men recently remarked that the age was becoming hysterical and every little while society took some new spasm of political, social or commercial hysteria. Certainly the religious world is threatened with a swarm of hysterical excitements. One of these, Dowieism, has just passed with the death of its founder. Another, Theosophy, has also lost its chief leader, Colonel Olcott of India, and has probably begun to wane. For a time Hindooism [sic] threatened to rob a lot of silly Americans of their senses. Christian Science is the most widely distributed craze of the generation, but it appears to be facing a serious, if not a fatal crisis. Just now there is much danger that the special gifts of the Holy Spirit shall be travestied to such an extent that rational Christians shall be turned away from the truly supernatural and divine manifestations of the power of God through the fear of the counterfeit. A wholesale condemnation of all supernatural and unusual manifestations of the Spirit is neither just nor effectual for the correction of these evils. The counterfeit always implies the genuine and it is only as we recognize the true that we shall be able to discern the false, and guard the honest seeker from its imposition. Just as the only way to meet spiritualism and Christian Science is to recognize the true Scriptural doctrine of the Holy Ghost and divine healing, so in these later developments of spiritual gifts and workings, we must have the spirit of candor as well as the spirit of caution, and while detecting the spurious, not fail to recognize the true.

There is no doubt that the gifts of tongues, miracles and prophecy were included in the Pentecostal Baptism, and as there is only one church and one Christian age, these gifts belong to us today, and we may expect their occasional manifestations as the Holy Ghost is pleased to exercise them, according to His sovereign pleasure, as the Apostle says, "severally as He will." There is no doubt also that we may expect special manifestations of the Holy Spirit in unusual and supernatural ways, as the end draws near and the Lord's coming approaches. The prophecy of Joel distinctly intimates that these signs shall lead up to "that great and notable day of the Lord." But just as Simon and others tried to mimic and prostitute the Pentecostal power and just as the evil spirits tried to take part with the Lord Jesus in His earthly miracles, so Satan would love to discredit the work of God in our own day by turning it into burlesque and making it ridiculous in the sight of sober and thoughtful men.

Happily the New Testament has left us sufficient tests and marks of distinction to enable us to prove all things and to discern between the false and the true. The Lord Jesus never was undignified, spectacular or ridiculous in His personal bearing and His earthly ministry. The ancient prophetic portrait given of Him by Isaiah, "Behold my servant whom I uphold, mine elect in whom my soul delighteth; He shall not strive, nor cry, nor cause his voice to be heard in the street," was literally fulfilled in the majestic picture of His human life. Not once did He resort to the tricks of the stage performer to attract the public. The calm dignity and resistless power of His presence and all His work, were sufficient to advertise Him, and again and again, even when He sought retirement, "He could not be hid." Surely if the example of our Lord has any weight with respect to the bearing and the deportment of His servants, we shall find little encouragement in the Master's example for many of our modern methods of attracting the multitude and manifesting the power of the Spirit.

When we turn to the day of Pentecost, it is true that the first manifestations of the Holy Ghost were inded startling and at first suggested to the astonished multitude that these people must be intoxicated. They were speaking with many tongues and the most vivid and extraordinary manifestations of the presence of God were certainly visible, but the Apostle Peter hastened to disclaim any mere natural excitement, and to say to the multitude how different this wonderful movement was from any mere excess of earthly stimulant, and indeed even the Pentecostal tongues were in no sense disorderly, for every man heard in his own tongue some message which he was compelled to recognize as the word of God, and the whole effect of the demonstration as well as the message of Peter was to produce the most solemn awe and profound conviction and lead to the most orderly and definite results in conviction of sin, conversion to God, and the public confession of the name of Jesus through the rite of Christian baptism. Indeed, it is distinctly stated in the later accounts of the Pentecostal Church that so far from extravagance and excess, their whole conduct was most beautiful and becoming, for it is added, "And they, continuing daily with one accord in the temple, and breaking bread from house to house, did eat their meat with gladness and singleness of heart. Praising God, and having favor with all the people. And the Lord added to the church daily such as should be saved." It is especially noted here that they had favor with all the people. A little later it is stated that such an awe and solemnity rested upon the gatherings, that "none durst join themselves unto them," who were not truly of them. In the story of Stephen's martyrdom all the frenzy is on the part of his enemies, while he himself is calm and dignified, and with a majesty, like his Master's, he passes through the gates from martyrdom to the arms of Jesus.

One especial epistle in the New Testament was written for the purpose of correcting abuses in connection with the supernatural gifts and the work and worship of the church. This is the first epistle of Paul to the Corinthians. It is to be noticed that the church to which it was addressed appears to have been more richly endowed with extraordinary spiritual gifts than any other, and at the same time to have been marked by greater faults, so that the possession of great gifts does not always involve great grace. In the very beginning Paul upbraids them with their divisions and strifes, and later denounces their unrighteousness, their spirit of going to law with one another, and their gross immoralities, worst of all the excusing of these things, and the failure to deal with them in righteous discipline.

Again he directs his strongest arguments to establish the true balance of spiritual endowments and to show them that the most valuable operations of the Holy Spirit are not those that are most showy and excite the greatest wonder. Among all the gifts of the Spirit he exalts prophecy to the highest place, because it is the most useful for edifying; and above all these gifts, even including prophecy, he exalts the grace of love as the queen of all gifts and graces, and the very crown of the bride of the Lamb. Even miracles he places below the ministry of the word, and the very last on the list are the gifts of tongues and the interpretation of tongues.

Further he insists that the supreme law which should govern the use of spiritual gifts is the principle of edification, and, he declares, that although he could speak with more tongues than all of them, he would rather speak one word to edification in a familiar tongue than ten thousand words is an unknown tongue.

Again, he appeals for order, decorum and propriety in all their assemblies and warns them against such scenes of confusion and wild fire as might easily occur through many persons speaking aloud at one time and in many languages, and "should one come in of those that are unlearned or unbleievers, will he not say ye are mad?" A little later he adds, "Let all things be done decently and in order." In another epistle, speaking of our conduct before the world, he says, "That he who in these things pleaseth God is accepted of God and approved of men." The New Testament never taught the ministers and people of Christ to offend public taste by defying the accepted standards of society. Probably this is one of the chief reasons why women were enjoined to wear their heads covered and observe modest silence in the public assemblies, because according to social customs "it was a shame" for them to act differently. There is a certain deference due to public opinion which a true Christian lady or gentleman will always show, and which constitutes our

Christian influence with our fellow men to a certain degree. This is not at all interfering with perfect liberty in the assemblies of Christ's people, and each one taking a proper part, for he distinctly says in I. Corinthians xiv. 26, "When ye come together, let every one of you have a psalm, have a doctrine, have a tongue, have a revelation, have an interpretation. Let all things be done unto edifying." This allows perfect freedom and fellowship, but at the same time demands perfect order, for should two brothers be moved at the same time to speak, let the one be silent while the other speaks.

And then he adds a very striking statement which illuminates the whole subject of the Spirit's guidance, and His relation to our individual minds: "For the spirits of the prophets are subject to the prophets." (I. Cor. viv. 32.) This clearly means that the Holy Spirit does not overrule our individual judgment and carry us off our feet in wild and reckless incoherency, but He holds His messages subject to our sanctified judgment and will, and permits us to act as rational and responsible beings, speaking or keeping silence as may seem to us most unto edification.

This teaching bears very distinctly upon some of the ideas we often hear expressed about abandoning ourselves to God. God does not ask us to give up our sanity and to become mere passive subjects of hypnotic influence, either from Himself or any other being. He has given to us our own rational nature and He acts in harmony with it. If we give ourselves up to spells and influences, irrespective of our judgment or reason, we are just as likely to be taken possessin of by evil spirits as by good. This is the very way in which the trance medium in clairvoyance and spiritualism becomes possessed with the spirit of Satan. This has sometimes been resorted to in what is known as trance-evangelism, and we have seen some of the fearful victims of this delusion. It is right to wait upon God for the fulness of His blessing, it is right to wait with an open heart and a listening ear, but God will never blame us for vigilance in proving the spirits and "discerning things that differ." If He has anything to say to us He will give us ample time to be sure that He is saying it. The Spirit of Christ is "the spirit of love, and power and of a sound mind."

In these days when the forces of heaven and hell are so intensely active, let us seek from God that gift which is of such practical value, the Spirit of discernment. We are raising no question about the reality of the gift of tongues as one of the manifestations of the Holy Spirit in the Christian age. Our warning is against the danger of exaggerating it, of seeking it for its own sake rather than seeking the Spirit Himself, and of exercising it in an extravagant and unscriptural way to the dishonor of Christ, the disorder of His work and the division of His people. We appeal for the spirit of sanity as well as the spirit of power.

It has been well said, that the element of proportion is indispensable, both in natural and spiritual things. The atmosphere we breathe depends for its wholesomeness upon the exact proportions in which the different constituents are mingled in the air. A little more carbon, a little more hydrogen, or a little more oxygen, would bring death in a single instant to the whole human race. It is because these elements are so perfectly mingled that the air we breath brings life and wholesomeness. It is precisely so with the gifts of the Spirit. The spirit of love alone will make us sentimental, unless it is mixed with power and wisdom. The spirit of wisdom alone will make us cold and hard, unless it is mixed with love. The spirit of power alone will run all the trains off the track, unless wisdom stands at the engine and directs the way. We have all seen Christian workers who suffered from such deformities and disproportions. God give us the blended fulness of the blessed Holy Ghost, the holy tact of the Master, who "increased in wisdom and in favor with God and men," and "the spirit of love, and of power, and of a sound mind."

Appendix 9

Gifts and Graces

A.B. Simpson

"But covet earnestly the best gifts. And yet I show unto you a more excellent way." I. Cor. xii. 31.

"Follow after love, and desire spiritual gifts, but rather that ye may prophesy. Wherefore brethren covet to prophesy, and forbid not to speak with tongues. Let all things be done decently and in order." I. Cor. xiv. 1. 39, 40.

The attention of the Christian church is being strongly directed at this time to the special gifts of the Spirit, and it is well that we should consider carefully and soberly the teachings of the Holy Scriptures on this important subject. It occupies a prominent and large place in this manual of the church, the first epistle of Paul to the Corinthians, almost three whole chapters being devoted to its discussion.

First of all let us carefully remember that the gifts of the Spirit here defined are quite distinct from the grace of the Spirit, and that our possession of these gifts does not affect our personal salvation and sanctification and our standing with God as subjects of His grace. This is quite apart from the Holy Spirit's ministry in leading us to Christ for salvation and in bringing us into union with Him through consecration and the baptism of the Holy Ghost. The most pernicious error abroad today in connection with these gifts is to make them a necessary test of our having received the Holy Ghost, and come into the fullness of Christ.

The following points are clear and important in connection with the teaching of the apostle regarding the *charismata* or gifts of the Spirit.

1. The apostle distinguishes gifts, ministries and operations of the Spirit. (Vs. 4-6.) By the gifts he means the special power communicated to the believer through the Holy Ghost for some special ministry. By the word administration he means the use of the gift in some actual ministry or form of service. And by the word operations he means the inward workings of the Holy Ghost in our individual experience as we receive this gift and exercise this ministry. It brings a corresponding experience to the heart as well as a more effective ministry to the life. We are not cold and passive instruments in the hands of the Master, but warm, living, responsive co-workers with Him, receiving in our own hearts the blessing which we are used in imparting to others. Now there are diversities of these gifts, ministries and experiences, but it is the one Spirit that works in every case. We are taught, therefore, at the beginning not to attempt to copy anyone, but to remember that God has a different method with every individual.

2. Every disciple of Christ ought to have some special manifestation of the Holy Ghost and some gift for Christian service. "The manifestation of the Spirit is given to every man to profit withal." (Vs. 7.) There is no place for idlers and drones, and there is no excuse for the fruitless Christian. God has power and work for all who will yield themselves to Him for His service and glory.

3. These gifts are conferred by the Holy Ghost Himself in His sovereign will according to individual fitness and for the completeness and profit of the whole body of Christ. He knows the gift that will best enable us to glorify Him and help others. No disciple can expect to receive all these gifts. It is preposterous to say that the gift of tongues, for example, is the criterion of having received the Holy Ghost. The apostle distinctly asks, "Have all the gift of tongues?" God adjusts our equipment to our natural temperament and ability, to our providential circumstances and to the special work which He has called us to do. We are represented here as various members of the body of Christ, and as in the body the different members have different offices, so is it in the body of Christ. The apostle asks with

graphic force, "If the whole body were an eye, where were the hearing? If the whole were hearing where were the smelling?" It is easy to make a figure still more vivid. Suppose a human face was all nose, or all ears, it would be a monstrosity. And suppose it were all tongue, and especially a foreign tongue, it would neither be attractive nor useful. Our business is to yield ourselves to the Holy Spirit for such gifts and ministries as He has for us, and trust Him for the enduement and the enabling.

4. The particular gifts of the Spirit are next specified. There are nine of them altogether. The first is the gift of wisdom. Wisdom is that quality which enables us to do the right thing and to avoid the wrong thing. It is the helm of life. Like salt in the natural world, often imperceptible and seemingly of little consequence, but absolutely necessary to life and health, so wisdom pervades every other quality and ministry, and rightly holds the first place as the pre-eminent gift of the Holy Ghost. We are very apt to overlook this quality in our search for the more brilliant and extraordinary manifestations of the Spirit, and the lack of wisdom often leads to the abuse of the very things we desire.

The second gift is knowledge. This is the knowledge of the truth, and especially the Word of God. Here it is spoken of as the Word of wisdom. It is not a general stock of crystallized knowledge laid up by mere human study, but it is a particular revelation as we need to use the Word for each occasion and service. "I have put My words into thy mouth," He says, "and covered thee with the shadow of My hand." "The Lord hath given me the tongue of one that hath learned, that I should know how to speak a word in season to him that is weary. He waketh morning by morning, He wakeneth mine ear to hear as one that has learned."

The next gift is the gift of faith. It is not saving faith, faith that justifies, sanctifies and brings to us every supply of divine grace, but it is the special faith which fits us for effectual service; the faith that removes mountains of difficulty, the faith that uproots sycamore trees of evil, the faith that knocks until doors are opened, the faith which equips the evangelist for the winning of souls and the worker for the accomplishing of great and mighty things in the pulling down of strongholds and the building up of the kingdom of God. No gift of the Holy Spirit is of more unspeakable value than the gift of faith. It was of this the Master said to His disciples, when they asked Him the secret of His own power, "Have the faith of God."

Following this come the gifts of healing. This does not mean some magic or some magnetic power possessed by some individuals, enabling them to remove disease by a touch, but at the same time a very real power to help God's sick and suffering children to know and receive Him as their healer and life. Just as God gives to some the special ministry of leading souls to Christ, so He gives to others as distinct a ministry in leading sufferers to receive the healing power of the Great Physician. And in these days of divine manifestation, when God has been for some years calling marked attention to the physical aspects of redemption, it is surely a time when we should call upon God for a mighty revival of the ministry of healing, and a distinct enduement of the workers who are called to it with the faith and power of God, even as in the days of old.

Next follows the working of miracles. These are distinguished from the gifts of healing, inasmuch as healing is not always or even usually miraculous, but rather on lines which, while distinctly supernatural, are more quiet, normal and even gradual. There are cases of miraculous healing, but there are many more in which the subject is led to receive the life of the Lord Jesus in a simpler way as the very element of his being and the habit of his whole life. The miracle is rather intended by its sudden and startling character to attract public attention, and to bear witness in some extraordinary way to the power and majesty of God. There is no doubt that the miraculous is an element of the Spirit's enduement, and there is no reason why it should ever have ceased in the history of the church. But here again we are not to be watching for the wonderful, but rather seeking the useful and helpful and leaving it to God Himself in His sovereign will to work miraculously when it pleases and glorifies Him.

The sixth of these gifts is prophecy. Ordinarily we associate this gift with the foretelling of future events. The Scriptural idea of it is different. It is rather a divine inspiration enabling the possessor to speak direct messages of the Holy Spirit for the spiritual profit of the hearer. "He that prophesieth speaketh unto men to edification and exhortation and comfort." All preaching ought to be to a certain extent prophetic in the sense of being God's immediate message to the hearer. This differs from the unfolding of the Scriptures and the teaching of doctrine. The prophetic message has more immediate reference to the particular condition of the hearer and the need of immediate spiritual help. This gift the apostle emphasizes above all the others as the one most useful and helpful. "Follow after love and desire after spiritual gifts, but rather that ye may prophesy."

The next gift is the discerning of spirits. It is quite remarkable that this gift immediately precedes the last two; namely tongues and interpretation of tongues. It would seem as if at this point there were peculiar need for the power to distinguish the false and the true. The gift of tongues above all others opened the way for scenes of much excitement and the possibility of Satanic counterfeits. There are languages spoken in hell as well as in heaven, and God Himself has forewarned us to "try the spirits whether they be of God, for many false prophets have gone forth into the world."

If God is really speaking He will not be impatient with us in our earnest desire to make sure it is His voice. There are several tests to which we shall allude later by which we may discriminate between the false and the true and regulate the public worship of God's assemblies.

Next comes the gift of tongues. There is no doubt that this is one of the special manifestations of the Holy Ghost in the apostolic church. It appears to have been specially prominent in the church at Corinth, and perhaps to have been cultivated and sought to the extreme degree by that people who were not noted for the very deepest spiritual life. There is always danger in unduly seeking the occult, mysterious and demonstrative. It is in this line that the adversary manifests his power through clairvoyance and spiritualism. But there was no doubt of the divine reality of many of these extraordinary manifestations, nor is there any reason why this gift should not appear at any time in the history of the church, and especially in these last days when we may expect the most remarkable outpourings of the Holy Ghost. It appears to have been a divine ecstasy, which lifted the soul above the ordinary modes and expressions of reason and utterance. As a profound German scholar expresses it, "Man contains three elements in his higher constitution; namely, the *pneuma,* the *nous* and the *logos.*" That is, the spirit, the mind and the language. The spirit is the higher element and in the gift of tongues appeared to overlap the mind altogether and find its expression in speech, quite unintelligible to the person himself and yet truly expressing the higher thought and feeling of the exalted spiritual state of the subject. It may be a human tongue, or it may be a heavenly tongue. For the apostle distinctly speaks of both the tongues of men and of angels. It was not always employed in the apostolic church as the vehicle of preaching to people of other languages, but rather was a channel of direct worship and adoration. "He that prophesieth speaketh unto men, but he that speaketh in an unknown tongue speaketh not unto men but unto God."

Finally, the gift of interpretation was the power to understand and translate the language spoken in the Spirit. It might more correctly be called the gift of translation. Sometimes it was possessed by the speaker himself, sometimes by another who gave the translation. Therefore the apostle says, "Let him that speaketh in an unknown tongue pray that he may interpret."

5. The relative importance and value of these various gifts is next brought out with great clearness. They are named in a certain order in the various places where we find them specified, and this order is practically uniform. In every instance the gift of tongues comes at the end of the list, and the gifts of wisdom, knowledge, faith and prophecy take precedence. In the most practical way the apostle commends the things that edify and help as compared with those that directly bless and honor the individual worshipper. He does not ignore the gift of tongues by any means, but recognizes it as the distinct mark of the divine power and presence, and a very glorious and blessed channel of direct fellowship with the heavenly world, and in some sense a real opening of the doors between the earthly and the heavenly. But he adds with very evident point, "Wherefore covet to prophesy and forbid not to speak with tongues." "Foras-

much as ye are zealous of spiritual gifts, seek that ye may excel to the edification of the church."

6. The spirit of decorum, propriety and order are next emphasized with great fulness. "Let all things be done decently and in order," he admonishes. "If any man speak in an unknown tongue, let it be by two or at the most by three, and that by course, and then let one translate, but if there be no translator, let him keep silence in the church and let him speak to himself unto God." "If anything be revealed to another that sitteth by, let the first hold his peace, for ye may all prophesy one by one, that all may learn and all may be comforted. For God is not the author of confusion, but of peace, as in all the churches of the saints." Then he unfolds a principle of the profoundest importance, "The spirits of the prophets are subject to the prophets." The Holy Spirit does not carry us away in wild irrational extravagance, but holds His communications subject to our sanctified judgment, and the order and edification of the whole assembly. It is the spirit of evil that rushes us and drives us to the excesses that bring dishonor and contempt upon the work and worship of God. How much cause we have to thank God for these wise and holy cautions and counsels! Let us be willing to heed and follow.

7. The pre-eminence of love. Above all gifts, above all ministries is the grace of love. That love that uses every gift and ministry, not to exploit its own greatness, but to glorify God and bless men. Not only is love here described as an end, but as a means. He says, "I show unto you a more excellent way," which is the way to reach the highest gifts of the Spirit, and God will entrust to us His most sacred ministries and most glorious manifestations in proportion as He sees that we will use them in the spirit of love and for the help of the souls that are to dear to the Shepherd's heart.

In conclusion let us not fear or ignore any of the gifts and manifestations of the Holy Ghost, no matter how extraordinary; but be prepared to expect God to reveal Himself to His people, especially in these last days in many signal and glorious ways.

At the same time let us not fear to exercise the spirit of discernment and to take ample time and measures to be sure that any alleged work bears the signs of God's approval and control. Let us especially watch lest even good movements become mixed with evil through the lack of discernment or carefulness. Let us not be afraid to exercise proper supervision and control in the Spirit over religious assemblies. And especially let us endeavor to keep these remarkable and supernatural manifestations of the Spirit from being handed over to unwise and reckless leaders and persons of doubtful character or spiritual qualifications.

Again let us not confuse the gifts and the graces of the Spirit. The work of the Holy Ghost in saving and sanctifying is entirely distinct from these special gifts. To say that the gift of tongues is the only proper evidence of having been baptized with the Holy Ghost is rash and wholly unscriptural, and places a mere manifestation of the Holy Ghost above His higher ministry of grace. Love, which is simply a grace of the Spirit, is placed above any of the gifts, and this love will surely keep us from judging one another.

Again, let us covet earnestly the best gifts, but chiefly the gifts of useful and effectual spiritual ministry.

Let us set ourselves against disorder, excess and extravagance, even though we may be criticized and denounced for hindering and quenching the Spirit. The Spirit Himself has given to us these divine tests and directions by which we may discriminate and direct. We are therefore obeying Him when we firmly yet kindly insist that the assembly of Christ's people shall be characterized by order, propriety, decorum, consideration for one another, and especially the spirit of edification, usefulness and helpfulness.

Finally, let us pray for love, let us cultivate love, let us take the Lord Jesus Himself to be our love, and let our deepest cry be

"Give me a heart like Thine."

Appendix 10

The Ministry of the Spirit

A.B. Simpson

We are living in the dispensation of the Holy Ghost. The Old Testament was in a sense the dispensation of the Father, the Gospel age was the dispensation of the Son, and since Christ's ascension the church has been under the administration of the Holy Ghost.

The presence of God on earth today is represented by the third Person of the Trinity, even as during the life of Jesus Christ God was represented on earth in the person of His Son. As the age draws to its close, we are justified in expecting unusual manifestations of the Holy Ghost and a more intense activity in the finishing of His work and the preparation of the church and the world for the coming of the Lord. How important therefore it is that we should fully understand the person and work of the Spirit, and to be ready to co-operate with Him and receive all His gifts and graces.

The Holy Spirit is a person. He is a living being as distinct and real as the Lord Jesus Christ in His earthly incarnation, only the Spirit is not embodied like Him in a human form, but makes His abode in the bodies of His people and the midst of His church. The Holy Ghost has all the attributes of an individual, personality, will, purpose. He loves, He suffers, He guides, He speaks, and He can be vexed and grieved as really as any human friend.

The Holy Ghost is a divine person, He is equal with the Father and the Son in the glorious Trinity. He is represented as the Creator of the universe, jointly with the other persons of the Trinity. He is the author of light, of life, of reason and of all the beauty and the glory of earth and heaven. Not a star that burns, not a flower that blooms, not an angel that sings, not an intellect that soars, but came from His creating hand. He was the author of Christ's miraculous conception, He was the power through whom all His miracles were wrought and all His marvelous words were spoken. He was the mighty Force that established the early church and sustained it through persecution and opposition until it conquered the world. He is the power through whom every converted soul is turned from darkness to light, every saint is sanctified, every sorrowing heart is comforted, every victory over sin and Satan is achieved, and every soul perfected and translated to the home above. There is nothing too hard for His power. There is nothing too intricate for His wisdom. There is nothing too complicated for His knowledge, and there is nothing which the heart of Christ would choose for His beloved which the love of the Spirit is not as ready to bestow.

The Holy Spirit is the administrator on earth of all the work of redemption. He is the Executive of the divine Trinity, the supreme Guide and Overseer of the church, and the sovereign Dispenser of all the gifts of the ascended Christ. Every grace which the Saviour has purchased and the Father is ready to bestow in His name must come through the hands of the Holy Ghost. As the Father committed all things to the Son, so the Son has committed all things to the Spirit, and it is through Him that we must receive the blessings which Christ died to purchase and lives to bestow.

He is the Spirit of Christ. He resided in His bosom during the three and a half years of His earthly ministry, and now He comes to us softened, colored, and humanized by the heart of Jesus, and really brings to us the Master Himself in all that was really essential to his character and ministry. In a sense therefore the presence of the Spirit is the presence of Christ. As Jesus never did anything without the Holy Spirit, so the Holy Spirit never does anything without Jesus. It is His supreme delight to make Christ real to us and take of the things that are His and show them unto us. "At that day," that is the day when He comes, "ye shall know that I am in the Father and ye in Me and I in you." It is His especial work to unite us to Christ and transfer to us from the Lord Jesus all the qualities and graces of His nature and enable us to relive them in our actual experience. He is the great artist that transfers the divine picture to the living tablets of our lives, so that "we beholding as in a glass the glory of the Lord, are transformed into the same image from glory to glory even as by the Spirit of the Lord."

The first work of the Holy Spirit in our individual life is convicting us of sin and of righteousness, and leading us to Christ in conversion. It is He that shows us our sin, especially the sin of rejecting Jesus. It is He that "persuades and enables us to embrace Jesus Christ freely offered us in the Gospel." It is He that creates in us the new heart and then witnesses with our spirit that we are the children of God. It is He that brings to us the peace and comfort of pardoned sin and enables us to utter our first cry of sonship and prayer, "Abba Father." While our thoughts are not occupied with Him, but rather with the person of Christ to whom He introduces us, while He stands behind the scenes and "rejoiceth greatly, because of the bridegroom's voice," yet it is through Him as the divine Agent that all this comes to pass, so that we are really born of the Spirit, or as the apostle expresses it elsewhere, "saved by the washing of regeneration and the renewing of the Holy Ghost."

The next work of the Holy Spirit is our sanctification. "After that ye believed ye were sealed with the Holy Spirit of promise." This is subsequent to conversion. The regenerated soul has the Holy Spirit with it, but not in it, even as the builder of a house may have constructed it by his own hand, but he has not yet made it his residence and his home. The baptism of the Holy Spirit marks the moment when the Spirit comes to dwell within the converted heart, and henceforth it becomes the temple of the Holy Ghost. This forms a distinct epoch in every consecrated life. It is the second chapter of Christian experience, corresponding to the second year in the ancient tabernacle, when the cloud that had moved before them and led them from the heavens or the mount, came down to dwell in the midst as the Shekinah in the holy of holies.

This brings to the soul a train of glorious blessings. The first of these is sanctification. "The Spirit of life in Christ Jesus hath made me free from the law of sin and death." "I will put My Spirit within you and I will cause you to walk in My statutes and ye shall keep My judgments and do them." Sanctification is much more than a cleansed heart, it is the indwelling of God and such a union with Jesus Christ as brings His life and righteousness into our life as the power of sanctification and holy obedience. It is not so much a crystallized state in which we are subjectively made sinless, as a new relation to Him, by virtue of which we continually walk with Him and He abides in us as our righteousness, sanctification and redemption. This is the work of the Holy Spirit. In accomplishing it He first gives us a divine conviction of our sinfulness and our need of divine holiness, and then He reveals to us the Lord Jesus as the secret of holiness and the source of victory. All this is finely unfolded in the seventh and eighth chapters of Romans, the seventh being a picture of the soul under conviction and struggling for victory in its own strength, while the eighth chapter reveals the victorious side through the life of Christ and the indwelling and inworking of the Holy Ghost.

Of course, this leads up, not merely to a momentary act, but to a life-long experience. The life of holiness is really a life in the Spirit, and in this life the Holy Ghost nurtures, teaches, guides and develops our spiritual experience just as fully as we will let Him, ever leading us on to "the measure of the stature of the fullness of Christ." It is of this that the Apostle James says, "Know ye not that the Spirit that dwelleth in us loveth us to jealousy? But He giveth more grace." Our gentle and vigilant Monitor and Mother is ever watching us with jealous care lest we come short of anything in God's perfect will. It is of this life in the Spirit that the apostle says in the first chapter of Ephesians, "God hath blessed us with all the blessings of the Spirit in heavenly places in Christ Jesus." In the same Epistle he prays that their eyes may be enlightened that they may know all the fullness of this inheritance of blessing which God has for them through the risen Christ and the indwelling Spirit. It is here that so many of God's children come short. They receive the baptism of the Spirit, but they do not "follow on to know the Lord." They do not walk in the Spirit and they are not filled with the Spirit.

But there is a still higher stage of spiritual blessing which the apostle describes by the phrase, "Be filled with the Spirit." It is possible to have the Spirit actually indwelling and yet not fully know or use all His attributes and resources. It is possible to have the Holy Spirit, but to confine Him to some isolated chamber of our being and not open to Him all our faculties, powers and interests. The Holy Spirit comes to fill every channel of our manifold being and every department of our diversified life, and He is grieved and disappointed when we keep back any part of our life from His control. He wants to come into our affections and our homes, into our business and our practical life, into our bodies and our physical infirmities, into our trials, temptations and hard places, as well as into our more distinctly spiritual and devotional experiences and our Christian work and ministry. Many people are looking for some extraordinary gift, or strained experience of the Holy Spirit, when He really wants to come to you in your simple everyday life and help you to be a better wife and mother, a more kind and helpful friend, a more upright and successful business man, a more efficient employee, and a more genial, loving and unselfish member of your household and social circle. The twelfth chapter of the Epistle to the Romans is God's picture of the Spirit-filled life in all its domestic, social and practical aspects and fruitions. It will be a life, not only of spiritual ministry, as the apostle there describes according to the gifts bestowed upon us, but of industry and liberality in our business life, of kindness and affectionateness, of long-suffering and forgiveness toward our enemies, and of sympathetic tenderness toward the troubled and the tried, and of all round efficiency in our earthly calling and station in life. Beloved, perhaps it is here that the Holy Spirit wants to come to you first before you have a right to ask Him for the gifts of prophecy, miracles or tongues. He knows better than you your place in life, the needs of those around you and the sort of grace and help best fitted to make you efficient for His glory. Trust Him and take Him for His wise and perfect and holy will and begin to practice the works of the Spirit according to the measure of the grace already given, and you will find that as you are faithful in that which is least, He will give you more.

Remember also that before all gifts, ministries and marvelous things, the greatest thing He can give you is love, and love just means the all round life of gentleness, goodness, helpfulness that we have already described. They tell the story of a mother who was so intent on getting some profound religious experience that she had no time or heart for the little child that was hanging to her skirts and crying because there was no one to listen to her baby sorrows or fix the little doll that had got broken in her hands. The mother was reading some saintly volume and praying for some extraordinary blessing, and the little girl at last lay down upon the carpet with her broken doll in her arms and fell asleep with her face all covered with tears. The mother prayed, but found no response, and as she wondered what could be the matter she saw the little baby face with the tears yet wet beneath her eye lashes, and her heart smote her, and the Lord spake to her and said, "The greatest of these is love. Though I speak with tongues of man and angels and have not love, I am become as a sounding brass or a tinkling cymbal." She threw herself on the carpet in tears and contrition. She asked God to forgive her blindness and folly, and awaking her little child, begged its forgiveness, and as she helped the little hands to mend the broken doll, lo, the heavens were opened and the Spirit came down and filled her heart with joy and praise.

Finally, there are gifts of the Spirit for special service. We are not expected to minister in our human strength or with our natural talents only. The baptism of the Holy Ghost includes the varied gifts described in the twelfth of First Corinthians. There are nine of these in all, which may be divided into three groups. The first three gifts are wisdom, knowledge and faith, and they are what may be called the more indispensable and universal gifts for all effective ministry. Nothing can surpass the value of these three gifts; wisdom rightly to direct our work for God; knowledge to speak the word in season and teach the Holy Scripture, and faith to claim the mighty working of God's power in all this ministry. Above all other gifts let us covet these and use them for His glory and the help of others.

The second group includes the more supernatural enduements of prophecy, miracles and healing. Prophecy is the power to receive and give forth the special messages of the Holy Ghost for edification, exhortation and comfort of His people. It is not so much the ministry of teaching as the special testimony from time to time along the line which the prophet describes as the "word in season to him that is weary." The miracles need no explanation and may be expected at all periods of church history as God's occasional and signal witness of the supernatural when some marked evidence of His working is needed. The ministry of healing is not always miraculous, but none the less supernatural and should also be valued and constantly exercised in the church. And at this time especially, when God is so abundantly pouring out His Holy Spirit, it is fitting that there should be much believing prayer for a distinct revival of this special and most helpful ministry for a suffering world.

The third group of supernatural gifts forms also a distinct class, comprising the more special gifts of discerning of spirits, new tongues and the translation of tongues. It is to be noted that before the gift of tongues is specified this important gift of discerning the spirits is introduced. There are dangers in connection with the gift of tongues, of false as well as true spirits, and therefore there was to be much spiritual discernment so as to avoid fanaticism and error. In like manner the gift of tongues is followed by another gift, a sort of companion ministry called interpretation or translation. Because it was most important, as the apostle says in the fourteenth chapter of this Epistle, that the gift of tongues should not become a mere show or spectacle, but be for profit and edification; therefore he says, "Let him pray that he may translate, or else let him keep silent and speak to himself and to God."

It will thus be seen that the supreme aim of the Lord in all the gifts of the Spirit is not so much to display His power only or attract attention to the instrument of the gift, as to really help, comfort and edify His people.

Let us not therefore be straining after strange things, but ask and expect the Holy Spirit to fit us for helpful ministry in the place where God has put us and for the work which lies next to our hand. In a word, let us keep the thirteenth chapter of First Corinthians ever sandwiched between the twelfth and the fourteenth, the two chapters which tell us about the gifts. If love is thus embosomed within them, it will give balance to all our life and work, and realize in our experience that fine symmetrical picture which the apostle describes in his letter to his son Timothy. "God hath not given us the spirit of fear, but of power and of love and of a sound mind."

In the beautiful poem of Sir Launfal, a Christian knight had gone forth with holy zeal in quest of that which represented in that age the most glorious gift of God. It was the Holy Grail, the identical cup from which the Lord Jesus and His disciples had drunk the sacred draught "on that night in which He was betrayed." As he passed out from the palace gate, a loathsome leper stretched out his festering hands for help, and begged him to take the filthy cup that was lying beside him, and bring him a drink of water from the flowing brook. But the knight waved him aside and swept on, for he was after higher things.

Years passed by, as he pursued in vain his weary quest over many lands and under scorching suns. His body was worn, his hair was gray, his heart was broken, his hopes had almost died. A worn-out wreck, he was slowly returning to his home with a crushed and disappointed heart, when once again a leper met him on the way and stretched out the same festering hands for the same loving ministry. Swiftly the knight leaped from the horse, picked up the repulsive vessel, and hastening to the stream, with profoundest courtesy and tenderest sympathy he handed to the sufferer the drink he had requested. In a moment the scene was changed, and the transfigured leper had become none other than the Son of Man Himself. The light of heaven shone around Him and the filthy cup became transformed into a shining vessel of silver; and as the Master handed it back to him it was indeed the "Holy Grail!" Yes, he had learned the "more excellent way," and the ministry of love had brought the gifts of power and glory, which otherwise he had sought in vain. So still we shall find that "he that humbleth himself shall be exalted" and he that would stand nearest to the Son of Man must, like Him, also come "not to be ministered unto, but to minister," and to give up his very life as a living sacrifice of love.

Though I speak with tongues of mortals,
  Or of seraphim above;
I am but a tinkling cymbal
  If I have not Love!

Though I reach the heights of knowledge;
  Every mystery though I prove;
I am nothing, less than nothing,
  If I have not Love.

Though I give with princely bounty;
  Yield my life my zeal to prove;
Vain are all my gifts and sufferings
  If I have not Love.

Blessed, gently, holy Jesus,
  Blessed, holy, heavenly Dove!
Give to me the Master's spirit,
  Fill my heart with Love.

Appendix 11

"Speaking In Tongues"—Some Words of Kindly Counsel

Rev. R.A. Jaffray, of Wuchow, South China.

The writer with a full, glad heart praises the Lord for the outpouring of His Spirit in the South China Mission of the Christian and Missionary Alliance and for his personal share in that time of refreshing. In a quiet Saturday night meeting the Spirit fell upon His children and many "spake in tongues as the Spirit gave them utterance." Personally I have never received such a spiritual uplift as when, a year ago last October, I received this blessed Baptism and spoke in tongues. The anointing then received "abideth" unto this day. There are a few of the many benefits that I would mention:

(1) A deeper love for, and understanding of, the Word of God than ever before.

(2) A knowledge of my utter strenghlessness and of the power of the NAME and the BLOOD of JESUS in prayer as never before.

(3) An unction in witnessing and preaching greater than ever before. (Unction is needed more than eloquence.)

(4) A control of the "unruly member" in daily life since the Lord took peculiar charge of my tongue.

(5) A clearer understanding of the mighty workings of the Holy Spirit and of evil spirits, in these last days of the present Age.

It is generally admitted that as we draw near to the close of the Age, and the Coming of the Lord Jesus, that in answer to the many prayers of God's people, the Spirit will revive the Church to some extent and restore to her the long lost Gifts of the Apolistic Age. Therefore all over the Christian world there has been a spirit of prayer for REVIVAL. Now that the Lord has answered prayer and the work begun, many fail to recognize the movement as of God because it does not correspond with what they had expected and hoped for. That the enemy has come in at the same time with his subtle counterfeit and imitation to delude and, if it were possible, deceive the very elect, cannot be denied. And that he has succeeded in deceiving many of God's dear children cannot be denied. But this deception is twofold:

(1) Some are deceived into the error that all supernatural manifestation is of God, and so are easily led off into extravagances and fanaticism and thus bring much dishonor on the work and the name of the Lord.

(2) Others equally deceived and misled declare that the whole movement is of the devil. They have seen some things that were not of God and therefore conclude that the whole thing is from below.

It is very easy to thus declare radically for or against; and Satan is well pleased if in any way he can mimic the work of the Holy Spirit and so cause the child of God to either call his work God's or God's work his. It matters little to him whether you call it all of God or all of the devil so long as you confound the workings of the two spirits. It is no new tactic of the enemy to imitate the work of God. He has always been a faithful attendant at all good Holy Ghost Revivals. So it is wrong to go to extremes and not be watchful and fall into fanaticism, etc., but it is equally wrong and sinful to only see the evil in this latter day movement and to be so rigid and opposed that we fail to enter into what God has for His people in these last days. From what I have heard some opposers say I fear that had they been present on the Day of Pentecost they might have judged the demonstrations and manifestations of that wonderful day were the works of the devil, too. Some on that day not only were "amazed" and "in doubt," but on account of the unusual actions of the Spirit-filled disciples mockingly said, "These men are full of new wine." There is a great danger, too, of fearing the works of the devil to such an extent that we shall lose all courage to seek earnestly for the true and full endowment of the Spirit for which our souls hunger. I have met some who are so prejudiced on account of what they have seen that they say they have no desire to ever speak in tongues, forgetting that "tongues" is one of the "gifts of the Spirit." Let us not allow the enemy so to drive us away from, and cheat us out of, the real blessings of the Spirit because he has counterfeited in some cases "the gift of tongues." We have no business to be afraid of evil spirits, for He has given us "power over all the power of the enemy," and He can give supernatural discernment of spirits.

Again, let us consider a few of the danger lines in connection with this movement. That it is accompanied with some of the most subtle dangers is not surprising. Every leader and seeker in such meetings should be willing to be warned, for almost all the teaching that the Apostle Paul gives us in I. Corinthians on these lines is called forth in the way of warnings to the Corinthian Christians because of the abuse of this gift of tongues. There is no word that ought to be more before us in connection with these meetings than the word WATCH. Jesus said, "What I say unto you, I say unto all— WATCH." Satan is going about as an "angel of light" mimicking the works of God. He does not appear as a red monster with horns and forked tail and cloven foot. Well did the old Scotch saint say, pointing to such a picture of Satan, "You devil would never tempt me." He comes in such subtle likeness to the Holy Spirit that it is impossible for any natural wisdom to discern. Perhaps, too, it is true, that of all gifts of the Spirit there is no other that is easier for the enemy to counterfeit than the gift of tongues. It has often been said that coming toward the end of the list in I. Corinthians it may be considered one of the least important. But it should never be forgotten that while last in the Epistle it is the first in order of experience in the Acts. May it not be that the Spirit usually gives the "tongues" first to test us and see whether or not we may be trusted with greater gifts of the Spirit which may be indeed of more value in the Christian ministry. There may be this reason also, that if the Spirit can get hold of a man's tongue He has what corresponds, according to James, to the bit in the horse's mouth and the rudder of the ship, and so in turn the whole body may be bridled by the Spirit of God.

Now, while I have said that it may be that the Spirit usually gives the sign of speaking in tongues first, as was generally the case in the records of the Acts, yet I do not at all hold that "speaking in an unknown tongue" is the evidence or sign of the Baptism of the Spirit. On the contrary, I believe that the teaching of this doctrine, so unfounded in Scripture, in connection with this movement, has done more harm than can be estimated. If it were true, surely Paul would have given in his Epistles at least one clear statement to that effect in connection with all his teaching on the Spirit. On the other hand he says clearly that "Tongues are for a sign, NOT to them that believe." (I. Cor. xiv. 22.) Some of our missionaries who were most wonderfully baptized and most profoundly blessed in the time of refreshing referred to above, never spoke a word in an unknown tongue, though their mouths were filled with singing in their native language!

There is a subtle danger of attaching too much importance to supernatural utterances and interpretations of tongues, considering that they are the very infallible Word of the Spirit of God. It is easy to say, "The Spirit says," etc. "The Lord told me so and so" when it is quite possible that it is a matter of our self-wilfulness. The Apostle Paul did not accept such leadings given through the utterances of others as the infallible will of the Lord for him. (See Acts 21.) Some would make the prophets of the Lord mere fortune-tellers. No, the Lord is able to lead each child of His in a plain path by His own Sure Written Word. How sad it is that some have found this message in the tongue to take the place of the Word of God, when it ought to inspire to a deeper love and reverence and obedience to that precious Book of Books. Tongues shall cease (I. Cor. xiii. 8), but the Word of the Lord endureth forever (I. Pet. i. 25).

Another sad effect that is very noticeable sometimes as a result of this movement is "schism in the body." The restoring of the gifts ought to bring about unity. This division is often caused by those who speak in tongues withdrawing themselves apart from the others, considering themselves "more holy" than others and constituting themselves a sacred, select few and meeting together for the purpose of "speaking in tongues" (I. Cor. xiii. 4, 5). One of Paul's chief messages to this Corinthian Church was that Christ was not divided and that His people should be one. (See Chap. I.) Personally, I always fear that prolonged, special, waiting meetings, if not very guardedly and wisely conducted are often a good opportunity for Satan to work and may be productive of evil more than of good. Of course when the Spirit of the Lord falls upon the people as was the case at Pentecost and in Acts 10 and 19: then crudities and unusual manifestations can hardly be avoided. When sinners cry out under conviction, or in the first stages, the people act as though full of new wine, these things for the time being may be allowable, but such ought not to be encouraged after the first gust of Pentecostal wind has passed. It is very noticeable that men as a rule love to talk and talk loudly and hear themselves talk and many seem to enjoy a noise, but let us be exceedingly careful lest this is not after all a fleshy enjoyment, or at least, that a good deal of the flesh is intermingled. Is it not possible that after all Self is exalted a good deal more than Christ in such stormy meetings (I. Kings xix. 11, 12). God dwells in utter stillness and "a meek and a quiet spirit is in sight of God of great price"; "Love doth not behave itself unseemly" (I. Cor. xiii. 5). Let us not be like the old soldier that snored so loudly that he drew on the fire of the enemy. I confess I have been in some meetings that reminded me more of "O Baal hear us!" and "sounding brass and tinkling cymbal" than anything else (I. Cor. xiii. 1). There is a danger of some playing with the gift of tongues as a child with a new toy, and judging from the context it is possible that it is this very thing to which Paul refers in I. Cor. xiii. 2: "When I was a child I spake as a child . . . but when I became a man I put away childish things." And again in I. Cor. xiv. 19 and 20: "Yet in the Church I had rather speak five words with my understanding that with my voice I might teach others also, than ten thousand words in an unknown tongue. Brethren, be not children in understanding: howbeit in malice be ye children, but in understanding be men."

The Apostle lays down certain clearly defined Rules and Regulations as to the Order in the regular Church meeting in I. Cor. 14:

(1) Only two, or at most three, are to speak in a meeting in a tongue.

(2) These are to speak one at a time or "by course."

(3) They must have an interpreter and if there is none they should not speak in the Church. (See I. Cor. xiv. 27, 28 and 33, 39 and 40.) "Forbid not to speak in tongues. Let all things be done decently and in order."

May I say that in the work in South China, by the blessing of God, these Rules of the Apostle were made a great blessing. Without using harsh force, but by prayer and teaching, a meeting has been saved from confusion and the loss of edifying and inspiring messages in tongues and interpretation by observing the rule to speak by course. When the season of special outpouring of the Spirit had passed; when, as it were, the wind had ceased to blow, we all felt that it was the right thing to settle down to our regular work in the schools and in the Church again and let the Spirit lead us to future manifestation of a special character. Furthermore, all of the brethren and sisters who had spoken in tongues felt instinctively that from that time on they were to use the tongue the Lord had given in private prayer and intercession. This we felt was according to the Scriptures. (See I. Cor. xiv. 2, 4, 18, 19 and 28.) I might say that more than once we felt led to read before the whole congregation chapters xii. 13 and 14 of I. Corinthians.

One lamentable lack in connection with this outpouring of the Holy Spirit has been the spirit of evangelism. Divine unction bestowed on a child of God should lead that one out to seek and save the lost as Jesus did. What we longed for in the South China work was that the Spirit of conviction would fall upon the heathen and that many souls would be saved as a result of the baptism. In this we were, for the present at least, disappointed. Perhaps the Lord wanted to prepare His own vessels first so that we might the more effectually witness for Him in power afterwards. So it has proven to be, at least in some small measure. Since the special meetings referred to, there has been more fruit gathered for the Lord than ever before in a given time, and we are confidently looking to the Lord that He will soon send another mighty wave that will sweep into the Kingdom many precious souls. But to gather together in small, select meetings and merely enjoy our blessing selfishly and seek for more is surely not God's plan. Let us go out and compel the lost to come in.

Again, it has been a great grief to my soul to find some who have received this baptism, backsliding in their missionary zeal. O if Pentecost means anything, dear brother, does it not mean witnessing? And it is witnessing the Gospel to the uttermost part of the world. That we should be so taken up with Pentecost, with a gift of God, with an unknown tongue, that we should fail of our duty in the work of the evangelization of the world is a sad inconsistency indeed. Such, a baptism ought to fill our hearts with love for the lost heathen and cause us to pour out our souls in prayer as never before for the perishing, and cause us to give with more earnest self-sacrifice than we have ever done before.

Then there are some who have taken up with independent missionaries in connection with this movement. A considerable number of young men and women have thought that they had a call to some foreign field and that the Lord had given them the Chinese or Japanese tongue. Without attempting to test or prove the tongue, they have gone forth to the heathen shore and so far as I have ever heard not one of these have been able to speak to the people in the native language. This is not to be wondered at, for we find in the Word of God no such precedent, no such promise, no such use of the "gift of tongues" mentioned. Such dear ones have been sadly misled and have either had to return home a failure or have in some cases become a burden and a hindrance on some good missionary on the field. What dishonor such mistakes bring on the Lord's cause and on this Movement of the Spirit! But not only have the men and women who have gone forth in this way been deceived, but also a host of others, who have stood back of them and supported them with their money, have been misled. They have given their money to a foolish cause and the enemy has laughed as the money has been lost to the Missionary Society that they had been accustomed to give it to.

Finally, I desire to say a few things about I. Cor. xiv. 32: "The spirits of the prophets are subject to the prophets." Only those who have been present and in the spirit of full sympathy with such wonderful meetings can know what power there is present upon those concerned. The very air seems charged with supernaturalism and the atmosphere is spiritual, and wonderful and blessed things are taking place all about one so that the tendency is that the "rushing mighty wind" would cause one to lose one's balance as it were. Some of us who were glad indeed when the wind blew, were glad also when the lull came, so that we could, as it were, get our bearings again. It is very easy for one who has had no such experience to coldly criticize one's actions who is under the power, but he knows nothing of what it means till he has himself realized the power of God. With such marvelous manifestations of the power of God on every side one becomes fearful even of his own thoughts lest he be guilty of a doubt or be a hindrance to the work of the Spirit. And here is just where the danger lies and where the enemy comes in to misguide. Through fear lest we doubt, our judgment and reason is withdrawn, and the result sometimes is that we may do and say things that under ordinary circumstances we should not deem proper. But here is where we need to remember that the spirit of the prophet is subject to the prophet and the Lord never wants us under the power of the Spirit to abandon our judgment or personal self control of ourselves; we must ever be masters of our own minds before and in the Lord. This absolute abandonment of one's self gives the evil spirits an opportunity that they ever avail themselves of. The work that originally is of God may soon be spoiled by the intrusion of false and lying spirits imitating and counterfeiting the work of the Holy Spirit so as to deceive, if it were possible, the very elect. The air is full of voices and it is impossible, in the natural wisdom of man, to discern the spirits. Only by a God-given, supernatural instinct, only by "trying the spirits" in the Scriptural way may we be saved from evil influences that fill the "air" in these last days. In order to try a spirit it is necessary that one be separated from and not in any sense under the influence of that spirit at the time of the trial. (Cf. John iv. 1-3.) It is no light or trifling thing thus to come into the very presence of supernatural beings,—"wicked spirits in high places," and meet them in the Name of Jesus of Nazareth, but it is something that I am persuaded the child of God has to learn in these last days of this dispensation. As the coming of the Lord draweth nigh, the wicked spirits of the "air" are, as it were, being forced down nearer the earth and this will continue more and more till when the Lord will have really come in person in the air for His saints, then Satan with all his host will have come to take up their abode on the earth for the tribulation period. Therefore it is for the man of God to be clothed upon as never before in these last days with the very power of God and to receive from the Lord the Gifts of the Spirit so that in the evil day he shall be able to stand. In one's own name one may well fear to stand. Any who have had experiences on these lines will know what I mean when I say that there has been a great temptation to fear the power of evil spirits. Personally I have seen so much subtle counterfeit and the deep devices of wicked spirits, which come at first as angels of light, and finally sought to lead God's holy children away into actual sin, that I found myself becoming afraid of the power of the devil to such an extent that I was drawing back and had not the courage to press forward and seek for a fuller endowment of power from on high. But, beloved, we have no business to fear the enemy. He is a conquered foe and Jesus has given us power over all the power of the enemy and He can so fill and empower us that we shall be as the Apostles of old, "able ministers of the New Covenant" and "abound unto every good work." It is not sufficient to say, "O the Lord will take care of His own dear children. He will not suffer them to be deceived," etc. It is a day when all need to WATCH and so be covered with the precious Blood of Jesus and so clothed upon by the Holy Spirit with power that we shall not only be able to stand in the evil day, but to go forth in the service of the Master conquering and to conquer.

Appendix 12

A. B. Simpson Books in Print

The following books by A. B. Simpson are currently in print. Christian Publications is committed to bringing back all of the 100-plus titles of Simpson's that are relevant to today's readers.

The Best of A.B. Simpson
The Christ in the Bible Commentary
(The original 26 volumes are being edited, Scripture quotations changed to NIV, and are being released in six clothbound editions with the final edition available summer of 1994.)
Christ in the Tabernacle
The Christ Life
Danger Lines in the Deeper Life
Days of Heaven on Earth
The Fourfold Gospel
The Gentle Love of the Holy Spirit
The Gospel of Healing
The Holy Spirit Vol. 1
The Holy Spirit Vol. 2
A Larger Christian Life
The Life of Prayer
Missionary Messages
The Self-Life and the Christ-Life
Wholly Sanctified